Global Culture/Individual Identity

Most people still think of themselves as belonging to a particular culture. Yet today, many of us who live in affluent societies choose aspects of our lives from a global "cultural supermarket", whether in terms of food, the arts, or spirituality and beliefs. So if roots are becoming simply one more consumer choice, can we still claim to possess a fundamental cultural identity?

Global Culture/Individual Identity focuses on three groups for whom the tension between a particular national culture and the global cultural supermarket is especially acute: Japanese artists, American religious seekers, and Hong Kong intellectuals before and after the handover to China. These ethnographic case studies form the basis for a theory of culture which we can see reflected in our own lives.

Gordon Mathews opens up the complex and debated topics of globalization, culture, and identity in a clear and lively style. His book will be illuminating and valuable for social and cultural anthropologists, their students, and the interested layperson.

Gordon Mathews is associate professor of anthropology at the Chinese University of Hong Kong. He is also the author of *What Makes Life Worth Living? How Japanese and Americans Make Sense of Their Worlds*.

0415206154

Global Culture/ Individual Identity

Searching for home in the cultural supermarket

Gordon Mathews

London and New York

First published 2000 by Routledge
11 New Fetter Lane, London EC4P 4EE

Simultaneously published in the USA and Canada
by Routledge
29 West 35th Street, New York, NY 10001

Routledge is an imprint of the Taylor & Francis Group

© 2000 Gordon Mathews

Typeset in Baskerville by BC Typesetting, Bristol
Printed and bound in Great Britain by
Clays Ltd, St Ives plc

British Library Cataloguing in Publication Data
A catalogue record for this book is available from the British Library

Library of Congress Cataloging in Publication Data
Mathews, Gordon.
    Global culture/individual identity: searching for home in the
cultural supermarket/Gordon Mathews.
        p.   cm.
    Includes bibliographical references and index.
    1. Group identity.   2. Culture.   3. International relations and
culture.   4. Acculturation.   5. National characteristics.
6. Ethnicity.   I. Title.
HM753.M37   2000
306–dc21   99-41333
                                                            CIP

ISBN 0–415–20616–2 (pbk)
ISBN 0–415–20615–4 (hbk)

To Yoko

Contents

Preface

This book is about cultural identity. Most people today tend to think of culture as belonging to a particular society: Japanese have Japanese culture, French have French culture, Americans have American culture, and so on. But today this has become confusing: we belong to our particular national culture, but many of us in today's affluent world also choose – or at least believe we choose – aspects of our lives from what can be called "the global cultural supermarket." You might eat raisin bran for breakfast, curry for lunch, and sashimi for dinner; you may listen to opera, jazz, reggae, or juju; you may become a Christian, an atheist, a Buddhist, or a Sufi.

One result of this is a profound contradiction that many of us in the affluent, media-connected world live within. We feel that we belong to our particular national culture, and believe that we must cherish our culture. But we also consume from the global cultural supermarket, and believe (albeit in large part falsely) that we can buy, do, be anything in the world we want – but we can't have it both ways. We can't have both all the world's cultures to choose from and our own cultural particularity. If you believe that you can choose aspects of your life and culture from all the world, then where is your home? Do you have any home left to come back to? Can home and roots be simply one more consumer choice?

I focus in this book on three groups for whom the tension between particular national culture and the global cultural supermarket is particularly acute: Japanese artists traditional and contemporary, American religious seekers Christian and Buddhist, and Hong Kong intellectuals in the shadow and wake of Hong Kong's return to China. Japanese traditional artists may claim that their arts represent the essence of Japaneseness, an essence that their fellow Japanese have lost. Some Japanese contemporary artists seek a return, through their rock or jazz or abstract painting, to their Japanese roots. But is the Japaneseness that the *koto* player in kimono expresses through her art really the same as the Japaneseness that the punk rocker with dyed blond hair expresses through his art? What in the world is Japanese?

Some American Christians believe that the United States is a once-Christian nation that has lost sight of God's truth; but many American religious seekers see religion as a matter of taste: "believe whatever makes you happy." Different versions of the United States follow each of these principles: Is the United States "one nation under God," a beacon of truth to the world, or is it a land of "the individual pursuit of happiness"? What in the world is American?

Some Hong Kong intellectuals see themselves as Hongkongese, an identity that emerged only in recent decades and that may now be slowly vanishing under the weight of the Chinese state since the handover on 1 July 1997. Others see themselves as Chinese, and revere the Chinese identity to which they now claim they have returned. But in the wake of colonialism in Hong Kong and communism on the mainland, is there any such Chineseness left to go back to? Or is it no more than a dream? What in the world is Chinese?

These three groups, and the personal accounts of people within these groups, are featured in the three central chapters of this book; but these particular investigations are framed within a larger argument over the meanings of culture in today's world, and the meanings of home. This book is about three particular groups of people, but it is also about all of us in the mass-mediated, culturally supermarketed world of today. Who in this world are we? This book will provide no clear answers to this question; but it will, I hope, stimulate you who read these words to think about our contemporary quandaries of cultural identity in a new way.

A brief note on names. Japanese names in this book are written in Japanese style, with surname first and given name second. Chinese names are also written with surname first and given name second unless the person referred to goes by a Western given name, in which case the surname follows the given name.

Acknowledgments

I am indebted to a number of people and institutions who greatly aided me in the writing of this book. The Research Grants Council, Hong Kong provided an Earmarked Research Grant (CUHK 145/96H) that enabled me, over successive summers, to conduct this research in Japan and the United States, and during the school year in Hong Kong between 1996 and 1998; it also made possible the hiring of some three dozen student assistants – students from Hong Kong, Japan, and the United States – transcribing taped interviews into what amounted to some 3,000 pages of transcripts in all. Some of these students also conducted interviews in Cantonese to supplement my own interviews in Hong Kong; others helped locate newspaper articles in Chinese, Japanese, and English; and others assisted me in my own efforts at translation. Space makes it impossible to list all their names, but these students were of enormous help. Without the funding of the Research Grants Council and the assistance of these student helpers, this book would have been far slower in its generation, if, indeed, it had been written at all.

I am also indebted to various students, friends, and colleagues who have read drafts of this manuscript, and argued with me about many of the points in this book. James and Rubie Watson, Viki Li, Sidney Mintz, Lynne Nakano, and Robert Stone all read drafts of the manuscript, and offered critiques that have been extremely useful. My wife, Yoko Miyakawa, read over this manuscript not once but twice, a true labor of love on her part, and caught numerous errors and infelicities; Yoko Miyakawa, Chow Man-wai, Shirley Lee, and Viki Li were of great help in checking over and in some cases providing translations of Japanese and Chinese materials. Conversations with Sidney Mintz and Joseph Bosco over the course of several years about the meanings of culture have much stimulated my thinking, especially since I disagree with them both – they will no doubt shake their heads over my obtuse stubbornness if they read these pages. I also should mention here the very helpful suggestions from three anonymous referees at Routledge, as well as the encouragement of my editor, Victoria Peters.

Portions of Chapter 4, on Hong Kong intellectuals, have appeared in the *Bulletin of Concerned Asian Scholars*, July–September 1997, "*Hèunggóngyàhn*: On the Past, Present, and Future of Hong Kong Identity." I thank its editor, Tom Fenton, for permission to reprint the relevant pages in this book. The section on names in this chapter appeared in slightly different form in *Dialectical Anthropology*, September 1996, "Names and Identities in the Hong Kong Cultural Supermarket."

Finally, I must thank my 120 or so informants in three societies, each of whom took time out from their busy lives to sit with me, most often a stranger to them, for several hours and answer my stupid questions for no recompense. Anthropology as a discipline could not exist if the people anthropologists talk to were not willing to open their lives to strangers. I hope that this book is worthy of the trust these people have placed in me.

1 On the meanings of culture

Culture has become a problem in today's world. Anthropologists have traditionally defined culture as "the way of life of a people"; by this usage, we can speak of "Navaho culture," "American culture," "Chinese culture." But do such labels, in today's world of global flows and interactions, really make any sense? Is there really any such thing as an American, or Japanese, or Chinese culture that defines all Americans, Japanese, Chinese in common, as opposed to non-Americans, non-Japanese, non-Chinese? If not, then should we discard the term "culture"?

In this chapter, I argue that culture does continue to be meaningful, if we can combine the earlier idea of culture as "the way of life of a people" with a more contemporary concept of culture as "the information and identities available from the global cultural supermarket" – culture, roughly speaking, as shaped by the state as opposed to culture as shaped by the market. I try to do this through a theory of the cultural shaping of self, and from there explore questions of cultural identity: How do we formulate – and have formulated for us – who, culturally, we are? This discussion sets the stage for our later chapters' examinations of Japanese artists, American religious seekers, and Hong Kong intellectuals in their different yet parallel efforts to define themselves against both their particular cultural background and the global cultural supermarket.

The rise and fall of "culture"

Before its anthropological incarnation, "culture" meant refinement. Culture, in the nineteenth-century humanist Matthew Arnold's words, was "a study of perfection . . . an inward condition of the mind and spirit. . . . Culture indefatigably tries . . . to draw ever nearer to a sense of what is . . . beautiful, graceful, and becoming."[1] Culture was "the *best* that has been thought and said",[2] an ideal that most of us, living our ordinary, unrefined lives, could never hope to attain. This idea of culture remains in use today: I am thought to be "cultured" if I can sit through an opera without falling asleep and can comment knowingly – or at least pretend to comment knowingly – on the subtleties of literature and art.

Cultural anthropologists have reworked the concept of culture to apply not just to a learned and sophisticated few, but to all human beings. In Clifford Geertz's words, "Culture . . . is not just an ornament of human existence but . . . an essential condition for it. . . . There is no such thing as a human nature independent of culture."[3] As human beings, we are all cultured.

The history of this reworking of culture is well known to anthropologists. Edward Burnett Tylor and Lewis Henry Morgan are often credited with founding the science of anthropology in the late nineteenth century; to simplify a complex process, they took Arnold's concept of culture as refinement and applied it to cultural evolution, which involved the progression of the human race, from, in Morgan's famous terms, "Savagery to Barbarism to Civilization." All human beings, in their view, however "primitive," had the potential to become "cultured," which seemed to mean like the Europeans and Americans of their day. Franz Boas, in the decades after Morgan and Tylor, is widely credited as being the first anthropologist to conceive not of "culture" but of "cultures" – to show that there is not just one universal culture that human beings are in various stages of attaining, but rather that each different society has its own culture, unique and coherent, cultures which cannot be judged against one another.[4] This view has prevailed for most of the past century.

The history of cultural anthropology since Boas have been full of arguments about the particular meanings of culture. To what extent does culture determine individual behavior, and to what extent are individuals free to use culture for their own ends? What is the relation of culture to social and economic structures? To language? To the natural environment? How can we understand the relation between cultural ideals and reality, between what people say they do and what they actually do? Is culture best understood as public or private – as within people's minds, or within the symbols that convey meaning between minds?[5] Underlying these disputes, however, one basic definition of culture has been adhered to. "Culture," this definition has it, is "the way of life of a people."[6] For all the differences in formulations of culture between different anthropologists, the assumption that all held in common was that culture consisted of bounded units, enabling

Clifford Geertz to write of the contrasting Javanese, Balinese, and Moroccan concepts of self, just as Ruth Benedict, almost half a century earlier, had so distinctly portrayed the cultural values of the Zuñi, the Dobu, and the Kwakiutl.[7] The assumption common to these writers is that there are discrete patterns of cognition, values, and behavior that members of each of these groups share in common, in contrast to members of other groups. This is what cultural anthropologists have studied, and have believed in; this has been the basis of the discipline of anthropology – at least in its American if not its British variant.[8]

Ruth Benedict, through her best-selling 1934 book *Patterns of Culture*, was most responsible for making "culture" in its anthropological sense into a household word. As Margaret Mead later wrote:

> When Ruth Benedict began her work in anthropology . . . the term "culture" . . . was part of the vocabulary of a small and technical group of professional anthropologists. That today the modern world is on such easy terms with the concept of culture, that the words "in our culture" slip from the lips of educated men and women almost as effortlessly as do the phrases that refer to period and to place, is in very great part due to this book.[9]

As Mead's words indicate, "culture" – and an array of accompanying concepts, such as "culture shock" – have entered the mainstream today: we can speak of "Japanese culture," or "French culture," or "Chinese culture," or "Mexican culture," or "African-American culture" with the taken-for-granted assumption that what this label refers to will be more or less understood.

It is ironic, however, that anthropologists, the bringers of the concept of culture to the larger public, are now themselves abandoning this concept. As one anthropologist has recently noted, in today's anthropological writing,

> While the adjective "cultural" continues as an acceptable predicate . . . such phrases as "culture" or "Kwakiutl culture" or "the culture of the Nuer" are of increasingly infrequent occurrence. . . . When the word "culture" does occur, it frequently bears . . . quotation marks . . . [showing] the writer's ambivalence, self-consciousness, or censure.[10]

Various anthropologists of late have sought to get rid of the term "culture" for a number of interlocking reasons, but one of the most pivotal is that, in today's world of massive global flows of people, capital, and ideas, a "culture" can't easily be thought of as something that people in a certain place on the globe have or are in common, as opposed to other peoples elsewhere. As Ulf Hannerz has written, "Humankind has . . . bid farewell to that world which could . . . be seen as a cultural mosaic, of separate pieces with hard, well-defined edges. Cultural connections increasingly reach across the world."[11]

According to some contemporary commentators (more often from the new, amorphous field of cultural studies than from anthropology), we have come to live in a world of culture as fashion, in which each of us can pick and choose cultural identities like we pick and choose clothes. As Jean-François Lyotard has written:

> Eclecticism is the degree zero of contemporary general culture: one listens to reggae, watches a western, eats McDonald's food for lunch and local cuisine for dinner, wears Paris perfume in Tokyo and "retro" clothes in Hong Kong; knowledge is a matter for TV games.[12]

Embodying such claims, a Hong Kong newspaper article describes members of a motorcycle gang in China as obsessed by Harley Davidsons and the American dream of freedom. When the reporter asks why, he is told, "Cultures . . . are like the dishes on a table. You just pick up what you like."[13] "Culture," in line with these formulations, may be defined as "the information and identities available from the global cultural supermarket."[14]

Both these concepts of culture have considerable truth to them, but neither is adequate to describe the culturally complex world in which we live. Let me first discuss culture as "the way of life of a people." Clearly there remain elements of a "shared way of life" in different societies in the world. Language undoubtedly molds the thinking of members of these societies in different ways; there remain distinct patterns of childrearing that shape distinct ways of thinking; governments shape the thinking of their citizens through public schooling; mass media in different societies serve to create their "imagined communities"[15] as opposed to those of other societies. The nationally shaped cultures of societies such as Japan, China, and the United States do indeed exist. Anyone who stands on a Tokyo street corner for more than a few seconds, watching how people behave toward one another, can't help but realize that this is Japan, bearing a distinct culture, unlike anywhere else; and the same exercise can be repeated on street corners the world over.

Indeed, it may be that this book underemphasizes culture as "the way of life of a people." I focus in this book on cultural identity – how people comprehend who, culturally, they are – more than on culture as studied by outsiders: anthropologists examining patterns of language, knowledge, and social organization that may shape the way of life of people in a society beyond their own awareness. By focusing on people's awareness of culture, we may see culture as more contested than taken for granted, as more chosen than given, even though the latter too may be of fundamental importance in understanding culture.

But despite this, it seems undeniable that culture as "the way of life of a people" is today problematic: there is so much diversity and inter-relation within each different society that we can no longer easily speak of "Japanese culture," or "American culture," or "Chinese culture" as unified, distinctive wholes, as opposed to other unified, distinctive wholes. What values do the Japanese college professor, laborer, house-wife, feminist, and punk rocker all share, as opposed to all their American counterparts? What behaviors do the American funda-mentalist Christian, lesbian separatist, inner-city drug dealer, yuppie stockbroker, Vietnamese immigrant, and Hasidic Jew all share, as opposed to all Japanese or Chinese? Might it not be that the Tokyo rock musician has more, culturally, in common with his counterpart in Seattle than with his own grandparents? That two New York and Shanghai executives linked through their Internet connections share more of a common culture than does either with the janitors that clean her office? Maybe not; but the very fact that these questions can seriously be posed reveals the erosion of culture as the way of life of a particular people in a particular place, as opposed to other people in other places. That concept of culture is not enough.

Our other concept of culture – culture as "the information and identi-ties available from the global cultural supermarket" – seems even more problematic. Clearly culture has become in part a matter of personal taste; to a degree, we seem to pick and choose culturally who we are, in the music we listen to, the food we eat, and perhaps even the religion we practice. However, our choices are not free, but conditioned by our age, class, gender, and level of affluence, and by the national culture to which we belong, among other factors. The way of life and social world within which we have been formed as human beings, as well as the ongoing social world in which we live – the different groups of people around us, whose opinions we can't help but pay great attention to – show that free choice is largely a myth. Despite such objections, how-ever, there is a degree of validity to this concept of culture. There is a sense in which we who live among the affluent 10 or 15 percent of the world's population do wander through a "cultural supermarket," choosing, albeit in a highly conditioned way, the identities we perform within our social worlds.

These two concepts of culture – culture as "the way of life of a people" and culture as "the information and identities available from the global cultural supermarket" – both serve to describe aspects of today's world, but neither is sufficient to enable a real understanding of what culture means.[16] One reason why they are each insufficient is that they represent two opposing forces shaping culture today: the forces of state and of market.

Culture, state, and market

Anthropologists traditionally conceived of culture on the basis of field-work in tribal societies; they could, to a degree anyway, speak on this basis of culture as "the way of life of a people." Today, however, there are very few tribes left, at least as anthropologists traditionally thought of them: as groups with their own separate cultures, largely isolated from the world. Members of tribes once studied by anthropologists may now work as construction workers and stockbrokers, and watch *Titanic* and *Baywatch*. Anthropologists sometimes now investigate how tribes enact their cultures before tourists for their livelihoods; one recent account discusses how the Maasai in Kenya perform their culture for busloads of first-world visitors. During their performance, the Maasai are not permitted "to wear their digital watches, T-shirts, or football socks, and all radios, Walkmen, metal containers, plastics, aluminum cans, and mass-produced kitchen equipment must be locked away and hidden from the tourist view."[17] Tribes such as this one now belong to the same world that the rest of us belong to.

However, culture as "the way of life of a people" does clearly continue to exist in today's world in large part because of states and their molding of their citizens. Almost all the land in the world today is controlled by states – as Clifford Geertz has remarked, virtually every "spot on the globe is . . . included in a bounded continuous stretch of space called the Republic of this, the People's Republic of that, the Union, Kingdom, Emirate, Confederation, State, or Principality of something or other"[18] – and so too almost all the people. Culture as "the way of life of a people" is in today's world almost everywhere shaped by national states.

Anthropologists, in their predilection toward tribal societies, did not study national societies until relatively late in the discipline's history. It was World War II that led many anthropologists to turn their attention to national societies. If Ruth Benedict's *Patterns of Culture* compared three tribal societies, her second great book, *The Chrysanthemum and the Sword*, dealt with Japan – an effort to understand "the mind of the enemy" that was influential in shaping American policy in its occupation of Japan after World War II.[19] "National character" studies of societies such as the United States and Russia were published at roughly the same time, analyzing the "way of life" of these societies partly in terms of their common patterns of childrearing. However, it has only been in recent decades that anthropologists and other social scientists have begun to look critically at the particular ways in which states shape "the way of life of a people" for their own ends. Books such as Benedict Anderson's *Imagined Communities* and Hobsbawm and Ranger's edited collection, *The Invention of Tradition*, show how "cultural tradition" is very much the product of the contemporary state;[20] "culture," books such as these show, is not intrinsic and primordial, but manipulated and perhaps invented by the state for the sake of its own legitimation.

Loyalty to nation seems new in human history. The matter is unclear, but it appears that the empires and kingdoms of past history did not, for the most part, breed mass loyalty: one's loyalty, for most people, was to one's village, possibly to one's religion or one's ethnic group, but not to any nation. Nationalism emerged as an ideology only in the late eighteenth century, in the period prior to the French Revolution; the German philosopher Herder was the first to assert that "each national group has its own *Volksgeist* or *Nationalgeist* . . . its own . . . customs, mores, beliefs, psyche, and worldview."[21] States over the last two centuries have used such idealized concepts of the nation to justify their molding of disparate groups of people into a common citizenry, accepting that molding as the natural order of things. States seek to justify and legitimate their pursuits of power, shaping the thinking of their citizens through public education and through mass media. How many times this century have we heard states justify their aggression by making such statements as "we must defend our way of life"?

This shaping is remarkably effective. To speak personally, despite having striven as an anthropologist to see through and become detached from my national moldings, I still find myself unwittingly moved by the "The Star Spangled Banner"; the mantra of "one nation under God," repeated every school day of my childhood in the Pledge of Allegiance, sticks to me yet. "My nation is special, divinely ordained": might I not still believe such a thing in some unexamined corner of my mind? This is the case not just for me: 77 percent of Americans in one survey say they would be willing to fight in a war for their country,[22] defending "the way of life of the American people" – this reflects the extraordinary power of the state's molding.

Patriotism is not always a delusion; there may be values in one's country that are worth defending, even dying for. Looking, however, at the wars fought in recent history, from the patriot fighting for Nazi Germany, to the American in Vietnam fighting "Godless communism," to the Serb righteously engaged in "ethnic cleansing," it is hard not to shudder at how wrong one's country so often is, and how deluded citizens so often have been in what they are willing to die for. The nineteenth-century American military leader Stephen Decatur once famously proclaimed, "Our country! In her intercourse with foreign nations may she always be in the right; but our country, right or wrong!" – in other words, "Even if our country is wrong, we should fight for her because she is our country." But why? Why should one stand up for one's country when one's country is wrong? That well over a hundred million people have died this century fighting wars for their countries indicates the power of the state's molding as to its holy rightness; "suppose they gave a war and nobody came" was a wishful 1960s' slogan and no more.

States may be more or less warlike, and more or less direct or subtle in their shaping of their citizens; but that shaping is today ubiquitous, and all but taken for granted. "The idea of a man without a nation seems to impose a strain on the modern imagination," writes Ernest Gellner. "A man must have a nationality as he must have a nose and two ears. . . . Having a nation is not an inherent attribute of humanity, but it has now come to appear as such."[23] States throughout recent history have culturally shaped their citizens to believe that state and citizen are one within "the way of life of a people," and citizens have for the most part believed this without question.

However, states' molding of their citizens into a common "way of life" is under challenge today. It is under challenge in part because of the resurgence of ethnicity and ethnic identity. Across the globe – from the Ainu to the Zulu, from the Hutu to the Quebecois – we see the re-emergence of ethnic identity apart from the state, as people try to assert identities not wholly subsumed by the state:

> For a long time it appeared that ethnic groups were slowly being absorbed into the nations in which they lived. They were viewed as holdovers from another era, and it was thought that gradually as the people modernized, they would naturally abandon their ethnic identity in favor of a national one. . . . Instead, ethnic identities have grown stronger in the modern world.[24]

In some places – Yugoslavia, Rwanda – struggles over ethnic identity are drenched in blood, as ethnicities struggle to carve nations for themselves, and to carve away all other ethnicities from that nation. In other places, such as the United States, ethnic identity tends to be seen more as an adjunct to one's existing national identity: many have come to see themselves as African-American or Hispanic-American or Asian-American today rather than simply American, a choice of identity that might never have occurred to their grandparents or parents. In any case, ethnic identity has emerged as a powerful force in today's world, a counterforce to national identity.

However, it is, I argue, not ethnic identity, but identity as proffered through the market that is finally the greatest force eroding national identity in the world today. Ethnic identity may be opposed to the existing state, but is fundamentally of the same conceptual order as the state – like identity as proffered by the state, ethnic identity is often based on the idea of a particular people belonging to a particular place. Market identity, on the other hand, is based on belonging to no particular place, but rather to the market in both its material and cultural forms – in market-based identity, one's home is all the world.

There are two forms of the market: the material supermarket, bringing a flood of products from all over the world into every corner of the world, and the cultural supermarket, bringing a flood of information and potential identities into every corner of the world. Probably the cultural supermarket, like the material supermarket, has existed in rudimentary form for as long as there have been human beings: trade goods travel far from their source; ideas also travel far and wide, as anthropologists have long known. However, the cultural supermarket has extraordinarily expanded, exploded of late. If cultural identity as found through the state, in its molding of "the way of life of a people," seems largely a product of the past two centuries, cultural identity as found through the market – the information and identities available from the cultural supermarket – is in its present expanded form a product of the past few decades. I argue that people throughout the affluent, mass-mediated world today may be as molded by the material and cultural supermarkets as by the state.

This manipulation is as powerful and as bizarre as manipulation by the state: is believing, at least subliminally, that one's new toothpaste will give one "sex appeal" any less extraordinary than being willing to die for one's country? But this manipulation may be more gentle in its means than manipulation by the state: a manipulation more of seduction than coercion, of the blandishments of advertising rather than the force of law. This manipulation has different meanings and implications depending on the degree of affluence of one's society and self – those who are affluent and plugged into media may have more room for choice than those who are not. But this manipulation is everywhere profound; today, the molding of the state is everywhere being eroded by the molding of the market.[25]

This erosion takes different forms in different places. North Korea has almost entirely shut out the market, to its ruinous economic detriment: its survival will depend upon its becoming more open to the worldwide market. Iran, with its spiritual police in search of satellite dishes, and its diatribes against "Westernization," until recently has set itself in clear opposition to the market's attempted erosions, but those erosions, judging from news reports, inexorably continue. China, embarking at present on what has been called "capitalism with Chinese characteristics," attempts to defend itself from the market with its "spiritual civilization" campaigns, but finds that most of its citizens are less enthralled by the state's occasional posters of warning against capitalistic decadence and spiritual pollution than by the lure of the shop windows' stereos and computers. Japan has become so open to and over-run with foreign – Western – cultural forms that conservative commentators write darkly of how Japan has lost its identity; but many Japanese consumers of these foreign cultural forms don't seem to care. The United States' Declaration of Independence, in its promise that every citizen has "certain inalienable Rights," among them "Life, Liberty, and the pursuit of Happiness," seems almost a template for consumer choice, and yet the conflict of state and market is readily apparent in areas such as religion, as we will see. In short, there is not a society in the world today that escapes the conflict of state and market in the molding of citizens' "way of life."

The gap between our two concepts of culture thus results at least in part from the conflict between the principles of state and of market. This conflict has been explored in a large-scale theoretical sense in a number of interesting recent books, some of which I discuss in Chapter 5, but has not often been explored in smaller scale, at the level of people's minds and how they construct their senses of identity. Who do we most deeply think we are, culturally? Do we feel that we are most essentially members of a particular society in contrast to other societies, whose particular way of life we cherish and defend? Or do we feel that we are most essentially consumers of culture, believing that we shape our lives from a worldwide array of cultural forms? If we feel, as probably do most of us, that we have both these senses of identity, how do we reconcile them – how do we resolve their contradiction? The state's underlying claim is that "you are a citizen of your country and should defend it and uphold its values," or more indirectly, reflecting states' appropriation of culture, "you belong to your culture, and should uphold its particular cultural tradition." The market's underlying claim is that "you can buy and do and be anything you want; you can pursue happiness in your own way, as you see fit," from whatever worldwide forms you find to your liking. How do we weave our senses of identity between the contradictory yet taken-for-granted propositions that "you should cherish and protect your own nation and culture" and that "you should be free to shape your life as you choose"?

This book is about how particular people in three societies struggle to formulate their senses of cultural identity within and between these contradictory principles – the principles of state and market as lodged within their minds. But before turning to the Japanese artists, American religious seekers, and Hong Kong intellectuals that make up the heart of this book, we need a theoretical structure to enable us more thoroughly to analyze their accounts of who, culturally, they are. Let me now offer a phenomenological theory of the cultural shaping of self, a theory focusing on how selves comprehend the cultural shaping of their identities.

The cultural shaping of self

We have discussed two very different concepts of culture set forth by scholars today, culture as "the way of life of a people" and culture as "the information and identities available from the cultural supermarket." Recent concepts of self show a similar conceptual dichotomy. Clifford Geertz, in one of the most famous anthropological statements on the matter, argues that the Western notion of the person as an independent, bounded, unique being is "a rather peculiar idea within the context of the world's cultures."[26] Dorinne Kondo writes of "seemingly incorrigible Western assumptions about . . . the boundedness and fixity of personal identity. . . . Contemporary anthropologists . . . myself included, are in the process of grappling with the difficulties and paradoxes of demonstrating the cultural specificity of selfhood."[27] Different cultures have different culturally shaped selves, she argues, that can't be equated; but Western anthropologists, trapped in ethnocentric assumptions, have failed to comprehend that up until now.

On the other hand, other thinkers of late have focused on a "postmodern" self unbounded by any specific culture. Robert Jay Lifton has written of "the protean self," whereby we endlessly shift and weave and recreate ourselves:

> We are becoming fluid and many-sided. Without quite realizing it, we have been evolving a sense of self appropriate to the restlessness and flux of our time. . . . Any one of us can, at any moment, have access to any image or idea originating anywhere in the contemporary world, or from any cultural moment of the entire human past[28]

through the power of mass media, and can shape ourselves accordingly. Madan Sarup has written of how, in today's postmodern world, "through the market, one can put together elements of the complete 'Identikit' of a DIY [do-it-yourself] self."[29]

These two ideas of self echo our concepts of culture: both self and culture are seen by some as belonging to a particular place, bounding and shaping the beings therein, and by others as radically open and free. This contradiction can best be resolved by considering self and culture in a common phenomenological framework: a framework based on how people experience the world.

I maintain that selves of different societies may be compared as physically separate consciousnesses experiencing the world in part through that separation. There is no doubt that selves are culturally shaped: selves of different cultural backgrounds clearly have different ways of experiencing the world. It also seems true that the fragmented postmodern self discussed by many analysts is to a degree empirically true in the world today. However, I argue that underlying these formulations there is a universal basis of self, as both interdependent and independent, as a part of and apart from other selves. The self universally is made of past memories and future anticipation linked to an ever-shifting present; selves tell themselves in an ongoing construction made of words; and selves live in a world of others ever present in mind, but that others cannot ever fully understand.

The cultural shapings of self occur at what may analytically be viewed as three separate levels of consciousness. There is, most deeply, what we might call the taken-for-granted level of shaping: our shaping by a particular language and set of social practices that condition us as to how we comprehend self and world. This level of shaping is for the most part below the level of consciousness. Because we think in language, we can't easily comprehend how that language shapes our thinking; because we live through taken-for-granted social practices (as signified by the concept of *habitus*, referring to the processes through which self and social world ever shape one another[30]), we can't easily comprehend how they lead us to live our lives in some ways and not in others.

How can learning a new language affect this "taken-for-granted" thinking?

This level is difficult to get to: by the very fact it is taken for granted, it is not spoken of. In my classes, I occasionally try to plumb this level by seeking to find what shocks my students. If I say, "God is dead!", few people blink; if I shout, "Democracy is a fraud!" most people only shrug; when I proclaim, in Hong Kong, "China be damned!" few people pay much attention. But when I pull a Hong Kong $100 bill from my pocket (about US$13) and rip it into tiny pieces (or even better, borrow a student's cash for the occasion, later to be returned), the entire class gasps in disbelief. This gasp indicates that the taken for granted has been touched, breached; I have, by my bizarre behavior, violated that which most people consider to be unquestionable, and can thereby bring the unquestionable up for questioning.

This level forms the bedrock basis upon which people live, even though we mostly don't realize it. A key basis for anthropology's traditional formulations of culture has been that the anthropologist, doing fieldwork in a society beyond his own, can apprehend the taken for granted that the society's members cannot – and may thereby unwittingly threaten that society's taken-for-granted realm, erode its unquestioned assumptions, and even endanger its cultural survival. The stereotypical classical anthropologist doing fieldwork in remote, "untouched" places with his jeep, his gun, his cans of food, could only have dramatically transformed the people he encountered (as the movie *The Gods Must Be Crazy* showed in its Hollywood fashion): after beholding the anthropologist's magic, those people could never be the same again, for the world, and knowledge of the world, had intruded. They could never again take their own way of life for granted as *the* way of life.

This exposure of the taken for granted is, however, true not only for remote others but for ourselves as well. The history of social science, from Marx and Freud to Pierre Bourdieu, Michel Foucault, and Ernest Becker, has been one of progressively uncovering the taken for granted of contemporary society. Marx showed how money was not natural but a human creation and fetish; Freud revealed that our conscious rationality is a thin film over the irrational unconscious that controls us; Becker explored how the meanings of life we unthinkingly live by are fictional. These thinkers were engaged in the exposure of the taken for granted, to render it taken for granted no longer; and yet an inevitable taken-for-granted realm always remains. We come to consciousness as children after we have been personally and culturally shaped: as Berger and Luckmann note, "language appears to the child as inherent in the nature of things, and he cannot grasp the notion of its conventionality";[31] as Becker writes:

Since the child is partly conditioned before he can manipulate symbols, he is formed without being able to put any distance between himself and what is happening to him. . . . The result is that the person acts out his hero-style automatically and uncritically for the rest of his life.[32]

We may, through the works of thinkers like these, intellectually come to understand the arbitrariness of our taken-for-granted realm, but this probably won't alter the hold of that realm over our lives.

A second, middle level of the self's cultural shaping is at what I call the *shikata ga nai* level. *Shikata ga nai* is a Japanese phrase meaning "it can't be helped"; "there's nothing I can do about it." This level is that at which we do as we must as members of our societies whether we like it or not: we must go to school and then go to work, pay our taxes, act like "men" and "women," retire at the appropriate age, and stop at stoplights, among many, many other things. This level of cultural shaping is experienced by the self not as underlying the conscious self, known only as it is forced into consciousness, but as extrinsic to the self: the social and institutional pressures upon the self that it can't fully resist. Whereas the taken-for-granted level can be approached only indirectly, since once it is touched upon it is no longer fully taken for granted, the *shikata ga nai* level is ubiquitous in the accounts of people of three societies I've interviewed – the very terms *shikata ga nai* (Japanese), *mòuh baahnfaat là* (Cantonese), "there's nothing I can do about it," indicate how readily this realm is recognized. "I don't like having to smile and be polite regardless of how I really feel/kiss up to the boss all the time even though he's an idiot/force my kids to study even though studying robs them of their childhood . . . but *shikata ga nai/mòuh baahnfaat là/*that's life."

This level of cultural shaping is more important than traditional analysts of culture have tended to recognize. Much human behavior is based not on the underlying values we hold, but on our compliance to the pressures exerted by the social world around us, which can be resisted only at a high price. Everyone lives by cultural and social rules whose existence they are well aware of, but that they can't resist; their social world mostly rules them, as it rules us all. In the explanations that the people in this book give of their lives, the dominant form that the *shikata ga nai* level takes is that of the world of other people. These may be other people at large in one's society, with general values that may differ from one's own but to which one must more or less conform, or other people in particular, the people with whom one lives in ongoing dances of sporadic challenge and frequent compromise. The Japanese

artists, American religious seekers, and Hong Kong intellectuals portrayed in this book are all immersed in their worlds of *shikata ga nai*,
within and against which they struggle to shape their lives and paths.

A third, most shallow and most fully conscious level of the self's
cultural shaping involves "the cultural supermarket." This is the level
at which selves sense that they freely pick and choose the ideas they
want to live by. In a given (affluent) society, one person may be devoted
to Western classical music, another to Indian ragas, a third to grunge
rock, and a fourth to reggae; one person may become a conservative,
another a liberal, another a fascist, and still another an anarchist; one
person may become a Christian, another a Buddhist, a third an atheist,
and a fourth a believer in a UFO cult. Unlike one's interest in music or
sports, one's political convictions or religious beliefs may not be seen as
chosen: "God chose this path for me." But to the extent that one was
not born into these convictions and beliefs but arrived at them consciously, then they must be considered choices of sorts. Despite latter-
day naturalizations, they represent one path out of many that might
have been taken, one selection out of many that might have been made
from the cultural supermarket.

Of course, as mentioned earlier, this choice of interests, values, and
identities is not really free. People pick and choose themselves in
accordance with their class, gender, religious belief, ethnicity, and
citizenship, as well as all the exigencies of their own personal molding,
from a cultural supermarket that heavily advertises some choices and
suppresses others; they pick and choose themselves in negotiation with
and performance for others. Choice is not free, but it seems to be free:
as if, from the vast array of available cultural choices as to what one
might believe, how one might live, we make our choices and live and
believe accordingly. For the most part, we shape ourselves in ways
close to home, in congruence with our membership in our home
societies. However, we may, to a degree anyway, also shape ourselves
from beyond those bounds: the cultural supermarket and the identities
it offers are global.

These three levels of the self's cultural shaping may be thought of
very broadly as (1) deep shaping taking place beyond the self's control
and beyond all but indirect comprehension; (2) middle-level shaping
taking place beyond the self's full control but within its comprehension;
and (3) shallow shaping taking place with what the self sees as full
control and comprehension. These levels are too simple, in that people
often don't make these distinctions clearly; but people do recognize
these distinctions once they are pointed out: the distinction between
what you do without thinking, what you do because you have to, and

what you do because you choose to. Each of these levels shapes the levels above it. On the basis of their deepest level of cultural shaping, selves more or less accept the coercions of the middle level of shaping; having been shaped at these two deeper levels of shaping, selves at the shallowest level, to a degree culturally shape themselves.

In terms of our two concepts of culture, it is, if not typical, at least stereotypical that culture as "the way of life of a people" is to be found at the two deepest levels of the self's cultural shaping, and culture as "the global cultural supermarket" is at the shallowest level. People growing up in traditional societies who then become exposed to the cultural supermarket stereotypically illustrate this pattern: the peasant who acquires a transistor radio and a taste for Coca-Cola might see the latter as the stuff of Western affluence she can consume, as against the backdrop of the still taken-for-granted ways of her traditional culture. But for many people in today's affluent world, it is the realm of the cultural supermarket which is taken for granted: not in terms of the self's actual choices, which are at the more or less fully conscious level, but in terms of the underlying assumption that one is free to choose aspects of one's identity. This is a pattern we will see clearly in the chapters that follow: people live within the global cultural supermarket, whose putative freedom of choice they take for granted; but they may long for a sense of home, a sense of fixed belonging that the cultural supermarket's aisles cannot provide. Thus they construct their sense of home from the cultural supermarket's shelves, and endeavor to forget that their cultural home is their latter-day construction of home.

But this gets ahead of our analysis. Let us now examine more closely the meaning of cultural identity.

Cultural identity

Dictionary definitions refer to identity as "the condition of being a specified person or thing"; in contrast to this, postmodern discussions define identity in a far looser way. "Identities," Stuart Hall writes, "are . . . points of temporary attachment to the subject positions which discursive practices construct for us" [33] – fixed identities, by this definition, don't exist. I think of identity between these two extremes: identity is neither as clear as the dictionaries claim (one's "specified person" containing, beneath the veneer of name, many contradictions, holes, gaps) nor as flimsy as the postmodernists claim (each of us being repositories of our own unique sets of memories and hopes, that define each of us as distinct, self-conscious beings). I define identity, after Anthony Giddens,[34] as the ongoing sense the self has of who it is, as conditioned through its ongoing interactions with others. Identity is how the self conceives of itself, and labels itself.

There is both personal and collective identity, the former referring to one's sense of oneself apart from others – one's sense of who one uniquely is as an individual – and the latter referring to who one senses oneself to be in common with others. The balance of these modes of identity widely vary. In many societies in the world, "finding oneself," the oft-claimed prerogative of Americans to quit one's job or leave one's family or embark on any number of quirky paths to find one's true identity, might seem absurdly irresponsible, given the social roles and collective identities that one holds, or is obliged to hold. Still, both modes of identity seem to exist everywhere. The elements of collective identity include gender and social class, both of which are essential to the way most of us conceive of ourselves. But in this book I deal with cultural identity, in all the ambiguities of that term: one's sense of culturally belonging to a given society, or, beyond that, to the global cultural supermarket. In terms of our previous analysis, we can think of cultural identity as a matter of how people conceive of who, culturally, they are through their choices on the cultural supermarket level on the basis of their shaping at the two deeper levels. As we will see, some people seek to justify their choices on the cultural supermarket level through their claims of a cultural identity imprinted at the two deeper levels. Others deny any deeper cultural shaping: who they are, culturally, is their own free choice, they claim.

A key factor in cultural identity is national identity: as I earlier discussed, most people in today's world are socialized and propagandized to hold a national cultural identity. It may seem fashionable for many in affluent societies to downplay national identity: I've been in a number of conversations with sophisticated young Japanese and Americans and Hongkongese who claim that national identity means nothing to them. Yet when the discussion turns to certain sensitive topics – the behavior of Japanese in World War II, or the high American divorce rate and shattering of American families, or the Chineseness of young Hong Kong students who have little relation to China – the senses of national identity of these young cosmopolitans may unmistakably emerge: national identity is of sufficient importance for them to get in arguments over, despite their claims to be free of any such attachments.

Yet, as we have also seen earlier, national cultural identity is being eroded by the cultural supermarket. What would appear to signify the infringement of the market upon senses of national cultural identity is readily visible and audible throughout the world: the American pop tunes on radios across the globe, the Japanese comics sweeping East Asia, the Walkman, Coca-Cola, McDonald's, and Michael Jordan as worldwide icons. But it is not at all clear what relation these market and media products have to their consumers' senses of who, culturally, they are. Let us consider this in terms of food. The vast majority of eaters of, for example, sushi in America and McDonald's hamburgers in Japan and China may have little sense of making any statements about cultural identity through their consumption. However, at least some of these consumers definitely are making such statements. I have sat in a Japanese restaurant in the United States with a young woman telling me of her love for "the Orient" – she felt she had been born in the wrong society, of the wrong ethnicity; being all too blond, she contented herself with studying Japanese art and religion and eating sashimi once a week. And I have sat in McDonald's in a provincial Chinese city trying to read a book, only to be interrupted first by hamburger-chomping high school girls and then by McDonald's employees, telling me that they hated China and longed to go to Hong Kong and then to the United States, to find more "free" identities than they felt they could find in China.

Most people eating foreign foods bring no such intensity of feeling to their gustatory pleasures; most, it seems, have no particular dream of a foreign place that accompanies the falafel or tortillas or lasagna they consume. But the very fact of consuming foreign foods – the fact that some people seek out foreign tastes, while others shun them – is itself at least an implicit statement concerning cultural identity, of belonging to a worldwide cultural supermarket, as opposed to a single culture and cuisine. This is probably all the more true for consumers of foreign mass media. The Japanese aficionado of American jazz or the American fan of Japanese *anime* (animation) would almost certainly not assert that they are not Japanese or American, respectively. But the very fact that they choose these forms to follow rather than those of their home societies indicates their status as sophisticated consumers from the global cultural supermarket.

In terms of our three levels of cultural shaping, states attempt to inculcate national identity at the taken-for-granted level; mostly they more or less succeed, but to the extent that they fail, national identity becomes a matter of *shikata ga nai,* an identity that, given this world, you have no choice but to affirm at certain points – immigration counters, patriotic holidays perhaps – rather than an identity you adhere to as "natural." Ethnic identity is often asserted as being more natural than national identity: "The government and schools tell us we're Spanish/Nigerian/Japanese, but really we're Basque/Ibo/Ainu."

However, in at least some cases, ethnic identity is not an identity into which one was raised, but is instead one that is subsequently assumed: for example, the American of Chinese ancestry who decides in college that she is Chinese despite having almost no knowledge of Chinese language or culture. The cultural supermarket level of shaping may, as earlier discussed, serve to undermine and replace senses of national and ethnic identity at the taken-for-granted level. This may mean that the realm of the taken for granted is shrinking. On the other hand, the realm of the cultural supermarket may be expanding, as the cultural identity that people are "naturally" given becomes increasingly conscious, and as the cultural identity that people can create from the cultural supermarket becomes more wide open with possibilities.

However, it seems that for many people within today's affluent world, the principles of both national identity and culturally supermarketed identity – the principles of both state and market – remain thoroughly taken for granted. "One should stand up for one's country and protect its cultural tradition"/"One should be free to shape one's life as one chooses" – we tend to believe both of these principles, despite the fact that they are contradictory. Can one be free not to stand up for one's country, but to choose what one wants instead? One reason why mass-mediated democracy has swept the globe as a means of legitimation is that it is the form of government that most mirrors the workings of the market, allowing the state a veneer of market legitimacy. One reason why human rights have swept the globe as a value is that a key such right is that of self-determination: the freedom to choose oneself, make oneself as one sees fit. These values, however laudable they may be in their own right, reflect the values of the market. People in affluent market-oriented states can't easily see the contradiction between state and market because both contradictory propositions underlie their senses of cultural identity. The contradiction is thus rendered largely invisible, but the contradiction remains, more or less, in all of us, as we will see throughout this book.

Let us now consider in more depth the cultural supermarket, and the illusion of free choice it may give to the selves who consume therein.

The cultural supermarket

The cultural supermarket bears some resemblance to its metaphorical root, the material supermarket. Just as the material supermarket has been transformed as to the scope of its goods in recent years – David Harvey has written that "the food market . . . looks very different from what it was twenty years ago. Kenyan haricot beans, Californian celery and avocados, North African potatoes, Canadian apples, and Chilean grapes all sit side by side in a British [or American or Japanese or any other affluent nation's] supermarket"[35] – so too has the cultural supermarket, thanks to television and computers. And just as in the material supermarket shelf space is unequally distributed – products like Coca-Cola being on the middle, easily seen shelves, other, less heavily advertised products being above the customer's head, and less noticeable – so too in the cultural supermarket. Those societies whose material goods are readily available in the world also have greater cultural influence in the world. "The United States," writes Robert Bocock, ". . . has come to epitomize the modern [worldwide] consumer's dreamland";[36] and certainly the world's cultural supermarket has more than its share of American "goods," in the influences of movies, music, and sports – America's celebrity culture, spread worldwide.

But the structure of the cultural supermarket is far more complex than this metaphor indicates; in its far-flung intangibility, it is more like a vast library than like a grocery store, more like the Internet than like a map of nations of the world. A key difference between the material supermarket and the cultural supermarket is that while in the former money is absolutely essential in order to consume its goods, for the latter, money is not necessarily required in order to consume. The goods in the cultural supermarket may be commodities, bought and sold, but they need not be: one may be profoundly influenced by a book or a television program despite, to a degree, the money one may or may not possess. Popular culture as broadcast and vended throughout the world is indeed disproportionately American, and yet one can find in the large music stores of wealthier societies the seldom-browsed bins containing Bolivian panpipes and Sufi chants; one can find in the largest bookstores books from the world over, at least to the extent that they have been translated. Yes, the shelves of the cultural supermarket are arranged in terms of money; but a multiplicity of information and potential identities can be found there. Every tome gathering dust in a library, every shortwave radio broadcast and Internet homepage, every T-shirt slogan are potential material for the cultural supermarket: all can provide a basis for the construction of one's cultural identity.

The information within the cultural supermarket may be categorized by its users in a number of different ways, but the two most readily available are (1) region of origin, and (2) realm of use. For most of the information in the cultural supermarket, we have some idea of where it comes from. This usually corresponds to culture as "the way of life of a people," as embodied in national culture: we refer to Indian music, Brazilian samba, French cuisine, and so on, in order to have a shorthand way with which to refer to these entities. These represent aisle signs, often of questionable validity but of considerable convenience, in labeling and dividing up the vast array of materials in the cultural supermarket for consumers' ease. As we will see, these claims may become particularly vital when applied to oneself; claims of "Japanese" art or "American" religion or "Chinese" values may seek to make what may seem a choice from the cultural supermarket into one's underlying essence – they may seek to make a choice not a choice.

There is also the realm of use. We fashion ourselves from the cultural supermarket in a number of areas, among them our choices in home decor, in food and clothing, in what we read, watch, and listen to in music, art, and popular culture, in our religious belief, and in ethnic and national identity itself: whether, in the United States, to identify oneself as Hispanic-American or as American; whether, in Hong Kong, to be Chinese or Hongkongese. These different shapings bear differing degrees of personal significance: one's choice of home decor, for example ("That Buddhist mandala in the living room? No, of course I don't believe in that stuff. I just though it looked neat"), may be of considerably less significance for one's sense of cultural identity than, for example, one's choice of religion, which may lie at the core of who one senses oneself to be. In this book, we will consistently see that the choices people make in the realms of artistic expression, religious belief, and cultural identity are of deep personal significance: we will find that choices from the cultural supermarket, unlike many choices from the material supermarket, are very often agonized over, for they may be of extraordinary importance to these people in defining what their lives are most essentially about.

The foregoing should not, however, be taken to mean that our choices from the cultural supermarket are free; rather, as earlier noted, our choices are restricted in a number of different senses. There is first of all the differential in receiving equipment for the cultural supermarket. One who is educated and affluent may possess optimal receiving equipment: access to and ability to make use of the repository of human thought contained in libraries, and access to the contemporary repositories of thought in the Internet and in mass media – the world assortment of newspapers, magazines, and compact disks available at key outlets throughout the world. A person with such advantages may make full use of the cultural supermarket, but many of the people in the world cannot – their access to the cultural supermarket is more limited, confined to whatever echoes of the cultural supermarket may reach their particular corner of the world. No doubt more people from rich societies than poor societies, and more people from the upper, affluent, educated classes in every society than the lower, poorer, less-educated classes have this optimal receiving equipment. It may be that the less sophisticated the receiving equipment you have, the more likely that you will be manipulated down the standard paths of Coca-Cola, Marlboro, Rambo, Doraemon, although there are certainly exceptions to this; and as anthropologists often note, how consumers in different societies actually interpret these various products may differ substantially from the plans of marketers.[37]

Beyond this, there is the fact that the choices each of us makes as to cultural identity are made not for ourselves but for performance for and in negotiation with others: we choose ourselves within the cultural supermarket with an eye to our social world. One's cultural identity is performed in that one must convince others as to its validity: one must have the knowledge and social grace to convince others that one is not an impostor. Efforts to this effect may be seen in many different social milieux, as we will discuss in later chapters, from the Japanese salaryman/rock musician who wears a short-hair wig to his office rather than get his hair cut, so that he can convince his fellow rock musicians that he is "for real," to the American spiritual seeker who pursues various religions despite the scorn of her husband, snickering that she "goes through religions like she goes through clothes," to the mainland Chinese woman in Hong Kong who wears expensive fashions but not with quite enough of a sense of style to disguise her mainland background from the disdainful eyes of Hong Kong people.

A wide range of cultural identities in this world is available for appropriation; but although culturally the world may be wide open, socially it is not. One's cultural choices must fit within one's social world, which is more limited. In a typical middle-class American neighborhood, I could probably become a Buddhist without alarming my neighbors, but I could not become an Islamic fundamentalist; I may study the Mbuti pygmies in an anthropology text, but were I to express beliefs such as theirs to my co-workers, I would at best be seen as eccentric, at worst as a lunatic. One's social world – outside one's mind, and more, as resident within one's mind – acts as a censor and gatekeeper, selecting from the range of possible cultural ideas one might appropriate only those that seem plausible and acceptable within it. One's social world particularly constrains one's choices in terms of such factors as class, gender, and age. The elderly woman who wears a miniskirt and the working-class kid who uses fancy foreign words are likely to learn quite rapidly, if they have any sensitivity at all to the cues of their social world, about the inappropriateness of their cultural choices.

Despite these strictures, there is often the effort to bring into one's social world what Pierre Bourdieu terms "cultural capital":[38] knowledge from the cultural supermarket that one can display to one's social credit, justifying and bolstering one's social position. One's interest, at least within some segments of American society, in Indian ragas as opposed to top 40 hits, or in Tibetan Buddhist writings as opposed to evangelical Christian tracts, is a way of advertising cosmopolitan discernment: my far-flung tastes may well be the servant of my local strategy of impressing the people around me. The matter of what from the cultural supermarket can provide status in a given social milieu is highly complex. Each social milieu has its rating system for information and identities from the cultural supermarket; individuals seek to attain maximum credit and credibility, not only through consumption within the existing cultural rating system, but also through bringing in new information and identities, whose high status they seek to establish. The criteria for the establishment of such status are thus highly specific and flexible; individuals play the game with an extraordinarily acute sense of its implicit rules and strategies.

But all this is not to claim that there is absolutely no room for individual choice from the cultural supermarket. Why does one person thrill to Bach, another to juju? Why does one person become a Christian, another a Buddhist? Why does one person revel in her ethnicity, while another spurns that ethnicity? Why does one person travel the world while another stays home? Much can be predicted about our choices by considering such factors as social class, educational level, income, gender, and age, as well as our personal histories, but not everything can be predicted. We are not slaves to the world around us, but have (in a social if not a philosophical sense) a certain degree of freedom in choosing who we are. This freedom may be highly limited, but it cannot be altogether denied.

The subjects of this book

The analysis of this chapter applies, I believe, to at least some degree to people in societies across the globe. However, it seems that many people in today's world don't think very much about the cultural supermarket and its impact upon their lives. To get a sense of this, try asking people where the food they buy at the supermarket comes from: "These bananas/papayas/mangoes/pineapples? I don't know, I guess they're from South America, or maybe the Pacific. I've never thought about it; I just eat them." "Where's this ice cream made? I don't know. Why do you ask? Why does it matter?" These people take for granted the array of worldwide foodstuffs available to them in their particular locale – they are highly unlikely to allow their choices to destabilize their senses of who, culturally, they are.

This seems also the case for the cultural supermarket: people may listen to reggae and practice yoga while stoutly insisting upon their identities as American, or British, or Japanese. I have discussed how cultural identity in today's developed world is underlain by two contradictory principles, those of the state and of the market. For many people in the developed world, these principles, because they are both nested in the taken-for-granted level, and because they are brought into play largely in different social contexts, are not seen as conflicting – people live with them both deep in mind. Most people in the affluent capitalist world live their lives immersed within the concerns of work, and family, and immediate social world, underlain by the assumption of a coherent national identity, and the assumption of the openness of the material and cultural markets from which they consume. These assumptions for most people need not be questioned; this is what I have learned from my interviews with a range of people in several different societies.

Some, however, do question. Immigrants may find themselves asking, "Who am I? Where, really, is my home? This new place where I live: can this be my home? Or will my home always be the place I've left behind?" Members of minority ethnic groups may find themselves asking, for example, "Am I American? Or am I African-American? Or am I African, exiled through slavery to a foreign land? Maybe I'm all these things at different times; but still, who, really, am I?"

Cultural identity may also seem problematic to those who are not necessarily immigrants or of minority ethnicity, but who are engaged in pursuits that somehow bring to consciousness the contradiction between home cultural identity and the cultural supermarket. Artists and musicians may create within what they have been taught is their own cultural tradition, but wonder, "What is the relation of that tradition to how I live my life today?"; or they may create within a worldwide array of cultural forms, and wonder, "Where is my own cultural background? Where are my roots? Do I have any roots?" Religious seekers may follow the dominant religious traditions of their own society, but wonder, "How can I know if this is true? If I'd been born in some other society, I might not think it's true"; or they may follow the paths of other religious traditions and face self-doubt as a result: "Why don't the people around me see the value of this path? What's wrong with them? What's wrong with me?" Intellectuals in non-

Western societies may struggle within the gap between their Western-based training and outlook, and their sense of belonging to their own societies: "If I'm Western in my professional outlook, what of my identity? Has that been Westernized too? Am I simply more sophisticated than my fellow citizens, or have I been intellectually colonized?" People such as these may painfully struggle to comprehend who they are between self as defined by national culture and self as defined by the global cultural supermarket.

In this book, I examine members of three groups that broadly match the categories described above: Japanese artists and musicians, traditional and contemporary; American religious seekers, Christian and Buddhist; and Hong Kong intellectuals, Chinese and Western in orientation. In Japan, the cultural supermarket's interplay with national culture is readily apparent in the arts. Traditional Japanese arts such as *koto* and dance have long been more or less in decline in Japan, with some traditional artists claiming to be the last guardians of the Japaneseness their fellow Japanese have lost. Some contemporary artists – rock and jazz musicians, abstract painters – view their Japaneseness as an unfortunate cultural obstacle, preventing them from excelling at their imported arts; but others seek, from within these arts, to rediscover and reassert their Japaneseness. But how can they convince themselves that they have found Japaneseness?

In the United States, the cultural supermarket's interplay with national culture is apparent in the realm of religion. American evangelical Christians may believe that the United States is "one nation under God" that has forgotten the truth of God, but other Americans may view their society as a land of the individual "pursuit of happiness," and may happily stroll the aisles of the cultural supermarket in search of any religion that suits their tastes. Still others dream of creating an alternative "Buddhist America," but how could such an alternative United States ever prevail as anything other than one more consumer choice?

In Hong Kong, the cultural supermarket's interplay with national culture is apparent in the realm of politics. Since 1 July 1997, Hong Kong's people have been expected to assume their national identity as Chinese. Intellectuals – journalists, teachers, political activists – are at the center of this identity conflict. Some proclaim themselves Hongkongese as apart from Chinese, proud of their own separate cultural identity, however fleeting; others proudly proclaim their new Chinese identity despite their misgivings about the Chinese state and their confusion about what Chineseness might mean; and still others seek no such particular identities, but wish only to remain free to wander the cultural supermarket. Are these wanderers, in their distrust of any state, eccentric refugees of colonialism, or are they precursors of us all in the world?

I have chosen these groups primarily for intellectual reasons. These groups represent three central forms of choice within the cultural supermarket today, those of art and music, of religion, and of cultural identity itself, and they reveal the structuring of these choices under the supermarket aisle signs of "East" and "West"; these groups illustrate in particularly acute form the tension between national culture and global culture that is this book's central theme. However, my choice of these groups is also personal, reflecting my own biography.

I grew up in the United States, and found myself, as a teenager, disillusioned by Christianity ("The American Pledge of Allegiance says that America is 'one nation under God,' but what kind of God favors one country over another? Who is he, some kind of national cheerleader?") and fascinated by Eastern religions; but when I went, as a college student, on Buddhist meditation retreats, I felt intrigued yet skeptical about the exotic ritual trappings, and, eventually, about the wisdom of the teacher ("Is he really any wiser than I am? Aren't we looking up to him because he's foreign, 'from the spiritual East rather than the materialistic West' and all that crap?") Is there any religion, I wondered, whose truth might lie beyond cultural bounds?

Later, in my twenties and early thirties, I found myself in Japan, learning Japanese *shakuhachi* (bamboo flute), and playing flute and saxophone as an amateur and semi-professional jazz musician. Some Japanese would tell me that although I might become good at *shakuhachi*, I would never really be able to understand and play *shakuhachi* because I did not have "Japanese blood"; and by the same token, my Japanese jazz musician colleagues would treat me with a respect that far transcended my limited musical abilities because I was American, and thus somehow "authentic" as a jazz musician in a way that they, presumably, were not – but what, I wondered, is the relation of ethnic or cultural background to the ability to play music? Is there any such relation? Can "whites" play the *shakuhachi*? Can "yellows" play the blues? Does music and art belong to any particular culture, or is it all the world's?

Later, in my late thirties and early forties, I found myself in Hong Kong, as a professor of anthropology at the Chinese University of Hong Kong. I discovered a wide range of views among my students and colleagues as to how they viewed the handover of Hong Kong on 1 July 1997, and as to who they felt they themselves were culturally. I found myself instructing students with a split in view: a few felt an estrangement toward me as a white foreigner teaching them in the English language about the colonial discipline of anthropology at *Chinese* University; but others seemed to feel a link with me, a fellow "first-worlder," that they never would admit to feeling toward their fellow Chinese up north. I too benefitted from my Westernness as a "privileged other" in a Hong Kong not yet culturally postcolonial. The question of Chinese cultural identity in Hong Kong, I began to feel, may have something to teach us about the meaning of cultural identity in the world as a whole: What does it mean to be Chinese? What does it mean, today, to belong to any particular culture or nation?

In mulling over, in the past few years, the recent shifts in anthropological concepts of culture – the shift from culture as "the way of life of a people" to culture as "the information and identities available from the global cultural supermarket" described in this chapter – I soon enough realized that these were not just abstract concepts, applicable in theory alone; they applied directly to people I had known in my life, particularly to members of these three groups that I had been exposed to. I decided to study these groups formally, and thanks to a research grant from the Hong Kong Research Grants Council, was able to begin interviewing members of each of these groups, both those I had known in my past and those I later came to know: Japanese artists and musicians in a northern Japanese city, Sapporo, in the summers of 1995 and 1997; American religious seekers in a western American urban area, Denver-Boulder, in summer 1996; and intellectuals in Hong Kong from 1995 through 1998.[39]

In each locale, I was able to interview for two to three hours each some 40 people about their senses of cultural identity. The interviews – conducted in Japanese in Japan, in English in the United States, and in both English and Cantonese in Hong Kong with the aid of student assistants – were taped and then transcribed by a league of paid student helpers, and closely studied. I was also able to interact with these people at jazz clubs, dance studios, and gallery openings in Japan, at church services and meditation retreats in the United States, and at social events and political gatherings as well as classrooms and offices in Hong Kong. Beyond this, I was able to study books and magazines in all three societies, reading Japanese popular and scholarly writings in Japanese and in English on traditional and contemporary Japanese arts and music, American popular and scholarly writings on Christianity and Buddhism in the United States, and Hong Kong popular and scholarly writings in Chinese and in English on who, culturally, Hong Kong people are at this historical juncture.

An important question that the foregoing may raise is whether the 40 people I interviewed in each society can really represent their societies' struggles over cultural identity within the realms I have outlined. I argue that they can. These people are often among the elite in their societies, and in the world as well, to be sure. Many of them have the education and the economic liberty to think about questions that less well-off people in their societies and in the world might view as an idle luxury. But they differ from their fellows as a matter of degree rather than of kind, I believe, and their struggles resonate throughout their societies, although I will show this only indirectly.

For each of the three groups I analyze, I use popular media and academic writings in each society to place the particular voices of these people within the larger cultural discourses swirling around them; at the same time, the voices of these 40 people give the cultural discourses a particular embodiment in real people. Mass media and scholarly writings show that these particular people are not merely idiosyncratic, but reflect larger cultural currents; these people give larger cultural currents life through their particular voices. In each of the three ethnographic chapters, I quote from many of the people I interviewed, interspersed with quotations from the mass media and scholarly works. I also present three people at greater length in each chapter, giving their edited accounts of who, culturally, they are, and analyzing their accounts: these people were selected because their words convey with particular vividness the larger themes of each chapter. I have condensed hours of interviews with these people into a scant few pages of text. In this process, I have tried to present the essence of what they said in a way that is sympathetic to their accounts of themselves and in a way that enables you who read to comprehend their narratives in as clear a way as possible; but my own editing might not exactly correspond to how they themselves might edit their accounts and lives for print.

The ethnographic method upon which this book is based is concerned less with the statistical representativeness of its sample than with what the people I interviewed say: the discourses they use in explicating their identities, and how these in turn reflect and explicate cultural discourses at large in their societies. I believe that the individual self must not be seen simply as the product of collective cultural forms, but must be considered closely in his or her own right.[40] This is all the more true in the context of cultural identity, which no one else can choose: who you think you are culturally, within all the constraints of your social world, all the various ways that others see you, *is* who you are. It is this subjective sense, as mulled over, wrestled with, resisted, and accepted by the unique individuals I interviewed, that I report upon and analyze in this book.

Interviews can never be transparent windows into people's minds, in that all interviews, and all conversations between people, are in some sense performances:[41] we tell ourselves in different ways to different people, in accordance with who we think they are, and how we want them to see us. I do not know the majority of the people I interviewed beyond our interviews of just a few hours. This chapter's earlier discussion of self and of identity can't fully be fleshed out by the people in this book, in that I know them only through what they told me: I can't get inside their heads, but can only focus upon their words. There is no way around this limitation, but it must be kept in mind: this book consists of words spoken in social situations rather than of windows into minds. Nonetheless, I believe, from all the Japanese and Hong Kong Chinese as well as Americans I know, that people are not merely chameleons; although self-presentations may subtly shift, people's basic senses of who they are do not shift from social situation to social situation. The people I interviewed are, to a large degree, anyway, who they say they are; to argue differently would be to insult them.

In the pages that follow, I first consider, in Chapter 2, the cultural worlds of Japanese artists, then in Chapter 3 the worlds of American religious seekers, and then in Chapter 4 the worlds of Hong Kong intellectuals, before returning, in Chapter 5, to a broader consideration of our middle chapters' findings. In each of the middle chapters, I seek to combine the larger picture, of the complexity of these collective identities within global categories of state and market, with a more intimate picture, of particular selves struggling to find their particular situated identities. I don't finally know how much these groups and selves transcend their particularity. But I suspect that the struggles of members of these groups resonates to a degree with the struggles of many of us in our increasingly culturally supermarketed world. This, I sense, is what makes their struggles of relevance, not just to themselves but to us all.

2 What in the world is Japanese?

On the cultural identities of *koto*ists, calligraphers, bebop pianists, and punk rockers

When one leafs through books, Japanese or foreign, on Japanese visual art or music, one will probably see wisps of ink depicting bamboo and prints of kimono-clad maidens; one will probably see pictures of *koto* and *shakuhachi* (bamboo flute) players performing on their instruments. But today, not many Japanese artists practice such forms; instead, they play electric guitars and paint abstracts in oil paint. The world of punk rock and performance art, John Coltrane, Jimi Hendrix, Andy Warhol, and Salvador Dali, is the world into which they have been born; *koto* and kimono may be as exotic to them as they might be to a passing tourist seeking, through her guidebook, the last remaining vestiges of "traditional Japan."

This situation is often described as Japan's Westernization. "Japanese have lost their own culture, and now merely imitate the West," goes an oft-heard line; "Japanese identity is gone." There is some truth to this view: the taken-for-granted realm for many Japanese, in artistic culture as well as in many other areas of Japanese life, is now rock and jazz and Beethoven, not traditional Japanese music; Picasso and Van Gogh, not Sesshū and Tessai; suits and skirts more than kimono, carpets more than *tatami* (matted floors), hamburger more than *hijiki* (seaweed). But does this mean that "Japaneseness" is dead? Perhaps not: for it may be that the "Japaneseness" of Japanese artists is not vanishing once and for all, but rather ever being reinvented. In this chapter we will see, in an array of Japanese artists, the ongoing loss, rejection, and attempted reconstruction from the cultural supermarket's shelves of "Japaneseness" and a Japanese cultural home.

On the history of Japaneseness

All nations to some degree invent cultural traditions in order to legitimate their national existence: belief in a common culture, rooted in tradition, serves to justify the nation. Japan is no exception. In the decades before World War II, the myth of the unbroken imperial line since 660 BC, directly descended from the Sun Goddess, Amaterasu, was taught as truth in Japanese schools. In fact, the Japanese nation is at least in some sense a creation of the late nineteenth century. Through the previous 700 years, Japan had been divided into feudal domains, with ordinary people's senses of belonging apparently lodged more within their particular family and village than in any abstract sense of Japaneseness. The leaders of the Meiji Restoration, seeking to modernize Japan so that it could catch up with Western nations in its development, felt the need to create a sense of Japaneseness that did not, for the mass of Japanese people, previously exist. This they did in part through the Imperial Rescript on Education, promulgated in 1890 and for half a century thereafter recited in schools throughout Japan. The Imperial Rescript on Education proclaimed that filial piety and imperial loyalty were one and the same – loving the state, through its embodiment, the emperor, was no different from loving your own parents. This master metaphor of nation-shaping, "state is family," was apparently of considerable effectiveness. As Robert J. Smith notes, "It has been much debated in Japan whether soldiers [in World War II] cried out for their mothers or invoked the name of the emperor as they lay dying."[1] To the extent that soldiers in their last cries may indeed have invoked the emperor, the state's molding was successful.

But it would be an exaggeration to say that Japaneseness is wholly an invention of the modern state. Japan, consisting of the people living on a set of islands relatively isolated from other lands, really has had a more or less natural basis for its existence as a separate and autonomous culture throughout its history. The consciousness of *wareware nihonjin* ("we Japanese") as a separate, distinct people may have been held by the learned elite far more than by the mass of Japanese toiling in their fields century after century; but nonetheless this consciousness can be seen in Japanese writings at many points throughout Japanese history. Japan throughout its history has self-consciously taken from the cultural supermarket of its day, reshaping and reweaving its choices over time to make them "Japanese."

Through most of Japanese history, the source of its cultural super-market was China, providing Japan with religion, writing, and art and music as well. In the seventh and eighth centuries, "Chinese and Korean [Buddhist] monks, carried across stormy seas by religious zeal, at the same time served as the carriers of superior Chinese culture."[2] But Chinese religion, writing, art, and music were gradually transformed

in Japan. Chinese written characters came to be combined with
Japanese syllabary over several centuries, to make a distinct Japanese
writing system; Buddhism came to be linked in many ways to the indigenous Japanese religion of Shinto; Japanese-style painting, *yamato-e*,
dealing with Japanese subjects and settings, arose in contrast to
Chinese-style painting in Japan, *kara-e*, which had been strictly imitative of Chinese art; Japanese musical instruments such as *koto* and *shakuhachi*, although their prototypes were introduced from China, took on,
over centuries, their distinctly Japanese forms. In art and in culture as
a whole, the pattern was one in which Japanese took various continental
influences and fashioned them into something Japanese.

Throughout premodern Japanese history, China and its culture were
admired and imitated in some eras and by some social groups, and
rejected in favor of Japaneseness in other eras and by other social
groups. This was true in the visual arts, with some schools and styles
being imitative of China (*kara-e* of the eighth century; monochrome
landscapes of the fourteenth century) and others (the *e-maki* narrative
scrolls of the twelfth century) largely distinct from any art produced in
China.[3] This was also true in religion and in philosophy; as the
seventeenth-century thinker Yamaga Sokō wrote:

> I once thought that Japan was . . . inferior in every way to China –
> that "only in China could a sage arise." This was not my idea
> alone; [Japanese] scholars of every age have thought so. . . . Only
> recently have I become aware of the serious errors in this view. . . .
> Wisdom, humanity, and valor are the three cardinal virtues of a
> sage. . . . When we compare China and Japan with these virtues as
> criteria, we see that Japan greatly excels China in each of them.[4]

Japan, as the above words indicate, did not merely assimilate Chinese
culture in one period, to subsequently make it Japanese; rather, Chinese
culture was imitated and transcended, admired and rejected, argued
over by at least a few in Japan for a thousand years of Japanese history;
and this was often done with a distinct national self-consciousness.

However, at the time Yamaga was writing, China was becoming
eclipsed by the West as the dominant cultural other, the primary
source of the cultural supermarket. Portuguese traders first arrived in
Japan in the 1540s; Jesuit missionaries came shortly thereafter, and
had considerable success in converting Japanese to Catholicism.
Within a century, Christianity had been effectively expunged through
persecution by Japan's rulers, fearful of a foreign faith eroding their
control, and Japan entered two hundred years of national seclusion.

Still, elements of Western influence remained; Japanese art, for example, never altogether lost sight of its earlier exposure to Western art. *Ukiyo-e*, woodblock prints, begin using Western perspective in the eighteenth century, subsequently blossoming into the eclectic and world-renowned works of Hokusai and Hiroshige: "Hokusai is an excellent illustration of cross-cultural exchange," borrowing from Western sources and in turn greatly influencing Western art, such as the French Impressionists.[5]

It was the arrival of Perry's "black ships" in 1853, forcing open Japan to the West, and the Meiji Restoration of 1867, leading to the extraordinarily rapid state-led modernization of Japan in order to close off the inroads made by the West, that brought the full-fledged influx of Western cultural forms into Japanese life. The exhortation *sonnō jōi* ("revere the Emperor, repel the [Western] barbarians") had served as a rallying cry in the mid-nineteenth century for fighting off the West; but this rapidly gave way within two decades to the completely opposite slogan of *bunmei kaika* (adopt Western "civilization and enlightenment"), as Japanese realized that they could not possibly repel the West but had to learn from it. By the 1870s and 1880s, this led to the wholesale adoption of Western forms, in art, music, and in many other areas of life. This view gave way, in the latter two decades of the nineteenth century, to a new cultural conservatism, as embodied by the slogan *wakon yōsai* (adopt "Japanese spirit, Western learning"): Japan needs the learning and the technology of the West, but must preserve its own Japanese spirit in order to survive and flourish. But if Western learning is wholly adopted, then will there be any Japanese spirit remaining?

Japanese cultural history of the twentieth century may be broadly read in terms of the interplay of these three slogans (even though the slogans themselves were mostly no longer used), each positioning Japan in different ways *vis-à-vis* the West. Japanese of the 1910s and 1920s came to enjoy a mass culture that was internationalized and Westernized: radio, for example, brought Western popular music to a mass audience. In the years up to the end of World War II, this international popular culture was heavily curtailed and suppressed in favor of expressions of state-sanctioned Japaneseness – being "internationalized," "Westernized," was thought to be traitorous – but even during this period, appreciation for Western cultural products remained: "by 1937, Japan had become the largest market in the world for [Western] classical records."[6] With the end of World War II, Western popular culture was again taken up with enthusiasm, all the more so as Japan became progressively more affluent: leading to the largely Westernized modes of Japanese life described in the opening paragraphs of this chapter.

What, then, is the Japaneseness of today's Japan? Robert J. Smith writes of Japaneseness as follows:

> I have known actors of the Noh theater, dedicated to the perfection of their incredibly demanding art, who off-stage delighted in pipe and tweeds, pizza and jazz. Who is to say that the combination of interests is specious, or that one is more genuine, the other more spurious?. . . Who is to say that Japanese culture today is more or less authentic than it ever was?[7]

Smith's point is that we cannot say that the traditional Japanese art of *nō* – a highly stylized form of Japanese drama developed in the four-teenth century – is Japanese, whereas pipe and tweeds, pizza and jazz, are not Japanese. This seems true: Japaneseness is not simply a matter of Japanese tradition, but of Japanese life as it is actually lived today. The problem, however, is that Japanese life as lived today ignores much of what we tend to think of as Japanese. For the vast majority of Japanese today, pizza and jazz (if not pipe and tweeds) are a taken-for-granted part of Japanese life: it is all but impossible to grow up in Japan today without being exposed to pizza and jazz, thanks to radio, television, and fast food outlets. *Nō*, on the other hand, is known as high Japanese culture, but has not been actually seen by most Japanese people, except perhaps on educational television for an instant before changing the channel. If we define "Japaneseness" as a matter of how Japanese today live – how Japanese people actually experience the cultural world that surrounds them – then it seems that pizza and jazz are Japanese, while *nō* theater is *not* Japanese, but foreign.

A number of anthropologists have commented about how traditional Japanese culture has become exotic in Japan today. Creighton writes that "as material goods and customs associated with the once-exotic West have become a routine part of life, the customs, goods, and habits believed to symbolize the timeless Japanese past have been embraced as the new exotica."[8] Ivy explores "discourses of the vanishing," the efforts of Japanese to preserve marginalized and disappearing senses of Japaneseness from an inescapable modernity.[9] One reaction to the estrangement of Japanese people from Japaneseness has been the emer-gence of a genre known as *nihonjinron* – "discourse on Japaneseness" – which at its peak in the 1970s filled shelf after shelf of Japanese bookstores, as to a lesser extent it does today.[10] The popularity of *nihonjinron* indicates the desire of many Japanese to preserve a sense of

unchanging Japaneseness: to hold a Japanese identity more fundamental than a shopping list of choices from the global (largely Western)
cultural supermarket.

The popular success of *nihonjinron* indicates that many Japanese do
indeed think about Japaneseness at least occasionally in their lives.[11]
If Japaneseness was apparently something that only a learned elite
thought about through most of Japanese history, today the mass of
Japanese, linked through mass media to both the global cultural supermarket and to the outpouring of theories as to "who we Japanese really
are," have the opportunity to consider their national cultural identities.
My impression, however, from talking to a range of Japanese people at
length about their lives is that for many Japanese, the pressures of their
daily lives preclude the idle luxury of such thought. But there are some
people who do so think. Returnees from overseas, especially young
people who have been raised in foreign countries, may wonder, "Am I
really Japanese?" Members of minority groups such as Koreans or
Ainu may wonder from within their ineradicably Japanese upbringing
who culturally they are. And so too – this chapter's subject – artists.

Artists are interesting in the investigation of Japanese cultural
identity for two reasons. First, artists may see themselves not merely as
consumers of the discourses of cultural identity swirling around them,
but as preservers, interpreters, and creators, through their work, of
Japanese identity: thus, they may be particularly self-conscious as to
what that identity may mean. (Whether or not other Japanese are
paying any attention to them in their endeavors is of course another
matter: most of the artists I interviewed seemed to feel neglected by
their society.) Second, artists, more than most other groups in Japanese
society, reveal the rapidity of change in Japanese senses of cultural
identity. Today, there are *koto* players and calligraphers insisting on
the essential Japaneseness of their traditional Japanese arts, but there
are also rock guitarists and avant-garde painters insisting on the essential Japaneseness of *their* arts. What these very different groups mean in
their claims of Japaneseness can tell us a great deal about the invention
and reinvention of Japaneseness in Japan today.

I lived in Sapporo, Japan for seven years in the 1980s as an English
teacher, jazz musician, and student of *shakuhachi*, and had the chance
to return in 1995 and 1997 to do research for this book. I interviewed
38 professional or amateur artists – *koto*ists, calligraphers, bebop
pianists, surrealist painters, and punk rockers, among others – asking
them, in Japanese, about the relation of their senses of Japaneseness to
their senses of their arts. I interviewed each for several hours, and
examined their work with them; I asked them about what being an

artist, and being a Japanese artist, meant to them; and I later attended their exhibitions and concerts, to observe how they presented and performed their arts to a larger Japanese public.

I define as artist one who pursues an art – whether *shakuhachi*, sculpture, or electric guitar – as their *ikigai*: what they feel is most important to them in their lives.[12] I focused on visual artists and musicians rather than on writers, in that for the latter with whom I spoke, Japaneseness seemed not much of an issue – "Of course it's Japanese: I'm writing in Japanese" – whereas for most of the former, Japaneseness was something they had much thought about in the context of their arts. This removes a fascinating area of inquiry – clearly there is a huge difference between the writings of, for example, the 1968 Nobel Prize winner Kawabata Yasunari, much of whose work seems to ooze "Japaneseness" from every page, and such contemporary writers as Murakami Haruki and Hoshi Shin'ichi, many of whose books could take place anywhere in the modern world, with hardly a reference to Japan – but this goes beyond the scope of what I can accomplish in this chapter.

The artists I interviewed, living in and around Sapporo, a city of 1.7 million people, tended to consider themselves "minor league" as opposed to the artistic stars in Tokyo, Japan's center in all respects. Indeed, I am not dealing with the elite of Japanese artists. This is a limitation – the Tokyo elite, had I the chance to interview them, would certainly have proved to be more internationalized than their fellow artists in Sapporo, and perhaps more self-conscious about "Japaneseness" and what it signifies – but was also an advantage, I think. The Sapporo artists saw me not as a foreign critic who might help or hurt their careers, as might have their more internationally visible fellow artists in Tokyo, but merely as an interested onlooker, with whom they were quite happy to discuss freely what they felt they were doing in their artistic pursuits.

I discussed in Chapter 1 how interviews can never be transparent windows into selves, and this may be all the more the case in Japan. I was, for some of these artists, one of the few foreigners they had ever spoken with: a foreigner asking them, as Japanese artists, about Japanese identity. This surely had some impact on how they spoke with me; there may have been a self-consciousness of themselves as Japanese that our interviews tended to sharpen. More than in this book's other ethnographic chapters, this particular circumstance may have had some significance in shaping what was said. I don't believe that this invalidates what was said – these people are, I'm sure, revealing very real aspects of themselves – but it probably did, to some degree, influence what was said.

Traditional artists: Japaneseness as roots

I interviewed 12 Japanese artists working in traditional forms, such as *koto*, *shakuhachi* (bamboo flute), *nihonbuyō* (Japanese dance), *shigin* (the singing of poems), *shodō* (calligraphy), and *sumie* (ink painting). These artists were mostly older, ranging from their forties to their eighties. Although these artists varied in their arts and ages, they held similar views as to what they were doing in their arts: conveying "Japaneseness" to students who need to be taught who, culturally, they really are. Let us first consider the words of a practitioner and teacher of traditional Japanese dance:

Ōkubo Yuki (56)[13]
Doing Japanese dance, and teaching it to Japanese so that they will cherish it, is the purpose of my life. Each movement of my dance must be filled with *yamato damashi*: "Japanese spirit." Wearing kimono is absolutely necessary in order to practice Japanese dance; once I put on my kimono in the morning, I have that Japanese spirit within me. Very few people wear kimono now, on a regular basis – most people don't even know how to put on a kimono. I ride the trolley in the morning and I get stared at: wearing a kimono has become that unusual. Even though this is the Japanese mode of dress, Japanese stare at me! My grandmother always used to tell me, "this is the dress of Japanese, that they should feel proud of!" The kimono has been transmitted for hundreds of years in Japanese culture, but now I get stared at! That's really sad – that's what's happened to Japan today. . . .

My mother died the day I was born; my grandmother raised me. She insisted that I go to Japanese dance lessons, but I hated it. I would skip my lessons and go play instead; if grandma found out, she'd get furious, and not give me my snack after school! That was just after the war. . . . When I got married, in my early twenties, I quit dance, and became an ordinary housewife; but my husband died after just a few years, and I had to make a living: I ran a restaurant. While doing that at night, I began studying dance again during the day, as a way of regaining my mental balance. Gradually dance became the center of my life: eventually I quit the restaurant, and became a full-time teacher of dance. . . . When I dance now, especially when I dance alone, I often think of my mother, who died so that I could live. . . .

Today, Japanese life is Westernized. I have some students who are older, but most are young women in their twenties. These younger students have never lived any kind of traditional Japanese life in their homes; at first, that tradition is like a foreign tradition to them. Lots of young students come because they'll be traveling overseas; they want to wear a pretty kimono and show foreigners about Japan. . . .

When young women take dance lessons, they have to learn to sit properly, kneeling on *tatami* mats; but they say that their legs won't become pretty if they have to sit that way – they'd rather sit on a chair. But I insist that they wear kimono and sit properly if they're going to study dance. I don't care what kind of music they dance to, whether it's Japanese or Western. *Koto* and guitar are similar. We can bring in Western music, and even Western ballet, and link it to Japanese dance. While we preserve kimono and traditional dance, we can bring in these new elements. . . . "It was like this in the past" – you can't just keep saying that; rather, you've got to teach so that today's twenty-five-year olds will be able to understand it. Yes, you've got to compromise. But of course, you also have to work to change these young people's way of thinking, so that they will understand and preserve the traditions. . . .

Why do so many young people not like Japanese dance? Why do they all like rock music? Well, the style of life has changed in Japan, and people's sense of rhythm has changed as well. . . . I don't feel resentment towards America for this "Americanization" – there are good things too: people have become more free. But Japanese are losing their spirit; Japanese need to return to their roots. If Japanese traditional culture vanished, maybe in the future people all over the world would become alike. Wherever you went in the world, it would all be the same; you couldn't tell the difference anymore. . . .

I want Japanese to keep having pride in their traditions. Of course, if foreigners study Japanese traditions, that's a very happy thing too. Japanese are too close to Japan; they don't understand the wonderful things about Japan. An 18-year-old American exchange student studied dance with me recently: she said, "Why don't Japanese take lessons in such a wonderful dance?" She didn't understand how Japanese could ignore their own cultural tradition. Yes, it would be good if Japanese dance spread all over the world. But on the other hand, tradition and culture are linked to blood. Maybe it will be a tiny minority of people studying – out of 150 million Japanese in the future, maybe only a thousand will do Japanese dance. But they can still succeed in preserving

Japanese dance. It's for that tiny percentage of students that I'm pouring out my heart in dance. . . .

The purpose of her life, Ms. Ōkubo tells us, is teaching Japanese dance, and thereby bringing Japanese to rediscover their roots – roots that have become estranged from contemporary Japanese life. The rootedness of Japanese in Japanese tradition, she indicates, is no longer taken for granted by her young students, for whom Japanese tradition is foreign – a tradition they may seek to learn only before they travel to foreign countries, and feel the need to display their Japaneseness, even though this is a Japaneseness that may be as exotic to them as it is to their foreign hosts. For Ms. Ōkubo, this Japaneseness is indeed a part of her daily life, as shown by the kimono she insists on wearing; but that very insistence makes her an oddity, worthy of stares in the society around her.[14] In her teaching, she is willing to compromise to some degree in conveying Japanese dance to her students, but only to a degree: for this is Japanese dance, that Japanese must preserve, even if only a few people continue the tradition. Japaneseness, she implies, will never again be at the taken-for-granted level, but at least it can remain a viable choice from the cultural supermarket – allowing Japanese to have the chance to preserve their Japaneseness, as against all the world's homogenization.

Ms. Ōkubo's idea of Japanese roots is, however, more problematic than she indicates. The kimono she extols was indeed the traditional dress of Japanese, but the kimono worn by most Japanese women through history has had as much in common with today's dress kimono as has a housecoat to a mink coat. The Japanese dance she teaches was through most of its history the province of men, dancing in *kabuki* theater,[15] a popular form of entertainment from which women performers were banned shortly after its seventeenth-century founding. In her own life, she hated dance as a child, and completely departed from dance once she got married, intending to become "an ordinary housewife." It was only her husband's death, and the stress of trying to live in its aftermath, that brought her back to dance.

In this sense, dance was never for her a taken-for-granted Japaneseness; it was as a child a matter of *shikata ga nai* – something she had to do if she wanted her after-school snack – and as an adult a chosen pursuit from the cultural supermarket, one of many she might conceivably have chosen, in the wake of her expulsion from the more typical Japanese female life path of mother and housewife. (Obviously the fact that she had studied Japanese dance as a child influenced her adult return to it, but her earlier study of dance, which she had hated, hardly preordained that return.) Ms. Ōkubo presents her choice as a return to her Japanese roots, roots that Japanese possess by virtue of their blood. However, these roots are not natural, not genetic, but cultural, and indeed, no more than a small part of the Japanese cultural world today and, to a lesser degree, in the past as well. In a very real sense, for all the heartfelt sincerity of her invocation of Japanese roots, Ms. Ōkubo is engaged less in the rediscovery of her underlying Japaneseness than in the ongoing invention of Japaneseness for display in the cultural supermarket.

The traditional artists I interviewed as a whole held views of their arts more or less similar to those of Ms. Ōkubo. For a few, the world of traditional Japanese arts was indeed the taken-for-granted world of childhood. A *koto* teacher in her fifties said:

> When I was a child, I had *koto* lessons every day. We wouldn't use sheet music like they do today; we'd learn the piece by ear – it would seep into your body bit by bit. Once you learned a piece that way, you'd never forget it. My mother was a teacher, so whatever I was doing, I always heard *koto* music in the house.

For this woman, *koto* was the world into which she was born; when she first went to school as a child, it came as a surprise to her to learn that for her classmates *koto* was not a natural part of their everyday lives, but something unusual. Today, when she speaks of how most Japanese have forgotten the meaning of being Japanese – "It's so that Japanese can say, 'I'm Japanese' that they practice traditional Japanese arts" – she is speaking of her own personal experience of growing up in a world of traditional Japanese arts that today few Japanese share (if indeed they ever did). For most of the traditional artists I interviewed, however, traditional Japanese arts were not a part of their taken-for-granted early lives; these arts were a choice they made in their young adulthood as to who they wanted to be, often a choice made in opposition to the prevailing values of their social worlds. A calligrapher in his sixties said, "I always like to do things differently from other people. So even though, when I was a young man just after the war, traditional Japanese culture wasn't very popular, that's what I was attracted to." This man was a salaryman for a large insurance company, who in his twenties began to like calligraphy more than insurance; and so, to the amazement of his colleagues, who apparently thought he was crazy, he left the security of the latter for the uncertainty of the former. A *shakuhachi* teacher in his forties spoke of how, "when I was 20, I heard someone playing *shakuhachi* on a subway platform. At that time, rock music was really popular; I was shocked by the sound of *shakuhachi* – I'd never heard anything like it before."

These traditional artists chose their arts from the cultural super-market that surrounded them in the Japanese social world of their young adulthoods. They could conceivably have chosen any number of artistic identities, or any other identities, as the core of who they wanted to be, but they chose, for complex mixes of personal, social, and cultural reasons, to make their pursuit of traditional Japanese arts the essence of their identities. Having made that choice and proceeded along that path, these artists are now no longer choosers of identity from the cultural supermarket but purveyors; no longer, to use the economic metaphor, buyers but sellers. They must convince at least some of their fellow Japanese – their prospective and present students – to pursue the cultural identities and adhere to the conceptions of Japaneseness that they proffer. A key way to do this is to emphasize Japaneseness not as one more choice of identity that one might make, but rather as one's very essence, which one has lost and must regain: "You are Japanese, and you can realize your Japaneseness through the study of a traditional Japanese art."

This is not to say that the traditional artists I interviewed proclaimed the Japaneseness of their arts cynically, or with anything less than full belief in what they professed. "I am Japanese and I practice *koto/shakuhachi/nihonbuyō/shigin/shodō/sumie* because I am Japanese" was the refrain I heard from virtually all the traditional artists I spoke with. But in fact – as alluded to in our discussion of Ms. Ōkubo's words – the vast majority of Japanese through history have never practiced most traditional Japanese arts. Many of these arts have historically been the preserve of the upper class; some schools within these arts have been invented only over the past hundred years. Japanese language perhaps involves to a degree an encompassing Japaneseness over Japanese history, something most Japanese have to some extent shared (although language too has changed); Shinto/Buddhist religion might involve such an encompassing Japaneseness. However, these Japanese art forms clearly do not.

But in terms of the present, this doesn't matter. At present, in a wealthy Japan in which people from all walks of life have the means to pursue previously elite arts, these arts can indeed be represented and proffered as "Japanese tradition." However, this effort, despite its promise of "a return to Japanese roots," often seems remarkably inef-fective. An assistant teacher of *shigin* (the singing of poems) in his sixties said this:

Young people aren't interested in *shigin*. They say it's too stiff. At our club, the teacher is 85; students are in their sixties and seventies; the youngest is in his forties. I'm worried about *shigin* dying out; the old students die off, and new students don't enter. If we don't think of some good methods, we won't get young people to join. When I look at young people, no longer interested in any of this, I feel that the Japanese spirit is becoming weaker. If Japanese traditions are lost, Japanese will lose their identity! . . . My teacher made up a flyer asking people if they wanted to participate in *shigin*, and put it in the mailboxes of lots of houses; no one joined. No one's interested.

As if to epitomize this lack of interest, this teacher corraled his 10-year-old grandson at the close of our interview, to ask him, "When you become bigger, will you do *shigin*?" "No!" was the reply. "Why?" "It's boring" (*tsumaranai*). "Maybe you'll do it, won't you?" "The chance is only .00001 percent!" shouted the boy, as he slipped outside to avoid his grandfather's entreaties.

Not all traditional arts are in such dire straits as *shigin*. Some – flower arranging, for example – are flourishing in Japan today. A painter of ink paintings spoke of how, with the rise of Japanese economic power over the past several decades, "Japanese ink painting has come back into its own – people are more interested in Japanese culture." Indeed, this may be the case for Japanese arts as a whole, as compared to, for example, the late 1940s and early 1950s, when Japan remained too poor for the widespread practice of the arts, and when traditional Japanese arts were to a degree tainted with the legacy of Japan's defeat in World War II.

Nonetheless, many of the practitioners of traditional arts I interviewed seemed to see themselves as beings from an earlier Japan, now living in a Japanese world whose indifference to their arts they find difficult to comprehend. Their artistic construction of Japaneseness, they believe, is the essence of Japaneseness, and so the fact that most Japanese have no interest in their arts must mean that they have lost their Japaneseness. This theme is echoed in Ms. Ōkubo's account, as we saw; it is also echoed in many Japanese scholarly tracts on traditional arts as well as in *nihonjinron*, the "discourse on Japaneseness" discussed earlier. "The things Japanese have forgotten" [*Nihonjin no wasuremono*] is the title of a recent book by the conservative critic Aida Yūji[16] – they have forgotten their Japaneseness, having become immersed in the values of the West. "Japan has become a musical colony of the West," thunders Kikkawa Eishi in the opening pages of his book *The Character of Japanese Music* [*Nihon no ongaku no seikaku*][17] – Japanese now can judge their own music and visual art only through distorted Westernized ears and eyes. Indeed, teachers such as Ms. Ōkubo feel that their arts can survive only by being linked to contemporary popular "Westernized" Japanese culture: "*Koto* and guitar are similar. We can bring in Western music, and even Western ballet, and link it to Japanese dance." Artists such as she are saying that Japanese traditional arts have become so alien to young Japanese that they must be sweetened with "Westernness," or at least with contemporary Japanese popular culture, in order to be made palatable.

In Chapter 1, we discussed the state's contemporary shapings of culture across the globe. The Japanese government does indeed seek to shape Japanese culture through public schooling, as can be seen, for example, in the ways that social studies textbooks emphasize the oneness and goodness of "we Japanese," minimizing Japanese aggression in World War II. But this shaping of Japaneseness has not extended to the encouragement of Japanese traditional arts. Since the Meiji Restoration, music and (to a lesser extent) art instruction in public schools have been Western: music has meant recorders, pianos, Western notation, not *koto, shakuhachi*, Japanese notation; art has meant training in perspective and color theory, not Japanese ink painting. "After I graduated from the university," a *biwa* (lute) player told me, "I began teaching music in high school, but it felt very strange. I was always wondering why, even though I was Japanese and my students were Japanese, I was teaching Western music. I kept thinking that I should be teaching Japanese music." Eventually this woman quit teaching in school, to devote herself to Japanese music, but even now she still teaches piano for her living, because she can find far more students who want to learn piano than want to learn *biwa*. "We're in the ironical situation that we're better off playing Western instruments than our own instruments." Indeed, only two of the traditional artists I interviewed could make a living from art. Five of the twelve practiced their arts in their off-hours from their full-time jobs working for companies or teaching school; several more were supported by their spouses (husbands), and several were retired from earlier non-artistic careers. The arts they lived for were reduced, within their economic lives, although not their artistic and spiritual lives, to the status of hobbies.

Traditional Japanese music and art have, in the past few years, made a limited entry into the school curriculum, with, I was told, at least a few pages of textbook now devoted to them.[18] However, given the climate of today's Japan, this may mean little, according to several of those I interviewed. "Yes, traditional Japanese music and art have begun to be taught in school," said the calligrapher. "But the songs on TV are all Western. The power of the mass media is a lot stronger than school education." As a music critic recently lamented,

> Huge record stores [in Japan] that carry CDs of the folk music of Madagascar, Swiss Renaissance lute music, or even contemporary solo flute works by Norwegian composers rarely have shakuhachi CDs. . . . Ask a clerk at a large Tokyo record store where the shaku-hachi CDs are and you are likely to hear laughter or receive blank stares. You may even have to explain what a shakuhachi is.[19]

In the cultural and material supermarkets of contemporary Japan, Japanese traditional arts such as *shakuhachi* have come to occupy a very small niche indeed.

The institutional framework of traditional Japanese arts, preserving the cultural niche that these arts occupy, involves what is known as *iemoto seido*, the *iemoto* system:

> *Iemoto* . . . refers to the main house, which supposedly has descended from the school's original founder and thus has inherited the secret principle and techniques unique to the school. . . . The apprentice-student, after receiving training and a license at the *iemoto*, is permitted to open his own school as a branch.[20]

Most of the traditional artists I interviewed devote most of their efforts to practicing and teaching the arts set forth by the founder of their artistic school. They tended to view the *iemoto seido* as a necessary evil: most expressed dislike for the system, but felt that they could not easily survive without it, since their students sought certificates of proficiency only granted through the *iemoto*, and might quit without such certificates. "*Iemoto seido* is finally a matter of money: issuing certificates and collecting money for the *iemoto*. I'm not interested in money but in art," said a *shakuhachi* teacher. "Music is living: we can't only adhere to music written long ago." As, however, the calligrapher said, "Yes, *iemoto seido* has lots of problems, but it's worked well in preserving Japanese tradition." One artist likened *iemoto seido* to the emperor system, hallowing Japanese tradition from time immemorial; another likened it to a 7-Eleven franchising scheme: a way for the direct descendants of the founder of a given school to sit on their hands and make a great deal of money.

As the foregoing implies, most of the traditional artists and teachers I interviewed were not artistic creators in the Western sense, but skilled interpreters of traditional forms. This, coupled with the fact that instruction consists primarily of students imitating their teachers over and over, gives the *iemoto seido* a reputation for stifling creativity. Some I interviewed disputed this view; as the calligrapher said, "*Shodō*, like other traditional Japanese arts, has *kata*, forms that everyone learns, but these *kata* are expressed differently by each different artist – creativity springs from those *kata*. People who say that Japanese traditional arts stifle creativity are completely mistaken." There are indeed avant-garde practitioners of virtually every Japanese traditional art, bending the bounds of their genre, including this calligrapher himself. I have been to his exhibitions, and have heard complaints from viewers like those one might hear at modern art exhibitions anywhere: "I don't understand any of this stuff!" Nonetheless, the dominant view in Japan remains one of Japanese arts as old-fashioned, as opposed to Western arts as innovative.

This disparaging view is due not only to the institutional locking away of Japanese arts within *iemoto seido*, but also to the cultural construction of these arts: if Japanese arts are conceived as involving a return to Japanese roots, then their conservative, unchanging nature is implied; one can't easily be rooted in innovation. The question faced by the teachers of these arts is whether their arts can survive in today's Japan, which seems to them estranged from these postulated roots. And this leads these artists to the question, "What is Japaneseness?" Is Japaneseness a matter of ethnicity, enabling one particular group on the globe, those who are ethnically Japanese, to be able uniquely to understand traditional Japanese arts? Or is the Japaneseness of Japanese traditional arts something that anyone from across the globe can conceivably acquire?

Can a foreigner understand Japanese traditional arts? When I first went to Japan in 1980 and began studying *shakuhachi*, I was told by several Japanese acquaintances that I would never be able to understand *shakuhachi* as a Japanese could. This view corresponds with that expressed in many works of *nihonjinron*, that "Japaneseness" is a matter of "blood" (*chi*). A *shakuhachi* teacher stated that if he were to listen to a recording of a Japanese and a foreigner playing *shakuhachi*, he would always be able to distinguish the Japanese "because of Japanese blood"; the *shigin* teacher said, "I think a foreigner could understand 90 percent of *shigin*, but not the deepest 10 percent." The teacher of *biwa* wondered, in turn, why some Japanese could excel at foreign arts: "There are people who, even though they're Japanese, can play the violin and be international soloists. These people must have European

DNA in their blood" – just as foreigners who can excel at Japanese arts must have Japanese DNA, she maintained.

These explanations for the Japaneseness of Japanese arts seem based on genetics – there is something in Japanese "blood" that makes those of Japanese ethnicity able to understand Japanese arts better than those who are not of such ethnicity (unless, presumably, they have "Japanese DNA").[21] Other explanations for the Japaneseness of Japanese arts are based in environment. Another *shakuhachi* teacher said:

> If a Japanese and an American were each playing the *shakuhachi* and I could hear but not see them, I could tell the difference. That difference relates to the kind of society they lived in before starting to play *shakuhachi* – the Japanese has grown up in Japanese society, as the American has not.

The calligrapher said that even though Japanese often misunderstand his calligraphy because they try to read it rather than merely looking at its lines, still,

> Japanese people can understand *shodō* better than non-Japanese, because of the environment in which they grow up. Japanese people are unconsciously more sensitive to line than foreigners. The rhythms of *shodō* are deeply rooted in Japanese people's daily life, just as, for Americans, the rhythms of jazz are deeply rooted in their daily life.

These two explanations, those of genetics and environment, are quite different in their plausibility. "Blood" and "race," if these are thought to mean cultural characteristics rooted in genetics, are a fiction. Genes don't shape culture, making Japanese different in their values and behavior from Americans or French or Indians. On the other hand, environments do indeed differ in different places. It seems at least plausible that the Japanese cultural environment might enable Japanese to understand Japanese traditional arts better than other peoples. Nonetheless, despite their difference in plausibility, these two explanations do have a clear similarity, in that both assume an underlying Japaneseness that Japanese share in contrast to other peoples. These explanations assume a taken-for-granted level of shaping that makes people of Japanese ethnicity or upbringing able to understand Japanese traditional arts better than other peoples.

As we've seen, however, most young Japanese are not interested in attaining any understanding of traditional Japanese arts, and this is the problem faced by these explanations. If Japanese are uniquely supposed to be able to understand and practice Japanese arts, why aren't most Japanese interested in these arts? And why, in turn, are foreigners so interested in Japanese arts? A recent prize-winning book in Japanese laments how Japanese are forgetting their traditions, but it is written by an American devotee of Japanese traditional arts.[22] A *shakuhachi* teacher, amazed to find that in the Tokyo area alone some 150 foreigners from all over the world were studying *shakuhachi*, writes of how he told a gathering of Japanese students, only half in jest, "if you continue not to study *shakuhachi* at this rate, soon enough you'll have a red-haired, blue-eyed *iemoto*!"[23] Another Japanese book, hardly sympathetic to Japanese traditional arts, contains the following passage:

> You who read this book wear Western clothes, eat Western food . . . know all about foreign literature and movies, and enjoy jazz music. . . . [Foreigners well-versed in Japanese tradition] might say "You're not really Japanese. We're more truly Japanese than you are." If you were interrogated in this way, how would you respond? How could you prove that you were genuinely Japanese? . . . "I can speak and write Japanese," you might say. But there are foreigners who speak Japanese better than many Japanese, and . . . write better Japanese than many Japanese. . . . There are many foreigners who know Japanese classics and history and Buddhism much more than you do. . . . It's quite easy to embarrass a strange people like the Japanese, who know nothing about their traditions, by saying, "You can't really say you're Japanese!"[24]

This situation seems to have led a few of the traditional artists I interviewed to disavow the idea of Japanese culture as the exclusive possession of those with Japanese "blood" or upbringing. The *koto* teacher said, "There are many foreigners who have more 'Japanese sensibility' [*nihonjin no yō na kansei*] than Japanese do; you can't say that this is music that only Japanese can understand." A *shakuhachi* teacher stated, "If a foreigner can understand Japanese tradition, history, ways of thinking, and music, then he may be the one who's truly Japanese. Japaneseness isn't a matter or race or place, but a way of thinking, a matter of heart, behavior, attitude."

To these artists, anybody in the world could conceivably become Japanese if they devote themselves to the task. Japaneseness, for them, is not necessarily at a deep, taken-for-granted level of cultural shaping but at the level of the cultural supermarket, as people across the globe consciously choose to pursue Japaneseness, as opposed to any of the other global cultural identities they might choose. This implies that in tomorrow's world Japaneseness and Japanese ethnicity might become all but unlinked: Japaneseness might be carried on by people across the globe who happen to have chosen, as part of their culturally super-marketed identities, the appreciation and performance of a traditional Japanese art. This may seem exaggerated: if a broader conception of Japaneseness is adopted, then surely Japaneseness will have a close relation to the people who live in Japan and speak Japanese. But if Japaneseness is defined in terms of traditional arts, then the logic followed by these artists seems difficult to dispute.

The traditional artists I interviewed shared in common a worry about the future of their arts, and thus, by their equation, the future of Japaneseness ("If *koto* dies, Japanese culture will die," said the *koto* teacher, in a not untypical comment). But those who confined Japanese-ness to ethnicity and upbringing, race and place, were most bleak in their views, seeing themselves as the last keepers of the flickering flame of true Japaneseness in the face of the ignorance and indifference of the no-longer-Japanese society around them. Those who saw Japaneseness in a global frame were a bit more sanguine. After all, of the billions of people across the globe, surely a smattering of each generation would continue to become interested in traditional Japanese arts; and this is all it would take for those arts to remain as one more flavor in the world cultural smorgasbord, one more kit of pursuits available from the global cultural supermarket.

Contemporary artists: Japaneseness as chains

I interviewed 26 contemporary artists in all – jazz musicians, rock musicians, blues musicians, realist oil painters, abstract painters, a sculptor, a dancer, and an orchestral composer, among other people. A few of these artists agreed with the traditional artists as to the tragedy of the loss of what they held to be traditional Japanese culture. This was most obviously the case for a young painter I spoke with at an exhibition of her paintings, which resembled those of the late Keith Haring. She said, "No, there's nothing particularly Japanese about my painting; I don't have any consciousness of being Japanese." But later in our conversation, she suddenly began lamenting the ways in which Japanese cultural tradition was being destroyed:

Japan has a tendency to imitate the West. For example, that new department store downtown is an imitation of the work of a European architect; there's no Japanese flavor to it. When I look at buildings like that, I hate them. They're nothing but imitation!

I then pointed out as gently as I could that her own paintings too had no Japanese flavor to them, and could be called imitations of Western art. At this, she became distinctly uncomfortable (but admirably honest in her words):

Yes, that's a contradiction, isn't it? I value my culture, but what I want to do in my art is different! I don't want to think about that! . . . When you live in Japan today, "Westernness" is naturally a part of you, and that's what's expressed in my pictures. But I guess it's true that if everyone painted pictures like mine, Japanese identity would die out. . . . People have their own likes and dislikes: some people do Japanese traditional arts and some don't. But I guess that may mean that Japan is no longer a unified country. Yes, since I have Western influences in my paintings, probably my sense of self-consciousness as a Japanese is weaker. But after all, I was still raised in Japan. Is it a bad thing to have a weaker sense of being Japanese? . . . But I *do* value my culture!

This young painter seems to take for granted that she can shape her art in any way that she sees fit; but she also takes for granted that she is Japanese, a member of a particular culture that must be preserved. She seems to see both these principles as central to her identity, and is disturbed when their clash is made apparent to her. In Chapter 1, we looked at the contradiction between national culture and the global cultural supermarket in the minds of many people today: the principle of the market being that "you can buy, do, be whatever you want to buy, do, be," and the principle of the state being that "you should cherish your nation's way of life"/"you should value your particular culture." In this painter's words, above, we see her sudden realization that if Japanese artists express themselves as they wish through forms of the global cultural supermarket, then Japan as a particular culture may no longer exist in an artistic sense.

Many of the contemporary artists I interviewed were more dismissive of traditional Japanese culture. A rock musician said, "If Japanese traditional culture vanished, it would vanish because nobody needs it. That would be kind of lonely, but . . . I don't like *shodō, shakuhachi,*

koto – let them vanish! I was drawn to electric guitar, not *shakuhachi*!"
Another rock musician said, "Today's Japanese aren't really Japanese;
they've taken in American and European and other cultures. There's
no need to preserve traditional Japaneseness. Yes, Japan in this sense
may vanish in a few years, but I don't think that's bad." Japan, for
these artists, does not represent a cultural heritage underlying their art
– that cultural heritage is going or gone, they believe. Rather, Japan,
many of them feel, is a society and culture that is hostile to their arts.
This view is expressed in the following account, by an artist – or
would-be artist, by his description – who feels frustrated by his cultural
upbringing as a Japanese:

Sasaki Norihito (43)
I'm a painter, but by day I work as a graphic designer. I run my
own business, and I'm really busy – I have a wife and two daughters
I have to support, so work has to take first priority. But I paint
whenever I can: I showed a new picture of mine at an exhibition
last month. I still have that deep desire to paint: I don't want to
regret how I've lived when I'm 80 years old! I also used to be a
jazz drummer, playing in various groups, but I quit that a few
years ago – I just didn't have time. In my mid-twenties, I was
truly an artist – I did nothing but paint for several years – but I
couldn't make a living that way, so I've taken this path. . . .

I always loved to draw as a kid – I drew whenever I could, instead
of studying! When I was in junior high school, I saw Salvador
Dali's paintings in the art textbook, and was amazed; Dali was a
huge influence on my painting. As for music – well, you can see
that I have John Coltrane's picture above my desk in this office; I
look at that every day, and listen to his music too sometimes while
I work. Yes, I've wondered why I've been so strongly influenced
by foreign music and art. When I was in junior high school, people
were getting into rock, the Beatles; I began to listen to that, and
soon enough got into jazz, Coltrane and people like that. Western
art too – that's what I was most exposed to. . . .

Traditional Japanese music and art doesn't ever really enter into
the lives of ordinary people. My painter friends do oil painting, not
Japanese-style painting; my musician friends have no interest in
traditional Japanese music: they like jazz and rock. Why are we
Japanese so interested in foreign things? It's connected to imagination – it seems to me that most Japanese don't have any originality.
Yes, there have been original figures in Japanese arts, but those
arts have been based on established forms and traditions: every-

thing is master–apprentice relations and all that, *iemoto seido*. You can't express yourself freely in Japanese art. Naturally, I was drawn to Western arts, because I could express myself there. . . .

I don't think that Japanese can fully understand Western oil painting and American jazz. They may have the technique to play concerts, but. . . . When you listen to Coltrane – Japanese can imitate him, and maybe come close, but finally it's just imitation: the rhythm is different. It's impossible for a Japanese to become a world-quality jazz musician. There are Japanese who are trying hard to get closer, but. . . . As for painting: at first, in my own painting, yes, I imitated, painted like the people who influenced me. But you can't just imitate in music or art – you've got to add your originality. In my work, I guess that even now there's no true originality, not yet anyway; but if I don't find it soon! . . . In Japan there's not much room for creative expression, so it must be taken from foreign cultures, but their creative expression is hard to understand deeply. In rock, your cultural background doesn't seem to matter so much, but in jazz, it does. For visual art, it's a little less clear – in painting, your individuality comes out a bit more. But for oil painting too, it's imitation – almost always, it's someone's influence on you that you paint from. . . .

Why don't Japanese make their own way of oil painting? Oil painting in Japan has a shallow history: Japanese have been doing oil painting since Meiji, for only a little more than a hundred years. But it's more than that: it has to do with the basic mentality of the Japanese. Yes, if I'd grown up in America or Europe, maybe I'd truly be an artist now. I wouldn't have been locked into a society based on nothing but educational credentials, as Japan has become now. Teachers teach children what's in textbooks, but can't teach them anything about the human spirit. Salarymen in Japan today – they're so polite! They have no minds of their own! If only I'd been raised in another, better way. . . .

Mr. Sasaki, like Ms. Ōkubo, as we earlier saw, views art in terms of a dichotomy of Japanese/non-Japanese: just as traditional Japanese arts are held by some traditional artists to be fully understandable by Japanese and by no one else, so too Mr. Sasaki holds that arts such as jazz music and oil painting can only be fully understood by Americans or Westerners, and not by Japanese. For Ms. Ōkubo, as we saw, Japaneseness is a precious but endangered cultural identity; through her art she seeks to preserve that identity. For Mr. Sasaki, on the other hand, Japaneseness represents a gross misfortune and insurmountable obstacle: because he is Japanese, he believes himself all but doomed to an artistic life of sterile imitation, whereas if he had been raised in the West, he might have been able to become a real artist. If Ms. Ōkubo believes Japaneseness to be at the taken-for-granted level of roots, albeit roots in danger of being lost, Mr. Sasaki sees Japaneseness at the *shikata ga nai* level of chains, constraints.

The realm of *shikata ga nai* – the realm of "what can't be helped" – is apparent in his day-to-day social world. He couldn't make a living as an artist, and now must spend most of his days working at graphic design in order to support his family (although, arguably, if he had truly wanted to be an artist, he would not have chosen to have a family). But the realm of *shikata ga nai* is also apparent in his shaping as a Japanese person, by his account. Traditional Japanese arts, Mr. Sasaki feels, make real artistic expression impossible, so Japanese artists like him must turn to Western forms; but because those forms, such as jazz and oil painting, are Western, Japanese can't understand them well enough to truly express themselves, but can only imitate. Japanese education and society as a whole exacerbate this problem by valuing only credentials, and devaluing the human spirit and human individuality, he feels: thus, real art is impossible. Japanese artists may have access to the global cultural supermarket – from paintings by Salvador Dali in junior high school textbooks to portraits of John Coltrane gracing office desks – but because they are Japanese, he is saying, these artists can never really comprehend their choices from the cultural supermarket, can never make those choices their own artistic possession. They are rendered artistic cripples by their Japaneseness.

This dichotomy of Japanese/non-Japanese arts and comprehensions seems of doubtful validity in today's Japan, just as it also is untrue that Japanese artists using Western forms are doomed to imitation, doomed to be second-rate. Nonetheless, because this dichotomy was so often invoked by the artists I interviewed, and in Japanese mass media and tracts on art and music, it must be taken seriously – this is the way many Japanese artists think about their arts. Let us now turn from Mr. Sasaki's account to look at Japanese contemporary artists as a whole, and their constraints within what they experience as the *shikata ga nai* of Japaneseness.

Shikata ga nai is, as we saw for Mr. Sasaki, most obvious in the day-to-day world of work; and this is true for almost all of the contemporary artists I interviewed, who struggle for economic survival – they must eat, in a world that does not reward them for their arts. Of the 26 contemporary artists I interviewed, three were fully professional. Most of the rest managed to make some part of their living from their arts –

playing in rock bands or selling their paintings or sculptures – but couldn't fully support themselves through their arts. Instead, they made most of their living elsewhere: designing advertisements, teaching art or music in secondary school, managing coffeeshops or clubs, or working at various kinds of free-lance work, or at jobs wholly unrelated to their arts.

We earlier saw how many traditional Japanese arts have far fewer students than contemporary arts: the *biwa* player discussed in the previous section had to teach piano for a living. Indeed, the traditional artists generally had even less success at making a living from their arts than did contemporary artists. Despite this, the traditional artists I interviewed seemed for the most part to be economically middle class. This is not because their teaching is well paid – it is not – but more, because Japanese traditional arts do not bear much sense of the artist in rebellion against middle-class society. There is not much tradition of "the starving artist" in Japanese traditional arts, and there is little sense of artistic merit in being poor. The contemporary artists, on the other hand, tended to be of middle-class background, but were often emphatically not middle class in their current economic circumstances: our interviews were sometimes conducted in hovels – their studios and homes – reeking of turpentine, canvasses stacked to the ceiling, empty bottles of liquor littering the floor. Time after time, painters and musicians would tell me of the jobs they had quit and careers they had forsaken so that they could devote themselves to their arts, which they felt a calling to pursue, despite society's disapproval. Many spoke of the pressures they felt from parents, friends, and spouses to "lead a normal life and bring home a decent income." Unlike most traditional artists, who seemed quite pragmatic, many of these contemporary artists discussed their refusal to "compromise": their refusal to take the middle-class jobs their background would have pushed them towards, so that they could instead "live for their art."

To be an artist, *à la* Chatterton, Poe, Van Gogh, Charlie Parker, the long list of Western artists who have through their short, impoverished lives helped to create the heroic myth of "artist," is clearly a choice of identities from the cultural supermarket; but many of these artists saw their identities not as matters of choice but of fate. In one painter's words:

> Why do I paint pictures? It sounds strange, but it would be against God's will if I didn't paint. Not the Christian god – maybe it's my own god! But I've got to paint; I've felt this way all my life. It's a mission.

For many, the identity they claim as artists seems linked to a sense of alienation from Japan. This is in part because the identity of "artist" is a Western import in Japan. More, it is because the structures of Japanese society mean that one who seriously follows an artistic path outside of an established institution such as a university is decidedly non-mainstream – as reflected in the lack of societal recognition experienced by most of these artists. Mr. Sasaki's claim of Japanese society stifling creativity was echoed by a dozen or more of the artists I spoke with, many of whom, like him, deplored the Japanese society in which they lived. As the artist with a mission quoted above exclaimed:

> I feel something close to hatred toward Japan, toward all those people leading conventional lives. . . . My pictures are expressions of anger at society – that's why they don't sell! I hate the exclusion in Japan of everything that's different; I hate the joyful and bright world that people believe in, ignoring the darkness!

Japan, for him, was the enemy of his art, a sentiment well expressed in his dark surrealist canvasses.

This man kept mainstream Japanese society at a distance from his life; but others, holding down jobs within mainstream Japanese society, had daily immersion in that society, an immersion that sometimes caused problems of identity. This is shown vividly by a rock musician/ civil servant, taking a personal stand over the matter of hair:

> I wear a short-hair wig for my work at the city office; for my rock band I show my own real hair. For the job interview I cut my hair, but then let it grow; my boss called me aside and said, "Hey, what's with the hair? Do something about it!" So the wig. My hair is long because in concerts it's important, the way you're looked at; if I cut it, maybe the other band members wouldn't think I took music seriously. But long hair is also my expression of myself, of my real identity as a musician. I intend to quit my day job and become a musician full time.

This musician has at least two different audiences in his social worlds, but only one real head of hair. Rather than keep his hair short and proclaim the primary importance of his daytime job, he wears a wig to work, to affirm that he is truly serious about his music. (Indeed, two years after this interview, he quit his city office job, to devote himself wholly to music.) His conflict is particularly dramatic, but most contemporary artists I interviewed felt such a conflict, in that the identity of artist and the identity of worker were at such odds. The latter identity was a *shikata ga nai* imperative, whose rules had to be followed; but as the people I interviewed were all too aware, if the latter identity infringed too much on the former, then the artist is no longer truly an artist.

One area of Japan as *shikata ga nai* involves the fact that artists have to work for a living at jobs that may separate them from their arts. A second area of Japan as *shikata ga nai* – one emphasized by Mr. Sasaki, as we saw – is the perception that being Japanese is itself a barrier to artistic excellence. This view was expressed especially strongly by some of the musicians I interviewed, particularly those who were older, in their forties. This is because they grew up in an environment in which the music they now live for was foreign and strange. Today, rock music is ubiquitous in Japan; but when it first emerged in Japan in the late 1960s, it truly was an exotic novelty. A rock musician described his discovery of the Beatles:

> I was in fifth grade. An older kid had an expensive electric guitar, and played "A Hard Day's Night" on it – it was a real shock for me; I'd never heard anything like it before. In sixth grade each student had to sing a song in front of the class. I sang a Beatles' song. The teacher objected, saying that I shouldn't sing a song whose words I didn't understand. I told him – I was a smart-aleck back then! – that people our age sing love songs and we don't know what they mean, so why not songs in English?

Subsequently, even though he played rock professionally for many years, this musician seems to have felt that the music he played was foreign, not really his; like Mr. Sasaki, he felt he could only imitate. He told me of how he used to watch black people on American television programs and do his best to copy how they walked – they had rhythm and could feel "afterbeats," as he, as a Japanese, could not, he felt. Once he spied a black person walking in the streets downtown – a rare occurrence, even in this large city – and surreptitiously followed him block after block, imitating his every move in the hope of truly being able to feel "black" rhythm.

It seems clear that the rhythm and melodic structures of jazz and rock were something foreign, that had to be learned by these musicians through imitation before it could be made a part of themselves; and it seems clear that for many, this was an extraordinarily difficult process. A bebop pianist told me of how once in his bath he found himself, to his horror, humming a Japanese folk song instead of the jazz he'd been studying all his adult life. He thereafter mounted a pair of speakers in his bathroom so that he could listen to jazz even there – so that the impurity of his Japanese cultural background would never again, within his bathroom, impede his pursuit of a foreign artistic ideal. This man was trying to replace his cultural taken for granted with his chosen art, but was having difficulty doing so; the taken for granted at unexpected moments got in the way.

However, it seems remarkable the extent to which this imitation of Western art forms, jazz in particular, has continued. Japanese in recent decades have often had the opportunity to be exposed to jazz more than Americans (jazz coffeeshops, where one can listen to recordings for hours over a single cup of coffee, are widespread in Japanese cities, and professional American jazz musicians have told me that their opportunities for performing are far greater in Japan than in the US), and there are superbly creative jazz musicians at work in Japan today, such as Yamashita Yōsuke. Yet Japanese jazz musicians in general may to some degree deserve the criticism of a Western critic that they tend to be "highly competent but derivative," with Japanese interest in them "centered on the extent to which they had mastered the jazz idiom rather than their ability to advance the music."[25] A recent history of Japanese jazz maintains that the reputation Japanese jazz musicians have for only imitating American jazz is due to the fact that in traditional Japanese arts, copying is seen as a legitimate expression of art;[26] but perhaps the most important reason for this reputation has to do with Japanese musicians' ongoing sense of inferiority (*rettōkan*) before foreign forms. That both Japanese jazz and visual arts seem in the last five decades to have often followed lockstep the latest European and American artistic fashions is due in part to the insecurity of Japanese artists in finding their own voices in what they continue to perceive as being foreign mediums.

Indeed, the attitude remains strong in Japan even today that Japanese jazz should be, in effect, a copy of American jazz in order to be real jazz. Howard Becker has written that after World War II,

> U.S. soldiers, some of them musicians, stayed for extended periods in many European and Asian countries. Local musicians who had studied jazz only from recordings could now hear and play with American players. The Americans need not have been exceptionally good players; few were. But they were unquestionably authentic. . . . The lessons made an astounding difference. Prewar recordings by Europeans are clearly by non-Americans. After the war, you cannot tell Americans from Europeans or Japanese.[27]

What made American jazz musicians "authentic" is an open question; but it seems clear that the attitude remains strong in Japan even now that Japanese jazz should be, in effect, a copy of American jazz in order to be real jazz. A middle-aged jazz musician I interviewed, as if updating by half-a-century Becker's distinction between prewar and postwar muscians, spoke with admiration of younger players: "When a Japanese musician of my generation plays jazz, we can tell immediately that he's Japanese. But today when I hear a young Japanese playing jazz, I can't tell whether he's Japanese or American." Nonetheless, my own experience as a jazz musician in Japan in the 1980s revealed that the foreign remains more "authentic" than the native in the realm of jazz. My band's Japanese members, until they realized otherwise, assumed that my flubbed notes during saxophone solos were creative excursions; MCs would say of our band, "This is completely new music; we've never heard anything like this before!", while all-Japanese bands, playing equally avant-garde music, would get no such comments. I was "authentic," and could get away with incompetence – a situation my fellow band members tolerated because my white face could bring us performing opportunities and pay packets that their less "authentic" Japanese faces could not (and who knows what minor peaks of Japanese jazz celebrity we might have scaled had I been black, and thus truly "authentic": one of the few areas in which being black in Japan might have served as an advantage).

Some of the artists I interviewed spoke in specific ethnic terms: blacks, or Americans, or Westerners, play a music that Japanese may or may not be able to play and fully understand – just as, as we earlier saw, foreigners may or may not be able fully to understand Japanese arts. A recent Japanese book on jazz clearly – if crudely – emphasizes the importance of ethnicity in musical expression:

> There is no doubt that blues feeling and musical sensibility is expressed from the inside of black people's bodies. Today, by using so-called blue notes, anybody can play blues-like or jazz-like music, whether they're white or Japanese, whether they have blues feelings in their bodies or not. . . . It's like fake crab meat [that can be bought in Japanese supermarkets]. When jazz fans listen to jazz, they need to be able to judge whether the performer's jazz really is coming from his insides.[28]

This passage implies that only African-Americans can play blues and jazz that spring from the heart; other Americans, and Japanese, can play the notes but can't have the feeling, so their music is bound to be no more than imitation. Paralleling Mr. Sasaki's words, this book implies that if you aren't of the right ethnicity, you can't really play jazz. The contemporary artists I interviewed, as well as Japanese mass media, often interpreted ethnicity culturally more than racially. An admired Japanese culture hero, succeeding in American jazz, is the pianist Akiyoshi Toshiko – it can be done, examples such as hers show: Japanese can excel at jazz. Still, the fact that they are of the wrong ethnicity sets them at a distinct disadvantage, a number of artists I interviewed believed.

Other contemporary artists thought of the arts they aspired to perfect as being not tied to a particular ethnicity, but universal. When I asked the bebop pianist if he ever considered playing a Japanese-derived jazz, he said, "A foreign sumo wrestler can't say, 'because I'm from a different culture, I wrestle by my own rules.' The same thing is true with jazz." By his logic, jazz has a single, universal set of rules that every player must master. But of course this set of rules is a Western-derived set of rules: American jazz and rock musicians presumably don't have to suppress their culture when they play their music, but Japanese musicians must. An intellectual rock musician justified explicitly the idea that West is best:

> Japanese music didn't develop; it's childish [*yōchi*], primitive [*genshiteki*], aboriginal [*dojin ga tsukutta*]. All music is basically aimed at the same thing, just as is science: a universal development; but European music advanced much more than Japanese music. Music theory enables mathematically the development of music: rock emerged from that. Unlike traditional Japanese music, rock and pops are complex, so that human beings everywhere can appreciate them.

The fact that this development has been defined by the West was due, this man felt, to the universal progress that had begun in the West and that the West still led.

This musician's views are debatable – scholars of traditional Japanese music would doubtless indignantly claim that its complexity far exceeds that of the latest top 40 hit on the radio – but his logic has a long history. Max Weber, in his celebrated work *The Protestant Ethic and the Spirit of Capitalism*, points out that chordal music and harmony – the basis of all orchestral music, as well as rock – traditionally existed only in the West.[29] His views also echos the long history of Japanese who have urged their fellow citizens to progress along Western lines. For example, the critic Okakura Tenshin describes the attitudes of some Japanese in the late Meiji era as follows: "To the advocates of the wholesale westernization of Japan, Eastern civilization seems a lower development compared to the Western. The more we assimilate the foreign methods, the higher we mount in the scale of humanity."[30] And it is reflected in the lack of cultural confidence felt by many Japanese artists today.

Several of the rock musicians I spoke with expressed the dream of seeing a Japanese band "make it" on the world stage: "A real culture hero, like the Beatles, arises only rarely. I really hope that a Japanese group like that emerges in my lifetime" said one. "When will Japan produce a great worldwide band?" asked a rock promoter:

> Well, it's about time! But it'll take, at the earliest, another 10 years! That's my dream. . . . I run a rental stage. Sometimes when I see people playing here, I think, "Maybe this is the next Beatles, or Springsteen – if only they could get a little better!"

Maybe the purported inferiority of Japanese in rock's universal medium will come to an end before long. As one booking agent recently said in a newspaper article, "We've been trying to break Japanese bands overseas for 10 years. . . . Now, finally we feel we're in the right time"; as an American music executive said, "I think the next Beck or the next Paul McCartney is going to come from Japan. . . . And I want to be the one to find him."[31] But at present this has yet to happen, and remains only the dream of the musicians I interviewed.

I often questioned rock musicians as to why American rock should be popular in Japan, while Japanese rock makes scarcely a ripple in the United States. As one answered, "This has less to do with music than with race and economics"; as another said, "Japan is culturally open to the arts of other countries, especially the West, but America is culturally closed; it doesn't accept other countries' cultures." (Indeed, as if echoing these words, one American music executive has stated that Japanese rock music will never succeed in the American market because "They look different than we do. They speak different than we do."[32]) The musicians I interviewed were well aware of the skewed shelves of the cultural supermarket, favoring Western forms; but despite this, they dreamed of success in those imported forms.

As we have seen, the underlying assumption of many of these contemporary artists was that their Japaneseness was an obstacle preventing them from excelling at their arts. Other contemporary artists, however, did not feel this: for them, Japaneseness was not a cultural obstacle, but simply an irrelevance.

Contemporary artists: Japaneseness and choice

There continues to be a degree of inferiority complex felt toward the West among some Japanese artists; but it may be that this inferiority complex is finally giving way, in at least some art forms. In the mid-1980s, it was argued in an art journal that:

> [In the past] . . . Japanese artists . . . never went beyond copying the European trends, and the results were Japanese fauvism, Japanese cubism, Japanese constructivism, etc. . . . But now there is a new generation of artists emerging who consider painting in its whole context and produce works based on theories and sensibilities that can be called truly contemporary to those of . . . Western artists.[33]

More recently, an executive at the Japanese broadcast network NHK, beginning a new Asian-based music program, stated: "For fifty years, since the end of World War II, most Japanese musicians tried to be like American or European musicians, but finally we have realized we are not American, we are not French, we are Japanese."[34] Some of the younger artists I interviewed stoutly maintained that they felt absolutely no sense of inferiority before foreign art forms.

These claims may "protesteth too much." To maintain that "We don't have to follow Western art! We have our own art!" might perversely be read as indicating the opposite: "We're still so influenced by Western art that we have to loudly proclaim our freedom from that influence." And yet, there is a sense in which forms such as rock and jazz music and contemporary modern art are at present not foreign but part of the taken-for-granted fabric of contemporary Japanese life. A middle-aged rock guitarist told me of how, while the music he had played in his prime was all imitated, borrowed from the West, his teen-age daughter could understand rock on its own terms, without any consciousness of its foreignness: "She and her friends were born into rock: it's natural to them – it's their music," he said, with more than a hint of envy. This attitude is reflected in a number of the artists I interviewed, engaged in rock music and avant-garde visual art; they felt their arts were as natural to them as they would be to any artist in Paris or Munich or Seattle. They belong to a world in which these arts are taken for granted as worldwide.

This attitude led some of the people I interviewed to downplay the importance of culture and cultural tradition in shaping art. An oil painter said, "a great painting is a great painting regardless; nationality and culture don't matter." "*Ongaku ni wa kokkyō wa nai yo*" – music has no boundaries, exclaimed a rock musician; rock has no cultural home, it is universal. Another rock musician said, "I like the music I like, hate the music I hate. Whether it's Japanese or foreign, I don't care. I don't think about it." An avant-garde dancer spoke more articulately about the transcendence of national culture:

> I think I'm expressing something basic in my dance, something shared by all human beings. Initially, in my twenties, I danced to express my individuality, but later it became something more and more universal. I don't dance as a Japanese; there's more to human beings than national or ethnic cultures. . . . A native American cried when he saw my performance. He said he saw in me the person who brought up him and died in the past. Maybe so: I believe in reincarnation. I may not have been Japanese in my past lives.

This woman was unusual among those I interviewed in her complete disavowal of any sense of Japaneseness (having watched her performance and been moved to tears myself, I can attest to the power of her art beyond any national bounds). She expresses a feeling that seems to be held increasingly among some Japanese artists, the feeling that national culture means little before the global cultural supermarket. To take just one example from mass media, a Japanese techno musician states, "I feel like I'm *mukokuseki* (nationless). . . . I'm quite happy feeling like I have no nationality"[35] – his music and his consciousness are purely global, he claims.

A key factor behind such assertions is that of globalization: with the world ever more interlinked, the boundaries of societies mean less. The business writer Ohmae writes of *The Borderless World*,[36] in which Japanese corporations can no longer think of themselves as Japanese if they are to succeed, but must take on a global identity; and a similar global identity may be emerging among many artists. The noted conceptual artist Yanagi Yukinori's "World Flag Ant Farm" consisted of sand paintings of flags of the countries of the United Nations, gradually dismantled by thousands of ants. As he later wrote, "Do the ghettos of nations, ethnic groups, and religions truly determine personal identities?"[37] – he would clearly say that they do not, as so too would the artists quoted above.

A major artistic school of the 1980s in Japan was that of appropriationism, whereby all the world's visual cultures are seen as free for the taking, to be utilized as one wishes in one's art. The Japanese art world of the past decade has been commenting on a Japanese postmodern society that seems, at least "on the surface . . . a vast amalgam of disparate signs, styles, and structures culled indiscriminately from world cultures, past and present."[38] Several well-known contemporary Japanese artists wryly comment on this cultural appropriation. Morimura Yasumasa recreates the Western canon of artistic master-pieces with himself at center stage, as, for example, the female nude in Manet's *Olympia*; he thereby offers a "stylized critique of Japan's cul-ture of appropriation and commodification."[39] His commentary refers to Japan's worship of the West; but it is also a commentary on the world cultural supermarket, in which there are no roots to constrain one, no ethnic or cultural shackles – all the world is free to be explored and exploited in one's artistic creation.

One man I interviewed, a rock musician and explorer of world musics in his early forties, well revealed this attitude of appropriation and its pitfalls. He played in a New Orleans-style rhythm and blues band, and also played Australian didgeridoo at the intermissions of dance parties:

> My dream is to play music of aboriginal peoples from the world over. I can be exposed to something universal by dealing with aboriginal peoples. This didgeridoo was given me as a present by my Australian aboriginal friend; I took it to mean that I was entrusted to perform this instrument, to convey it to Japanese. The sound it makes is real, deep, from the body, not like other instru-ments. I play this music to explore the aboriginal part in myself; the ultimate question is "Who am I?" . . . If someone were to ask me why I steal music from aboriginal cultures, maybe I'd apologize! But if you want to play any of the world's musics, go ahead – it's no one's possession.

As he had learned to his regret, however, "music is not just music; it involves politics." He was interested in the culture and arts of the Ainu;[40] he had recorded the song of an old Ainu woman, and subjected it to a progressive-rock computer remix, to "bring Ainu music to a wide audience." However, problems emerged, since he himself was not Ainu, and his recording could be construed as exploiting Ainu music for his own ends. In disappointment, he voluntarily withdrew the album from circulation after several hundred copies had been distributed.

We saw earlier how some Japanese traditional artists may feel uneasy about Westerners playing traditional Japanese music, as if their own music was being appropriated; but here we see the reverse – Japanese not having their own music appropriated by others, but themselves appropriating others' music, not as the musically colonized but as the colonizers. This artist had believed that from the cultural supermarket, everything may be used – music is no one group's possession, but belongs to all the world. Some Ainu, however, believed otherwise, that their music was their possession, their roots, to be played by no one but themselves. This artist acceded to that argument – being well aware of the power differential between wealthy Japanese and impoverished Ainu and other aboriginal groups, he was acutely conscious that even music created with the best of intentions could be seen as exploiting these groups. However, in the long term, the argument of music as belonging to particular ethnic groups seems doomed. The sense of all the world's cultures as open, to be appropriated from as one chooses, is becoming inevitably more and more widespread, due to the ready availability of all the world's recorded musics:

> Once a sound is recorded, it's abstracted from its original time and space, and that makes it available for any new context. . . . It's no longer a wedding song or an age-old lament; it's just another chunk of information. . . . Snippets of Arabic and Tibetan chant, of the vocal polyphony of Corsicans or Central African pygmies and of the drums of Brazilian carnival bands or Moroccan healers can all be heard floating across the electronic soundscapes of recent releases.[41]

Sampling increases this disembodiment: sounds from across the globe may be appropriated as one pleases. Globalization and technology create a world in which everything in the world may be created from.

I interviewed only a few artists who seemed fully comfortable pursuing their arts as world citizens in the cultural supermarket – only a few for whom artistic Japaneseness truly didn't matter. But I suspect that there may be more and more Japanese artists of this ilk in the future.

Contemporary artists: the reinvention of Japanese roots

While the artists discussed above welcomed their membership in the global cultural supermarket, a number of the contemporary artists I interviewed seemed to recoil from it: they sought to pursue their arts not just from an uprooted cornucopia of all the world's forms, but from a place, a home, roots. They sought to assert their arts as Japanese. Bands interviewed in recent popular Japanese rock magazines sometimes proudly proclaim that they are *Japanese* rock musicians, and so too some of the musicians I spoke with, saying, albeit more diffidently, "We don't need to compare ourselves to Western rock; we have our own Japanese rock." An orchestral composer I interviewed said,

> I don't support the idea of cosmopolitanism. It's good for different groups to get along well with one another, but every culture, every ethnic group must have something different, to distinguish itself. . . .
> I compose *Japanese* music – for Western instruments, but it's *Japanese*.

An interesting question is of course what makes these artists' expressions and identities Japanese. Let me explore this question first in terms of music, and then visual arts.

The orchestral composer told me that he could convey the Japaneseness of his music simply by composing through a traditional five-tone scale rather than the Western musical major and minor scales. His audience would intuitively understand this music as Japanese, he maintained. Some jazz musicians spoke of the free jazz movement of the 1960s and 1970s, in which musicians such as Moriyama Takeo and Yamamoto Hōzan used melody lines that recalled Japanese folk music and classical *shakuhachi* music. Even though Japanese jazz musicians have turned away from such expressions of "Japaneseness" of late – following the American conservative jazz turn in recent years, Japanese jazz musicians have turned to playing 1950s' American bebop instead – some jazz musicians I interviewed could assert on this basis that "Japanese jazz does exist."

Rock music's Japaneseness is straightforward in at least one sense, that of language. Rock in Japan used to be sung in English, and a long-running argument was waged as to whether Japanese was a suitable language for rock.[42] From Japanese bands of the 1970s mouthing songs in English whose meanings they didn't understand, to bands like the Southern All Stars in the 1980s, singing in a stilted American-sounding Japanese as if to subordinate the rhythms of the Japanese language to the Western rhythms they felt to exist in rock, to Japanese bands of today, singing rock in a Japanese that sounds more or less like Japanese, we see a distinct linguistic Japanization of rock. As the Beatles-loving middle-aged rock musician cited earlier stated:

We used to try to sing Beatles tunes and be happy with that; but young musicians today write and perform their own music in their own language. Rock means you have to be able to express yourself, and for that, you need to use your own language.

But this is not enough in asserting the Japaneseness of Japanese rock. For rock truly to be Japanese, this must be reflected in the music itself, and this seems more problematic. "We're Japanese, and we play rock music, so it's Japanese," said some of the less reflective musicians I interviewed, but others were more doubtful: "For rock, you can make the lyrics Japanese, but the rhythm, melodies, and instruments can never really be Japanese: it's just too different." One musician said:

> No, I don't think that there's any real Japanese rock – it's all borrowed. The rock that Japanese musicians come up with is written on the basis of their having listened to foreign music: there's a lot of stealing. Of course blues and soul were once black, stolen by white musicians. Maybe, since everything is stolen anyway, we really can say there is Japanese rock!

This is a very astute statement, reflecting the reality of the culturally supermarketed world we live in. But the question remains, what could make rock *Japanese*?

Traditional Japanese musical forms – *koto* and *shakuhachi* – have been on occasion mixed with rock by Japanese bands, but this was dismissed by the musicians I interviewed as being contrived, even silly, so great was felt to be the gap between the two forms: "*koto* and *shakuhachi* don't fit in rock!" exclaimed one. The scales and melodic structures of such music, used to create "Japaneseness" by the classical composer, were dismissed by the rock musicians I interviewed as being either "old-fashioned" and "boring," or as simply incompatible with rock. Another marker of Japaneseness could be *min'yō*, Japanese folk music: not the traditional high culture of *koto* and *shakuhachi* but *shomin bunka*, "ordinary people's culture." However, this too was acknowledged by the musicians I interviewed as being extremely difficult to merge with rock. The city of Sapporo sponsored a dance festival while I was there, whereby competing troupes would perform to their own musical compositions; the one requirement was that these compositions feature a traditional *min'yō* tune thought to symbolize the city. It was fascinating listening to the synthesized compositions: most consisted of 10 minutes of rock and disco interspersed with a few awkward seconds of *min'yō* so as to meet the festival's requirement.[43]

If the Japaneseness of Japanese music were no more than a matter of technique, of using certain scales or melodic structures to evoke Japaneseness, then the matter would be simple: of course jazz and orchestral music, and even rock, can be Japanese. There are a number of recordings of the *shakuhachi* player Yamamoto Hōzan, to take just one example, in which *shakuhachi* is combined with jazz in a way that is faithful both to the timbres and textures of traditional *shakuhachi* and to the rhythmic propulsion and complex melodic and chordal structures of jazz.[44] However, the matter is more complex than this, in that Japaneseness is not simply a technical problem of how to insert certain sequences of notes, and rhythms, and textures into one's music, but a cultural problem: what *is* Japaneseness in today's world? I discussed near the start of this chapter how, for young Japanese today, jazz and pizza may be more a part of the taken-for-granted world in which they grew up and live than are traditional Japanese arts. This seems to apply to music as well. Neither five-tone scales nor (to a lesser extent) *min'yō* folk music are prevalent forms within contemporary Japanese society: can we thus claim that they are truly Japanese today, as other forms are not?

A rock guitarist said to me, "Yes, maybe it would sound strange to put a *min'yō* song into rock, but . . . I'd like to do that in my music. These are our roots [*rūtsu*]. We're Japanese, and we want to show that we're Japanese." This musician indeed grew up hearing *min'yō* as the background music in noodle shops and at the summer festival *bon-odori*; but he also grew up hearing the Beatles, reggae, and Afropop, he told me. What makes *min'yō* his roots as opposed to all these other musics? When I asked him this question, he answered in terms of Japanese history; but in terms of his personal history, and all the different musics he has been exposed to, there is little basis for his claim. If one has, within one's own experience, never been rooted within a tradition, then the claim of returning to one's roots doesn't really make sense except on an intellectual level, as a matter of conscious choice from the cultural supermarket.

In a number of recent books, critics have exhorted Japanese artists to escape their Western shackles, to return to Japaneseness. The jazz critic Yui Shōichi compares Japanese to African-Americans: Just as African-Americans have adopted white European culture, which has infected their jazz, so too have Japanese discarded their own culture to take up European culture, he maintains.[45] His hope is that just as African-Americans have thrown off Western cultural domination to play their own jazz in recent decades, so too can Japanese jazz emerge from under its Western shadow: "How in Japanese jazz will the ethnic individuality [*minzokuteki kosei*] of Japanese come to be expressed?"[46]

But where is any such artistic "ethnic individuality" to be found at this point in Japanese history? As the noted rock musician Hosono Haruomi has said, "There's a cultural chaos here in Japan. We're bombarded with music from everywhere. . . . And we don't know what to do if we don't know who we are."[47] In a Japanese world in which the taken-for-granted realm has increasingly become that of the global cultural supermarket – albeit a supermarket many of whose forms continue to be seen as foreign – it is difficult to see how "ethnic individuality" and "Japanese roots" could be anything but a latter-day invention from the cultural supermarket. But to understand this matter more fully, let us turn to visual arts.

Contemporary visual arts seem more developed in their efforts to express Japaneseness than jazz and rock music, largely because of their longer history in Japan; whereas jazz and rock have existed in Japan only in recent decades, oil painting has been around since the Meiji Restoration, and abstract painting virtually since its Western inception. However, the same kinds of questions – "Where is the Japaneseness of contemporary Japanese art?" – continue to be asked and struggled with. Japaneseness, the critic Wakabayashi Naoki argues, connotes for Japanese today a traditional world that some people may cherish but in which nobody actually lives – "Japanese people are trying to be proud of Japanese tradition . . . but contemporary Japanese life is far away from that tradition."[48] Only through transcending the distinction between "traditional Japanese art" and "modern Western art" can a vital Japanese art emerge, he asserts. Wakabayashi is saying that a modern Japanese art must be created, in clear distinction to both Japanese tradition and Western modernity.

Wakabayashi's heroes are the artists of the *mono-ha* school of the late 1960s and early 1970s, who used unprocessed natural materials such as stones and wood to create forms that sought to "make the mind and nature one,"[49] and who sought to create an Asian art theory distinct from Western theory. The *mono-ha* artists strove to embody in their work a "logic of the East" as opposed to a "logic of the West," and thereby to create an alternative version of modernism, one rooted in Japan's Asian identity. One person I interviewed, a Korean-born painter, echoed this view: "Japan is rooted in Asia. Today, more and more young people are looking to Asia for their identity." This is to a degree true – it has been fashionable in some circles in recent years to proclaim the Asianness of Japan – but underlying this is a deep ambivalence about Japanese identity in relation to Asia. A movie released a few years ago provides a fascinating if caricatured glimpse into Japanese attitudes toward their fellow Asians. It depicts a Japanese gangster struggling to evict Asian (Filipino, Thai, Pakistani) workers from a decrepit dormitory in Tokyo. He tries every possible method to get them to move; in a climactic scene, the lodgers confront him, to say, "We're all Asian, aren't we?" The gangster replies with the extraordinary words, "We . . . We're not Asians. We Japanese – we're white!"[50] This is meant to be funny, and indeed it is, but it also illustrates an ongoing fact of Japanese life: for many Japanese, and certainly for almost all the artists I interviewed, the West, not Asia, was their reference point, the focus of their envy, longing, disdain, or sense of competition.

It seems fairly clear that there is no underlying "logic of the East" – Asian societies are different enough in their underlying values to make any such assumption of commonality difficult to give credence to. Beyond this, it seems debatable that there is even any underlying "logic of Japaneseness" apparent in the work of Japanese artists: in a culturally supermarketed, fragmented Japan, what might such a common Japaneseness consist of? Contemporary avant-garde Tokyo artists, influenced by theories of postmodernism, argue, as we've seen, that there is no such Japaneseness, in their appropriation of all the world's forms; but some of the artists I interviewed believed that there is such a Japaneseness, albeit threatened. Let us now consider at length the words of one such man.

Kobayashi Jōji (37)

I paint pastel and watercolor paintings sometimes, but my heart lies in *sumie* (Japanese ink paintings). I go to the performances of a free dancer and paint his movement. It takes only 30 or 40 seconds to do one of these paintings, but it's really difficult – the lines has to be as expressive as possible. Sometimes my pictures have just two or three lines in them: I want to paint not a body, but the flow of energy. I don't do traditional *sumie* – that's too restrictive; I dislike tradition. I turned to *sumie* because I want to portray free modern dance, in all its quickness – I use Japanese ink because it lets me depict motion. . . .

Except for my own exhibition once a year, I don't exhibit my work; I don't advertise, I don't want to be famous! At my exhibition I can only sell three or four paintings, enough to pay the exhibition fee. If you think of making money from your work, you won't be able to create what you really want. . . . For 10 years I worked for a printing company. But when you're in a company, you've got to kill your sensitivity; I'd come home and not know what to paint. I was reading too much art theory, thinking about being an "artist" – it became a barrier. Then I saw dance, and really wanted to paint again. I was asked by a friend to manage an apartment building; I'd have time to paint, he said. Actually I have even less time now than I had as a salaryman! But I feel better in spirit – my sensitivity has returned. . . . (If I were free 24 hours a day to paint, maybe I couldn't paint anything! All my experiences in life – meeting people, dealing with problems of tenants, taking care of my children – it all fertilizes my painting. If I didn't have those experiences, I'd paint boring pictures!)

My son once said about my dance paintings, "Dad, even though you can paint really good pictures, why do you exhibit only bad ones?" But I don't want to exhibit skillful pictures, I want to move people's hearts! Anyone, with training, can paint technically good pictures. . . . I think that foreigners might understand my pictures better than Japanese can, because they don't have preconceptions; they can look at my work with a fresh eye. Many Japanese think of *sumie* and look for mountains and rivers. Their thinking is stiff. Japanese who like my work aren't painters, but dancers and musicians. I'm outside the standard genres of the Japanese art world – I'm not recognized by that world. . . .

I was raised in Western painting – that's what I was taught in school. I've thought much more about Western culture than Japanese culture. (I went to a *koto* concert recently, and thought it was great, but maybe that's because the composer was very much influenced by Western music!) When I was 20, I imitated Picasso; also Egon Schiele, a student of Gustav Klimt; his work amazed me. . . . Whether a picture is good or not transcends the cultural tradition it comes from; it transcends ideology, race, cultural tradition. I was in Spain, and saw Picasso's *Guernica*. I knew nothing about its historical background, about the event it depicted; but when I saw the painting, I was overwhelmed; tears came to my eyes. The painting exists on its own. . . .

Japanese today talk about "culture," but there's no natural feeling for that culture. "Japanese culture" is preserved simply to show tourists and foreigners. Yes, I think that Japanese culture – the high artistic culture, anyway – may simply vanish. Looking at young people today, I think it probably will vanish. But Japaneseness will continue. Japanese people have Japaneseness not in their words but in their bodies. Inevitably, in my work, my Japaneseness comes out: in my mind, I have Western culture and arts; but when

I paint, my body expresses my Japaneseness. Sometimes when I paint, I draw *ojizō-san* [Buddhist statues representing the guardian deities of children], not consciously, but it comes out that way. That's inside me, maybe from my early experiences – I wasn't raised in traditional society, of course, but I draw what I've experienced in life. Even if Japanese aren't conscious of it, their Japaneseness, created over two thousand years of history, comes out. "Japaneseness": it's in such words as *"iki," "wabi," "sabi"*[51] – those aren't just matters of traditional culture; those are in the Japanese temperament, that foreigners can't fully understand. However much Japanese culture becomes mixed in with other cultures, that sense will remain, however vaguely. . . .

To be honest, when I was in my twenties I hated the Japanese, kow-towed to foreigners. But then I went to Europe, and began to see the good points of the Japanese. I found, in Europe, that the smell of *sumi* [Japanese ink] soothed me. . . . As for my paintings, though, people don't need to see Japaneseness. Whether people see *ojizō-san* or ghosts or snowmen, all I want is to move them, excite them, stimulate their sensitivity. . . .

Mr. Kobayashi grew up studying Western art; that artistic world was his taken-for-granted artistic realm, the artistic world he understands best, he tells us. He chooses to work using *sumi*, Japanese ink, only because *sumi* suits his artistic purpose, of rapidly painting the motion of avant-garde dance; he dislikes Japanese tradition, and enjoys a *koto* concert, he tells us, perhaps because of the Western-influenced tastes of the composer. Art transcends culture, he says: his own work can perhaps be understood better by foreigners than by Japanese. On the basis of his Western artistic training and exposure, he chooses his own particular artistic path from the world's cultural supermarket of forms he might have chosen.

And yet, the *sumi* that he first claims merely as a practical means for the pursuit of his art, he later tells us is more: in Europe, where his attitude toward Japaneseness shifted from hatred to acceptance, it was the smell of *sumi* that soothed him, apparently assuring him of his Japaneseness. If intellectually his taken-for-granted artistic world is Western, at the level of the body, it is Japanese, he maintains. Japan, for him, seems implicitly to have shifted from being in the realm of *shikata ga nai* – the society he had to live within in pursuing his unrecognized art (which even members of his own family can't understand); the culture and society he disliked having to be a member of – to the realm of roots. These roots he sees as extending throughout Japanese history, roots that, even though "'Japanese culture' is preserved simply to show tourists and foreigners," can in some sense never be destroyed. His own art may be interpreted in multiple ways, all of which make him happy as long as its viewers are moved; but his art does reflect his ineradicable underlying Japaneseness, he maintains.

Perhaps it does. Mr. Kobayashi did not directly discuss it, but his work, in its spare use of line and of blank space, does indeed have much in common with traditional calligraphy, as well as *sumie*; while he may dislike traditional Japanese arts for their restrictions, his own contemporary work may share with traditional Japanese arts a degree of *iki, wabi, sabi*, those aesthetic virtues that, he tells us, are hallmarks of Japaneseness. But are these really a matter of unconscious Japaneseness, the accretions of history that come welling up in his work, or are they instead a matter of conscious aesthetic choice from the cultural supermarket? Mr. Kobayashi speaks of *ojizō-san* as emerging from his ink sketches; and *ojizō-san* are a distinct cultural form within the Japanese visual environment: this is what he has seen and internalized in Japan. But he has also seen and internalized many other cultural forms, from Disneyland to McDonald's golden arches – why don't these forms also emerge within his art? (When I suggested that the shape in his ink painting that he believed evoked *ojizō-san* and thus his Japanese roots also resembled the McDonald's golden arches to be seen just a few blocks from his house, Mr. Kobayashi seemed less than pleased.) I suspect that *ojizō-san* represent not his rooted unconscious, but rather his subsequent interpretation of rootedness – not his underlying unconscious Japaneseness, but rather his conscious construction of Japaneseness. I can't know this – who, after all, am I to interpret whether other people's senses of their roots are genuine? – and yet, given the extraordinary cultural mix and flux of Japan today, it's not altogether clear how artistic roots can exist for most Japanese.

Mr. Kobayashi's views echo a number of recent books on contemporary Japanese art, seeking to establish the Japaneseness of that art. One book, by the critic Sugawara Norio, discusses Japaneseness in terms of the common "ethnic memory" (*minzoku koyū no kioku*) it claims is held by Japanese.[52] This "ethnic memory" creates the Japaneseness of contemporary Japanese art, Sugawara claims – Japanese artists may not be conscious of it in their work, and may have no intention of creating Japaneseness, but it's there all the same, its author writes. He discusses a painting of the abstract painter Yamada Masaaki:

> This is clearly a work created by a Japanese. This is shown by its
> atmosphere. . . . In the same sense that Matisse was a French artist
> and Pollock was an American artist, this work suggests Japan as its
> place of production. And this is something that we [Japanese]
> should definitely feel proud of.[53]

The premise that Japaneseness is apparent in the works of contemporary Japanese artists seems debatable – other artists discussed by
Sugawara in this book claim that there is no such Japaneseness to
return to.[54] Nonetheless, several painters I interviewed spoke of a
rooted sense of Japaneseness in ways that seemed convincing: there is a
unique physical world of Japan that their paintings reflect. A surrealist
painter spoke of Japaneseness as the lights of *pachinko* parlors – the
bright pinball arcades that dot the Japanese urban landscape – which
appear as the backdrop of several of his paintings; and indeed, *pachinko*
parlors form a distinct recognizably Japanese feature of Japanese life
today (notwithstanding the fact that many of the proprietors of these
parlors are in fact Korean). This artist grew up next to a *pachinko*
parlor, he told me, and used to stare at it out the window as a child; the
lights of the *pachinko* parlor, we might say, form his personal Japanese
roots. A realist painter, a man who grew up deep in the countryside,
spoke of Japaneseness in terms of climate and landscape,

> the forests, the mountains; the snow of Hokkaido[55]. . . . Because I
> live with that, I paint as I paint. . . . As Japan loses its natural
> features, becomes nothing but buildings, maybe Japanese will
> become just like people in other countries. But if Japanese nature is
> allowed to remain, Japaneseness will remain.

This last artist's expression of Japaneseness is tinged with melan-
choly; his rooted sense of Japaneseness seems tenuous, just as it seems
tenuous to the traditional artists earlier discussed. I brought up this
possible death of Japaneseness with a rock musician, who said, "All
over the world now there's Coca-Cola and McDonald's, but this doesn't
mean that all the world has become nothing but Coca-Cola and
McDonald's. People's ways of eating all are different in different
places." This seems true enough, as recent anthropological work has
attested;[56] but if Japaneseness comes down to no more than differences
in eating McDonald's hamburgers, then the Japaneseness of Japan
somehow seems awfully small and tenuous.

But perhaps such pessimism is misplaced. We earlier saw how,
throughout Japanese history, Japanese have taken foreign cultural

forms and made them Japanese; a similar process is clearly taking place today as well, as we've seen. The global cultural supermarket in all its contemporary ubiquity makes the idea of belonging to a particular artistic and cultural home increasingly problematic; what Japanese arts might consist of in a culturally supermarketed world is an open question. However, what finally counts as Japaneseness is less a matter of objective validity, despite the carping of anthropologists like me, than of what people can be persuaded to believe in. All that it takes to recreate artistic Japaneseness in Japanese music or visual art is the imaginative choice of and creation from forms within the global cultural supermarket and the ability and luck to convince the Japanese world at large, and, to a degree, the world at large, that one's creation is indeed Japanese, whatever Japaneseness is construed to mean. This is a huge task, but to the extent that the past is any guide, it will indeed eventually be accomplished.

Conclusion: what in the world is Japanese?

One way to consider the different ideas of Japaneseness among the artists we have examined is in terms of different generations. The artists using traditional forms who see Japan as a threatened culture that must be saved were more often than not in their fifties or older; the artists using contemporary forms who see Japan as a barrier to artistic creation within a universal or non-Japanese standard were more often than not in their late thirties or forties; the artists using contemporary forms who see Japaneseness as irrelevant to their global choices, as well as those who seek to reassert their Japaneseness through their global choices, were more often than not in their twenties or early thirties. This generational division is hardly surprising: older artists grew up in a prewar Japan in which Japanese traditional arts were more readily visible and open to experience than today; middle-aged artists grew up in a postwar Japan immersed in American and Western cultural forms, Japanese arts having been discredited by defeat in war; and younger artists grew up in a Japan becoming more confident of itself in its affluence, a Japan in which Japaneseness could indeed begin to be reasserted. Although these individual artists' choices and paths were by no means determined by their generational placement – why is one man in his forties a *shakuhachi* player, another a jazz pianist? – their generational placement clearly sets their horizons and colors their worldviews.

But beyond the generation gap, it seems clear that the different versions of Japanese cultural identity we have examined echo throughout Japanese history. Consider again the three nineteenth-century slogans mentioned in the first section of this chapter. The exhortation *sonnō jōi* ("revere the Emperor, repel the barbarians") seems to some degree to apply to the artists working in traditional forms lamenting the Westernization of Japan and dreaming of a resurgence of their Japanese arts, the Japanese "roots" that they see as having been lost. The exhortation *bunmei kaika* (adopt Western "civilization and enlightenment") seems to apply to the contemporary artists we considered who see their Japanese cultural background as a barrier to their pursuit of artistic excellence in foreign – Western – forms. The exhortation *wakon yōsai* (adopt "Japanese spirit, Western learning") corresponds to some degree to the contemporary artists who seek, from within their wholesale immersion in Western, worldwide artistic forms, to rediscover their Japaneseness.

However these forms of identity are not merely reflections of history: they also reflect the unique situation of Japan today, a hypermodern society flooded by the cultural supermarket. Some traditional artists, as we saw, view Japanese identity as a primordial ethnic essence, Japanese traditional culture as the inherent product of Japanese "blood." Some contemporary artists see Japaneseness as a provincial barrier to their pursuit of their foreign artistic forms; others see Japaneseness as simply irrelevant to their membership in the global cultural supermarket. Still other contemporary artists see their arts as involving the construction of a new sense of Japaneseness within supermarketed cultural forms. The first and the last of these groups both proclaim the Japaneseness of their arts, but there is a huge gap – the cultural supermarket intervenes. The earlier primordial sense of Japaneseness cannot be returned to, at least artistically, but only reinvented from the cultural supermarket's array of forms.

But this is difficult to admit to. Some contemporary artists I interviewed seem to construct Japaneseness from the cultural supermarket, and then assert that what they have selected is not merely one more supermarketed choice, but roots, home, where one primordially belongs. These artists can no longer live in the homes of the traditional artists, but can only build new homes from bits and pieces of the cultural supermarket. They can only imagine home from the supermarket's aisles; and perhaps with some sleight of hand and rhetorical persuasiveness, the cultural supermarket of today's Japan may yet be transformed into their particular Japanese cultural home.

Or, perhaps, on the other hand, for a new generation of Japanese artists, no such home will be needed. All the world will be home; and perhaps this attitude will come to transcend these artists to include Japan at large, and all of us in this world. The implicit conflict in this chapter between those who seek a particular cultural home from within the cultural supermarket, and those who spurn any such home, is the case for Japanese artists, but also for those in worlds beyond, as we will explore in the chapters to come.

3   What in the world is American?

On the cultural identities of evangelical Christians, spiritual searchers, and Tibetan Buddhists

The United States has seemed to many observers during its history to be a God-fearing nation; and indeed the vast majority of Americans today say they believe in God. But who or what is this God? Christian preachers regularly proclaim that the United States is a Christian nation founded on divine principles, and urge Americans to accept the Christian God as their saviour. On the other hand, religious groups from the Unitarians to the Mormons to the Christian Scientists each have their own different ideas of God; and in what may be thought of as "the Easternization of America," there are hundreds of thousands of Buddhists in the United States today, as well as many adherents to Islam and Hinduism. The coins and bills Americans use proclaim "In God we trust" – but what God? whose God?

The different religious orientations in the United States today may be thought of as different formulations of "America."[1] Is America "One nation under God," as the Pledge of Allegiance declares, a Judeo-Christian society entrusted by God to be a beacon of truth to the world? Or is America a land of the individual "pursuit of happiness," as the Declaration of Independence declares: America as a cultural supermarket of world religions, from which Americans are free to pick and choose as fits their particular attitudes, lifestyles, tastes? We saw last chapter how, for some Japanese artists, Japan represented primordial roots now all but lost, for others a cultural impediment to the pursuit of art within the global cultural supermarket, and for still others a cultural home that must be recreated from the cultural super-market's shelves. In this chapter, we will see a broadly similar pattern, in the realm not of art but of religion. For some American religious seekers, America is a Christian nation that has now forgotten its Christian essence; for others, America represents the cultural super-market, and the principle that one may choose from its shelves what-ever in the world might make one happy; and still others envision the emergence of an alternative "Buddhist America," an alternative American essence. As in last chapter's Japan, albeit in a different register, we see in this chapter an ongoing loss and recreation of "America."

Two concepts of America

Religion has been a central aspect of American life since its beginning. Eastern North America was settled in the seventeenth century by members of diverse Christian groups, from Quakers in Pennsylvania, to Puritans in Massachusetts, to Catholics in Maryland. However, it was the Massachusetts Puritans whose religious impact was most to shape America's religious sense of itself. Scholars writing about American religion tend to see "in American Puritanism the first statement of America's self-consciousness as a divinely appointed 'redeemer nation'";[2] the Puritan discourse of America shaped American consciousness throughout the nation's subsequent history, of "the American self as representative of universal rebirth."[3]

By the late eighteenth century, the strict religiousness of Puritanism had given way in some quarters to the values of the French Enlightenment, and belief in a more abstract God allied with Reason and Nature. The God of America's founding fathers was not so much the personal Christian God, damning humans to hell for their vanity (the God in the writings of Jonathan Edwards) but rather a principle of benevolence, aiding humans in their self-improvement (the God apparent in the writings of Benjamin Franklin). Yet the founding fathers too sought to keep the language of the Bible in American life, and sought to keep the idea of America as a redeemer nation divinely ordained, an exemplar and guide for all nations. How much this was a practical effort at divine legitimation for a new and shaky nation, and how much was genuinely believed by the nation's founders, is an open question (no doubt there was a degree of both). In any case, although the first amendment of the US Constitution guaranteed freedom of religion, and the separation of church and state, Christianity and its book, the Bible, continued to serve as the basic narrative of American life. "The Old Testament is . . . so omnipresent in the American culture of 1800 or 1820 that historians have as much difficulty taking cognizance of it as of the air people breathed";[4] "On the face of it, it would be hard to imagine a nation more thoroughly biblical than the United States between the American Revolution and the Civil War."[5]

Over the course of the nineteenth century, by many accounts, the United States became progressively less immersed in Christianity.

James Turner has written of how Darwinism served as the trigger for the emergence of agnosticism as a viable option in American life:

> America in 1840 was a Christian nation. . . . Within twenty years after the Civil War, agnosticism emerged as a self-sustaining phenomenon. Disbelief in God was, for the first time, plausible enough to grow beyond a rare eccentricity and to stake out a sizeable permanent niche in American culture.[6]

While Protestant revivalism continued to be powerful, such revivalism, in an increasingly commercial United States, became more and more a matter of selling religion: "Revivalism . . . shoved American religion into the marketplace of culture. . . . The intention was to save souls, but in a brassy way that threw religion into a free-for-all competition for people's attention."[7] Competing for such attention, a host of new religions begin to emerge: Mormonism, Christian Science, Theosophy, and many other creeds.

Turning to our present century, a number of scholars have written of America's secularization ("No student of modern American culture could seriously say, as did English traveller James Bryce in 1888, that Americans are basically a religious people"[8]); yet today, according to recent surveys, 98 percent, or 95 percent, or 84 percent of Americans claim to believe in God.[9] There are grounds for skepticism at such high figures – it may well be that many Americans feel social pressure to proclaim belief in God to a pollster while in fact hardly ever thinking about God[10] – but clearly Americans claim religious belief to a far greater extent than members of other contemporary affluent societies. In American public life, presidents Reagan, Bush, and Clinton have continued regularly to invoke God in their rhetoric, not just because of pressure from a newly emergent politicized Christian Right over the past 20 years, but more, in continuation of the American "civil religion."[11] This civil religion is apparent in the speeches of Washington, Jefferson, and Lincoln, proclaiming America as providentially guided by God – a religion that while often not specifically Christian in its rhetoric, does seem to be a direct descendant of the divine invocations of the Puritans.

Despite this, however, it seems clear that the erosion of the taken-for-granted Christian beliefs of the American past has continued to a marked degree. Those 90-or-so percent of Americans claiming to believe in God often have very different conceptions of what God is. "The most singular fact about religion in the United States . . . is diversity. Perhaps no other industrial nations have such an amazing variety of religious groups"[12] – in the words of a person I interviewed, "if you take a busload of people in America today, the chances are good that there won't be two people on that bus who believe the same thing."

This is certainly true of "homegrown" religious conceptions – between Southern Baptism, Unitarianism, Mormonism, Jehovah's Witnesses, and Christian Science, there are real chasms in conceptions of the ultimate – but is also true because of American exposure to world-wide religions. "Eastern spirituality" has long held a small place in American life, since the days of Emerson and Thoreau (who marveled at the wisdom of the Hindu classic, the *Bhagavad Gita*); but the beginnings of widespread exposure really began in the late nineteenth century, as symbolized, for example, by the World Parliament of Religions in Chicago in 1893. In this century, particularly in the post-World War II era, Buddhism began to enter into American life at large. Figures such as D. T. Suzuki and Alan Watts brought their depictions of Eastern religions to American mass media; Allen Ginsberg, Jack Kerouac, and other beat writers brought Buddhist themes to their American literary voices. The social upheavals of the 1960s created an American generation receptive to Buddhism and other non-JudeoChristian spiritual practices as never before: a generation who often sought an alternative to "grubby American materialism" and "moralizing American religion, with all its rules" (to quote several people I interviewed) in "the spiritual wisdom of the East." Today, Zen and Tibetan Buddhism, as well as other "Eastern" religious paths, have become well established in the United States. In any large and many small American cities, one may go to dozens of different meetings of all different worldwide faiths, and one may take classes explicating and espousing virtually every one of the major religious beliefs held in the world.

With such a smorgasbord of world religions available from the cultural supermarket – as well as the choice of not believing anything at all, but focusing one's energies on other matters, from one's career to one's love life to one's vacations – all these religions must sell themselves in the marketplace as never before. This is true of the newly imported Eastern religions: as one Korean Zen master recently said, "We Buddhist teachers – those of us who came from Asia – are like transplanted lotuses. . . . Here we find ourselves in the marketplace – as dharma [Buddhist teachings] peddlers, you might say."[13] This seems equally true of Christianity: "We have a better product than soap or automobiles. We have eternal life," said the televangelist Jim Bakker in his fundraising appeals.[14] Christian books, music, greeting cards,

T-shirts, and so on, form major segments of the American market, and so too the Christian religion itself, which, according to one scholar, "has become an ordinary commodity."[15]

There are, it seems, two basic contradictory principles at work in American religion; these contradictions underlie America's cultural conceptions of itself in past and at present as well. One principle is that of the Christian religion in its singular truth, a truth shared by no other religion. (Buddhists may also make claims as to the truth that they particularly hold, as we will see, but not nearly as strongly.) This is the truth proclaimed by Christian evangelists, but also in less specifically Christian form, in America's civil religion: the "in God we trust" of our currency and the American Pledge of Allegiance's claim of America as "one nation under God." This religious formulation of America is that which is rooted in the Puritan tradition, rewoven into "the American way" and "justified even into the 20th century by a long procession of evangelists from Billy Sunday to . . . Billy Graham and Jerry Falwell."[16] If there is a "God we trust," if America is indeed "one nation under God," then Americans had better follow that God.

The other side of America is that enshrined in the Declaration of Independence: human beings have "certain inalienable Rights," among them "Life, Liberty, and the pursuit of Happiness." One is free, by this promise, to pursue one's happiness down whatever path one chooses. In Chapter 1, I quoted Bocock's words: "The United States . . . has come to epitomize the modern consumer's dreamland";[17] and what is true for material consumption seems true for cultural consumption as well. "It's my life; I can do what I want," is a common rejoinder in the United States. The United States, by its founding charter, is the home of the cultural supermarket, and this of course includes religion. America is "the land of the free," in which you are free to believe whatever makes you happy.

These two formulations of America broadly correspond to the two conceptions of culture we discussed in Chapter 1, and to the opposing principles of state and market – culture as a particular bounded way of life, and culture as information and identities chosen from the global cultural supermarket. America as "one nation under God" corresponds to the first of these principles, and America as "the individual pursuit of happiness" corresponds to the second. In fact, historically speaking, these two sides of American cultural definition seem, in some respects, not to have been directly opposed. The founding fathers of the United States were not evangelical Christians but deists, basing their ideas of God on the religious ideals of the French Enlightenment; this God could, without contradiction, preside over the multitude of paths through which free human beings might pursue happiness. Nonetheless, from the Puritans through to evangelical Christians of the present, the American God has been interpreted by many as the Christian God. An oft-declared contemporary Christian belief is that of a once Christian America now lost to the evils of secularism:

> The United States of America, founded as one nation under God, has truly betrayed its heritage. . . . We have become a nihilistic, hedonistic, self-centered, humanistic nation. The Lord has blessed this nation so greatly. . . . No other nation has been so blessed, yet, like the ancient Israelites, we have become proud and haughty. We don't thank God for our blessings. We take them for granted. That, my friends, is always a sure recipe for disaster with God.[18]

More historically informed Christian writers point out that the God of the founding fathers was not necessarily the Christian God;[19] but it does seem to be the case that in the United States today a struggle is being waged between adherents of these two principles: a struggle between the one God of universal truth, and a multiplicity of gods, representing individual taste.

In his 1991 book *Culture Wars: The Struggle to Define America*, James Davison Hunter examines this struggle at length: the conflict of cultural definitions of America in such areas as politics, law, family, education, and the arts. As he depicts this struggle, it is between Christian fundamentalists, Orthodox Jews, and conservative Catholics as against more secular liberals and progressives for control of American culture. "Relativism is the American way," the historian Arthur Schlesinger Jr. has written. "The American mind . . . is by nature and tradition skeptical, irreverent, pluralistic and relativistic." As opposed to this, there is Jerry Falwell's argument that "only by godly leadership can America be put back on a divine course";[20] there is Pat Buchanan's call for an America based on Christian culture; there is Gary Bauer's claim that "We are, in the words of 'The Star Spangled Banner,' 'a heav'n-rescued land.' We should teach these patriotic values because we have a higher responsibility than other countries."[21]

Hunter's thesis of a culture war has been criticized for presenting an American society more polarized than it actually is; in fact, most Americans are in the middle, between these extremes of belief. But in a deep sense, this depiction of polarization is apt, for it is an argument over the nature of truth, for which a middle ground may be difficult to find. Is there a single ultimate truth, true for all Americans and all human beings, whether they accept it or not? Or is truth relative, no more than a human construction? The evangelical Christian may pray fervently in her church on Sunday, but on Monday deal amicably with her non-Christian friends; but if her religion is true, then those friends may be doomed to hell if she does not persuade them to become Christians. To keep the peace and keep her popularity within her pluralistic social world, she must keep her belief in the absolute truth of her religion to herself, but this may be a violation of the tenets of her religion. The American Buddhist may fervently maintain the relativism of all truth, and see meditation as no more than a form of this-world therapy; but when a visiting teacher, fresh from Tibet, claims that a certain meditation practice will lead to liberation in seven lifetimes rather than sixteen lifetimes, he may squirm uncomfortably for a moment – "Can reincarnation and relativism both be true?" – before shrugging and reasserting his relativism: "After all, who knows what's ultimately true? . . . But then, why am I practicing Buddhism if I'm not sure if what it says is true?" Both these people, like most religious Americans, find themselves in the midst of an all-but-irreconcilable contradiction over the nature of truth.

The dispute can be summed up as one of "truth vs. taste" – is there an ultimate religious truth that everyone in common should follow? Or is one's religious pursuit more akin to a hobby, a personal pursuit of one's own truth that others need not share? This dispute, this confusion over the nature of spiritual truth, is linked to contemporary conceptions of American cultural identity. "Truth vs. taste" corresponds to the idea of a spiritual national culture – "America as God's country" – versus the cultural supermarket – "America as one's own pursuit of happiness."

In the pages that follow, I explore these two realms, those of "truth vs. taste," in conceptions of American cultural identity by considering the words of 44 religious seekers – almost all of whom considered their religion to be the most important aspect of their lives – interviewed in Denver-Boulder, Colorado in 1996. I chose Denver-Boulder for personal reasons – I have lived there and have friends and relatives there – but also because, like many American cities, it has a range of religions, from evangelical Christianity to New Age groups of every stripe; and Boulder, in particular, is a center of Eastern religion in contemporary America. The people I have interviewed are by no means representative of all American religion: I barely begin to scratch the surface in this chapter of the diversity and depth of American religious belief.[22] However, the words of these people do serve to illustrate some large-scale patterns in contemporary American senses of cultural identity in conjunction with religious belief, and illustrate a particularly American variant of the conflict we explore throughout this book, that of particular national culture vs. the global cultural supermarket. This theme, I should note, could also have been explored in other areas of American life, such as ethnic identity (What leads one person of African – or Asian or Hispanic – ancestry to identify herself as African, another as African-American, still another as American?). I focus on religion because it embodies vividly the conflict of truth vs. taste that I see as pivotally linked to that of particular culture vs. global cultural supermarket.

I interviewed people of various religious convictions, but to make the contrasts I seek to draw most apparent, I focused primarily on several different groups – evangelical and liberal Christians, "New Age" spiritual shoppers, and Tibetan Buddhists. In interviews with these people, I asked about the nature of their religious beliefs and practices, and the relation of their religions to their lives as a whole; and I asked about the relation of their religions to their senses of America and of being American. Beyond this, I prayed with some of the Christians and meditated with some of the Buddhists; and I attended Christian and New Age church services and Tibetan Buddhist ceremonies, and hung out in Christian, New Age, and Buddhist bookstores, some of their stock of books and periodicals from which I quote in this chapter. Let me now discuss what I have found.

Evangelical Christians and American truth

I spoke to 18 Christians at length, 11 of whom were evangelical, in the broad sense that they believed that salvation could come only through faith in Christ and the Christian God; almost all of these evangelical Christians considered themselves to be born-again, in their experience of a spiritual reawakening of their faith as teenagers or adults. These Christians included a schoolteacher, a policeman, a psychologist, a college student and her teacher at a Christian university, a librarian, several homemakers, and several small businesspeople; these people, white, Hispanic, and black, fit the statistical profile of more or less average Americans. Where they departed from their less fully believing fellow Americans was in the fact that the Christian God was more real for many of them than anyone or anything else in their lives. In one person's words, "I'm always praying to God. Even when I'm sitting here talking with you, I'm praying. God is a continual presence for me, by far the being I'm closest to in my life." In another's words, defining the importance of God by God's occasional absence:

> I catch myself all of a sudden at three o'clock – I haven't thought about God for three hours! It's just my nature to wander off into my own little world, and forget that God is with me every second, taking me by my hand, and guiding me.

God was the single most important being of these people's lives.

Let us now consider at greater length the words of one born-again Christian:

Carol Martin (52)
I've been married for 30 years, and raised three children. Now I work in the city office, and play classical piano. But the real center of my life is my faith in God. I went to Lutheran parochial schools as a child, but I drifted away: went to college, dropped out, got married. It was when my kids were small that I rediscovered my faith.

At that time, I'd go to church sometimes, but it just wasn't sinking in. But I saw that my kids, especially my son, had a need for guidance, spiritually. And my husband's drinking was getting worse. I was depressed, in a fearful state. . . . I had a sister-in-law who was trying to convert me, and I hated it. She was into speaking in tongues: I was pushed into one of her meetings, and I just didn't know what was going on – I was making these weird noises, and I felt awful. Afterwards, I felt so bad that I thought about killing myself. . . . Eventually I realized that I needed a commitment to God more than anything else, but a commitment following my own path to God. I'd gone to parochial schools all my life and sang millions of hymns and been in church a lot, and I still had no idea who God was. I felt that I needed to know the Bible: I begin taking Bible study classes, and after studying for several years, I made that commitment to God. In my life ever since, I've been trying to know God better. My husband Bill went through a stage where he hated me becoming Christian. He thought, "You weren't like this when I married you. I'm not gonna have a wife like this." But eventually, he too made a commitment. . . .

Some Christians say that "Those who don't follow the word of Jesus Christ will burn in hell." I would never come close to making a judgment like that. I don't know where other people are. But I do have to say that I think Christ is essential to salvation. A person who asked for forgiveness and was open to God would definitely go to heaven. Someone who does good things, but not because they love God – I don't know if they would go to heaven, because they haven't accepted God and Christ into their lives. But I don't know: that's up to God. . . . You say that God seems unfair; but God gives us so much mercy and grace! Man was in need of a saviour, and God gave man that saviour. We don't choose this religion intellectually; we accept it on faith. It's all because of God: He imbues you with the holy spirit. If we got what we really deserved in this world, we'd be in terrible trouble. The way we respond to God in this country is with disobedience and indifference, instead of making Him the center of our lives. . . . America may have been a Christian country in its past, its founding, but it's not a Christian country anymore. Do I think that America will ever become a vibrant Christian country once again? It sure doesn't seem like that. It seems to be going further away from that in a lot of ways.

I really hate the intolerance of some American Christian groups today. There's a lot in the Bible about not judging people. Until I could become open-minded about other people, I couldn't go to church without being terribly upset because everyone was a self-righteous asshole but me! The Bible study group I belong to really tries to get you to tell people about your faith, bringing people into the faith. I hate doing that. I'm cowardly, because I know that God wants me to be so grateful for His love that I would want to communicate that to other people. I guess I don't want people to view me as a fanatic. I do carry my Bible around. But I hated it when people were telling me, before I became Christian, that you should be more like me because I'm right and you're wrong. . . .

What it comes down to is that each person has to explore this word of God and respond to it in their own way. I don't think you can go into a church and be converted, and from then on, you're a Christian. I think you have to keep growing in the Word of God. A lot of Christians have hardly ever read the Bible. They just want to call themselves Christians. It's easier to say that than to really work at it. I'm not saying I work at it nearly as hard as I should, but. . . . God cares about me, about every aspect of my life. The psalm that I was reading this morning said that I am always with God: His counsel is always with me. That's true, as true as anything I know in this world.

Ms. Martin grew up in a taken-for-granted Christian environment as a child, of church, parochial schools, and hymns; but she drifted away from that, she tells us, and returned to God through her own personal commitment. A God that is merely taken for granted is a God not properly worshipped, she maintains: one must make a full and conscious commitment to God, and continually work on that commitment. In this sense, she is the opposite of some of the traditional Japanese artists of Chapter 2, such as Ms. Ōkubo – if some of them claimed that their choice from the cultural supermarket represented their Japanese roots, she asserts that Christianity can't be just taken-for-granted roots: it must be one's own conscious choice. Ms. Martin does so choose: of all the varieties of Christian paths within the cultural supermarket, she chose the one that most suits her: not the emotionality of speaking in tongues, nor the formality of mainstream churches such as those of her childhood, but Bible study in her own particular group. However, she also resists the idea that this is but her own choice: "It's all because of God." Her religious commitment she sees as her response to God's call, not a matter of her own consumer taste but of ultimate truth. It is as if she seeks to assert choice over roots, the cultural supermarket over the taken for granted on the cultural level, but to reassert her ultimate rootedness on the spiritual level: God chose her rather than her choosing God.

The *shikata ga nai* world in her account seems represented by the people in her social world to whom she must pay heed, even if she finally overcomes them, people trying to mold her to fit their views – her sister-in-law pushing her to speak in tongues; her husband scorning her new-found religious beliefs. This *shikata ga nai* in a larger sense is America, apparently once a Christian nation, but a Christian nation no longer. Today, this America of *shikata ga nai* seems bifurcated in her account: on the one hand, it is today's secular America, ignoring God, and on the other hand, it is the land of today's intolerant, judgmental American Christians. In Ms. Martin's account, we see her struggle between formulating her religion as a matter of ultimate truth, as opposed to a matter of her own personal taste as a consumer from the cultural supermarket. Her God is not merely her own God, but rather the only path to salvation, she tells us; but she squirms when asked if non-Christians will burn in hell. She hates proselytizing, although she criticizes herself as cowardly – she should spread God's Word to others, but she is fearful of being seen as a fanatic. She seems wedged between two mutually exclusive conceptions of her faith, and of America. Is there one religious truth, that the "intolerant" American Christians loudly proclaim? Or is religion a matter of one's personal taste, as most more secular Americans would say? She dislikes both views, but finally seems closer to the former than to the latter. In a sense, she is attempting both to have her cake and eat it too, by maintaining the ultimate truth of her religion, yet not expressing that truth in the social world around her, for fear of offending those who believe in other truths, or in no truths.

Ms. Martin is struggling to balance truth and taste, her own spiritual certainty with social pluralism. But turning in general to the evangelical Christians I interviewed, some were not so concerned with such a balancing of their spiritual and social worlds; rather, they were proud to proclaim from the rooftops that Christ is the one and only truth. With these people, one key question of mine was that of how their truth could be believed in a world of so many competing truths. How, in a world of the cultural supermarket and the cultural relativism that this entails, can anyone claim to know the singular truth of the world?

Like Ms. Martin, these people felt that their relation with God was not the product of their upbringing, not merely a matter of the taken-for-granted culture in which they grew up; rather, it was a product of their adult re-conversions. Indeed, almost as a rule, the born-again Christians I interviewed came from families that were not born again: their relation to God and Christ stemmed from what they felt to be God's grace visiting them as adults – or, as I would put it, their own personal choice from the cultural supermarket. As thinking, cognizant adults, they chose to give their lives to Jesus Christ: theirs was an explicit denial of roots, background, belonging to any group: all was their own individual choice of God. However, these people did not see their status as born-again Christians as matters merely of personal preference. Christianity may be chosen from the cultural supermarket, but it infinitely transcends that, the people I interviewed maintained. The religious choice of the Christians I interviewed, we might say, was the only choice; all other choices were false. These people, reflecting Ms. Martin's words, were often ambiguous as to the extent to which they had themselves chosen God as opposed to being chosen by God in the granting of grace; but all uniformly agreed that God must remain consciously apprehended, rather than being allowed to sink into the merely taken-for-granted realm of consumer choice, and thus, as we have seen, not sufficiently appreciated.

These evangelical Christians steadfastly maintained that there was but a single religious truth in the world as presented through the Gospel. In one Christian's words, "Only God, through Christ, offers salvation, eternal life. That's the bottom line." Extrapolating from this, an evangelical text says:

> Take . . . the fact of the deity, death and resurrection of the Lord Jesus Christ. Christianity affirms these facts as the heart of its message. Islam, on the other hand, denies the deity, death and resurrection of Christ. On this very crucial point, one of these mutually contradictory views is wrong. They can't simultaneously be true, no matter how sincerely both are believed by how many people. . . . Christianity alone offers *assurance* of salvation.[23]

The evangelical Christians I interviewed explained that no one could know for sure who would be saved and who would not; like Ms. Martin, a number expressed distaste for any human attempt at such judgment. Several stated that "anyone who doesn't accept God is going to hell. Absolutely"; but others emphasized that only God can see into people's hearts: "I don't know who's going to be saved. Only God knows. But I'd guess that some people within the church will not be saved and some people outside the church will be saved." Some of the more worldly of these Christians hastened to add that hell wasn't flames, just as heaven wasn't clouds and tinsel-winged angels. Rather, "Heaven is being with God, and hell is the absence of God." But nonetheless, these people emphasized that there is only one God and heaven, true for all people throughout the world, if only they have the wits and chance to choose, and the grace to be so chosen.

I myself attended Christian Sunday school as a child, and remember exasperating my teachers with my arguments (stemming from my parents, who had left the Christian faith of their childhoods, but who felt guilty enough about their lapsed faith to want to give their children an exposure to Christianity): "Gandhi wasn't a Christian. Isn't he going to heaven? What about Buddha? He was a good person, wasn't he? My parents don't pray. They only send me here because 'it's part of my education.' Are they going to heaven?" Perhaps I've developed little, spiritually, since that time, for in my interviews with evangelical Christians, I often argued with them from the standpoint of cultural relativism:

> The world has all these different religions. If you were born else-where in the world, you might believe in a different religion. But you were born in America, in your particular family, going through your particular cultural experiences, and so you believe in Christianity. How can you know that it's true, but every other religious path is false?

Consider the following exchange:

G   If I had been talking to you in Pakistan, you'd be saying, "Oh, I found Allah. I found . . . "

M   It's not possible for me to be in Pakistan. There's only one of me. I'm alive right now. And I found God.

G   How do you know that you're right and other faiths are wrong?

M   I only know my own existence, my own life.

For this man, abstract arguments mean nothing before his own experience. For him, God is so overpoweringly real within his own experience, that logical objections are beside the point. But the question is not only one of logic, but of fairness. After all, some people have more access to the Christian God than others: why is it that the American Christian will go to heaven, while the third-world Muslim, Buddhist, and Hindu, not hearing the Christian message, are doomed hell?

Several of the evangelical Christians I interviewed argued that "Jesus always said life wouldn't be fair." One Christian accused me of gross arrogance for presuming to judge God by my own puny human standards: "Who are you to say how God should think? Who are you to judge God?" That God happened to have made the Jews his chosen people, that Christianity happened to have been the religion of the West was God's plan, not to be questioned by humans like me, who are guilty of trying to make God fit their own limited human standards.

In any case, I was told, Christianity has become known all over the world, beyond any cultural bounds: "As the world gets closer and closer together, Christ becomes more and more available to everyone." "You can get free Bibles all over these days. If you were raised a Buddhist, somewhere along the line the word of God would be preached. Somewhere you'd have the chance to hear it. So there's no excuse." These people are saying that in today's world, people will not be doomed for never having heard the word of Christ; rather, their doom will come because they have heard the word of Christ but have rejected it. Christianity has left the realm of national cultures, to become instead a full-fledged item of the cultural supermarket, available for everyone – but one whose choice determines one's fitness for eternal life. If the Japanese artists we earlier discussed saw their traditional arts as the essence of Japan, these American Christians saw their faith as transcending national culture, as the faith of all the world, if only the world would pay heed.

Indeed, most of these Christians felt that America could not be considered a Christian nation. The vast majority of Americans may believe in God, but the number of Americans who are Christians along the lines of these evangelicals is far smaller. Several of those I interviewed, like Ms. Martin, expressed scorn for what they called "cultural Christians," those who follow the accepted pattern of Christian belief in America, but don't truly believe:

> You have a lot of people say, "I believe in God, I go to church, therefore, I'm a Christian," based on the concept that "we're a Christian nation, so if I do what society does, I must be a Christian." They believe they are, but they're not: they've been led astray. . . . I see a lot of Christians in America just half-baked. It hurts me that some people who claim they are Christians can't look you in the face and say, "I will die for Christ."

American politicians still regularly talk of America as a Christian nation. As President Bush said, in 1992, to an audience of Christian broadcasters, "I want to thank you for helping America, as Christ ordained, to be a light upon the world."[24] But the dominant message among the people I interviewed was not of America as a Christian nation, but of a nation that is Christian no longer. As one young Christian I interviewed said,

> Will America become a Christian nation once again? I would love to see it. I'll keep praying for it. But probably, instead, you're going to see some UFO stories, you know, 50 million people, five million people lifted away, a UFO came and took us away.

America, by this vision, has become too corrupt to be any longer the land of God and Christ; because America can't be redeemed, it must be divided, with the minority of truly Christian Americans, and presumably of other countries as well, being swept off the earth, away from their damned and doomed fellows, to reconstitute a pure Christian realm off in heaven. In keeping with this vision, America on this earth was often identified by its secularism. This resembles the traditional Japanese artists we considered, in their denunciation of contemporary Japan, but is often far stronger. As one person said,

> I think the United States is the false prophet spoken of in Revelations. The movies, the music, the pop culture – it's a net that wants to catch me, drown me. . . . Satan is behind that. . . . You have to turn on the TV every once in a while, so that you can understand that it's all wrong, that you need God. Then you can turn it off.

America is, by her words, the epitome of evil. But the purity that this woman – a homemaker living off a dirt road high in the mountains – was able to attain, in contrast to America's secular evil, was unattractive to others of the Christians I interviewed. As one fervent young Christian businessman said, "I'm into video games; I'll still put in a CD, listen to some Eric Clapton. I'm not going to get into all that weird isolation. I love going out to eat and see a movie." "Despite my Christianity, I'm still a mainstream American," he seemed to be saying. This man urged me to attend his church: I did, and was startled. The preacher sounded little different from many other evangelical preachers I've heard, but the music, sung by a skilled gospel choir, had the congregation of well over a thousand, black and brown and white, swaying and all but dancing in the aisles together as one. The music was the stuff of Saturday night parties, but the Sunday morning lyrics were not about love of man and woman, but love of God and Christ.

This church seemed to recognize that the secular world was the world that most Christians live in; it was successful in bringing so many different hues of people to worship together perhaps because of this recognition. Most of the evangelical Christians lived very much in the midst of the secular world, if not necessarily within their families then definitely at work; they thus faced the major issue of how to present their Christianity to that secular world. One socially uncompromising Christian I interviewed admitted that his stand might lose him friends, but stated clearly why he had to proselytize:

> One of my favourite sayings is, "I love you so much, I don't want to see you go to hell." I'm going to try and get you to sit down and talk about Jesus. Yes, maybe I'll lose friends that way. But that doesn't bother me. I'd rather live alone and know that I'm doing God's will to get the word out, than to know that my mom and my brother, or this person next door didn't get a chance to hear about God before they die. After all, this world passes by, but heaven and hell are for eternity!

Indeed, this man closed our interview by praying with me for my soul. For him, the social world very clearly comes in second before the spiritual world, but others were not so sure. The contradiction between social and secular was resolved by some through the idea that "it's not by my power that I'm going to change people's hearts. God is the one who will change their hearts." In other words, one needn't struggle too hard to save one's secular friends: that's God's work. Others vacillate. As one admirably honest professional woman said,

I imagine that if [a non-Christian friend] . . . came to me and said "I'm a Buddhist and this is what I do. Do you think I'm going to heaven?" I would say, "Here is the Bible, here's what it says – that Jesus was the son of God who was crucified for our sins. Now, that is what I believe. You have your system of belief. I sure don't think God is going to be unfair in any way, but personally I wouldn't want to deal with your system". . . . And then I would say, "Are we going to fall out about being friends here?"

This tension between the spiritual and social is apparent in evangelical writings. "When a Christian asserts that Jesus Christ is the only way to God . . . he or she is not suggesting that Christians think they are better than anyone else,"[25] as one Christian tract states: as if to say, "Christianity is true and other religions are false, but don't let that get in the way of the American credo that all people are created equal, or else you'll alienate all the non-Christians around you." Surveys have indicated that close to half of evangelical seminary students feel that to tell people they would go to hell if they did not repent was "in poor taste"[26] – it may be spiritually true that they are going to hell, but it is a social *faux pas* to bring up such indiscreet matters in a socially and spiritually pluralistic America. Even to many of these future professional evangelists, spiritual truth may be one, but the American social world's truths are many; and in social behavior, anyway, the latter's relativism is what wins out. America, even for them, is not God's country but rather the land of the individual pursuit of happiness.

Many contemporary Christian writers storm against such relativism. In one writer's words:

> Americans are confused about moral and social issues because they no longer believe in a firm foundation of reality. . . . Since relativism and subjectivism . . . deny that universal objective knowledge is possible, every religion is equally "valid," and none could ever be criticized as being false. . . . Our only option is to wander through the giant supermarket of religions and spiritual beliefs guided only by a shopping list that merely reflects individual desires and feelings.[27]

In another evangelical Christian writer's despairing words, "Not only the question of truth is neglected, but the very concept of truth seems to have been abandoned. 'Religion' has been reduced to a mere mood, a choice, or a lifestyle. Truth is no longer an issue."[28] In today's America, as the theologian Martin Marty has said, "as far as the fabric of the culture is concerned, [one's choice of religion] is about as decisive as whether you like Bartok or rock music. Individuals are on their own quest."[29] The cultural supermarket has taken over – an American can be a Christian within the American cultural supermarket, but can never again return to an American Christian home: if, indeed, such a home ever existed.

Liberal Christians and spiritual searchers in the American cultural supermarket

The evangelical Christians I interviewed saw their truth as the only truth, a truth that secular America, wallowing in its relativistic super-market of cultural forms, has spurned. Many of the other Christians I interviewed were less certain about truth; some of them welcomed the cultural supermarket in all its spiritual choices.[30] In a Catholic nun's words, "My house is eclectic – African, Asian, Indian, Western art. This Indian Kachina doll, 'morning singer,' helps me get going in the morning; it's not my culture, but why shouldn't I appreciate it and learn from it?" She used various different worldwide religious scriptures and meditational practices in her worship as well, applying the cultural supermarket not just to her household possessions, but to her spiritual life: "In order to get in touch with the feminine, you can have a picture of Mary, but then Mary can also be Mother of the Universe. . . . I'd still consider myself, I guess, a Roman Catholic – just don't question me too closely!"

For a few of the people I interviewed, the acceptance of diverse cultures and beliefs was arrived at through anguished Christian reflec-tion: "How could a loving God damn those of other cultures?" For others, both Christians and non-Christian spiritual searchers, this view signified an explicit pan-culturalism: "All the world's religions and cultures offer different paths to cosmic awareness. They all can be useful, depending on where you're coming from." This latter attitude came to connote, for some non-Christian spiritual searchers, the abdica-tion of all ideas of truth before the freedom of individual taste in the cultural supermarket: "I need to choose the religion that best suits my lifestyle." Let me first discuss liberal Christians: a half-dozen people who define themselves as Christians but who recognize truth in other religious traditions.

Liberal Christian writers often argue against the idea expressed by evangelical Christian writers that there is but one religious truth in the world, that of Christ; Christianity bears truth, they maintain, but so too may other faiths. As the philosopher of religion John Hick writes,

"The great world faiths embody different perceptions and conceptions of, and correspondingly different responses to, the Real or the Ultimate."[31] Some of the Christians I interviewed spoke similarly, in acknowledging the cultural relativity of their views. In one devout Catholic's words:

> As I understand it, Jesus died for all men. But of course I have to take into account my cultural biases: I've grown up a Catholic. . . . What I would say is that when you get to the higher level of spirituality, when you get through all the cultural constraints and biases, that you kind of rise up towards God and these differences become a lot more transparent. Thomas Merton said that a good Christian would be a good Hindu and good Hindu a good Christian. It's only down in the muck that the differences seem so insurmountable.

For this man, as well as for several other more pluralistic Christians I interviewed, the culture in which they lived represented not the under-lying basis of truth – "America as God's country" – but rather an inevitable cultural coloration of truth, and sometimes impediment to truth. In Chapter 2 we saw how some contemporary Japanese artists saw their Japaneseness as an impediment to their pursuit of their arts; but many of these American religious seekers saw not just American culture but any culture as such an impediment. Cultural shaping is what makes God appear not as God, but in distorting cultural trap-pings: in one person's words, "I'll die and go, 'man, that's not how I thought it was going to be,' just because I was in this cultural thing, and couldn't see the awesome reality of God." In another person's wry words, "Of course, God is culturally derived. God is not going to appear to me with a bone in His nose, because that universal thing comes in a cultural form."

A problem raised by these convictions is that if the form God takes is culturally derived, then what about God itself? God has been invoked since America's founding; a huge majority of Americans claim to believe in God, far more than in any other industrialized country. Part of the cultural baggage of being American, we might say, seems to be belief in God. If a liberal Christian acknowledges the role of culture in shaping her beliefs, then it seems that she would have to acknowledge not simply that her conception of God but that the very idea of God may be a cultural artefact. But can a God beyond cultural shaping ever be discovered? Can religious truth ever be found apart from one's cultural molding?

The liberal Christians I interviewed answered this question in several ways. One deflected my question with dry wit: "Who knows what's true? This truth thing is highly overrated – especially when you remember that God has a sense of humor!" Others cited personal experience: "Yes, my imagining of what God is is culturally shaped. But I know that God is real. I've felt Him – or Her or It – in my life so many times." Several others justified their belief in God in terms of what they saw as universal human experience: "Cultures throughout history have had religious beliefs, and have believed in divinity. That means something!" In another person's more informal words, "People shouldn't get all whacked out about Buddha, Mohammed, Jesus – it's all God!" But it's not all God: these faiths fundamentally contradict one another. Assertions such as these run the risk of assuming the universality of one's own cultural beliefs, as if to say, "We believe in God, so they must too, in their own way." It is sometimes said that Americans tend to believe that all the world is like America; perhaps some of the liberal Christians were assuming this in the realm of religion – that a taken-for-granted belief in God born of their particular cultural shaping should be a matter of universal truth.

A number of the liberal Christians I interviewed associated America not with any taken-for-granted Christianity but rather with the political actions of America's government, actions that deeply disturbed them: how can they believe, they said, in the God of a country that behaves so barbarously? "We went to war with Iraq, a country of seventeen million, five million of them children, and we did this in the name of God?" asked the Catholic nun. Another person I interviewed, a former Christian missionary in Okinawa, said this:

> I often say that if I make it to heaven, wherever and whatever heaven is, I'm going to be very lonely, unless some of my Buddhist friends are there. One of my closest Japanese friends is an activist against the US military bases in Okinawa. The reason that he has not become a Christian is that he has seen actions by our so-called Christian nation that have degraded and showed disrespect to Okinawa. It was very difficult for me to speak about forgiveness and peace when my own country had policies that were so awful.

Given America's behavior in the world, America cannot be God's country, these people maintained; and their own Christianity they sought to dissociate from the American nation. Other liberal Christians were less overtly opposed to American political and military positions, but they too were well aware of secular history in its many shades of grey. In one woman's words:

> Is America a Christian nation? . . . Morally is America meant to be the "city on the hill"? My belief is that we are a Christian nation, but lots of things fit into that. Was it God's divine invention that we had bright men to start with? That they were all white and they had slaves? I have to really grapple on this one. I think part of the reason is that we are a Christian nation is that we have tremendous resources in this country. We can afford to be nice.

What makes America "chosen," she is saying, may perhaps be due less to the innate virtue of America than to the historical circumstances of America's development, not to mention the injustices Americans have perpetrated upon the rest of the world – America's money helps it to be a spiritual haven, she tells us. Nonetheless, she was one of the few Christians I interviewed who felt able to say forthrightly that America was indeed a Christian nation today as well as in the past.

As a whole, the liberal Christians I interviewed were as skeptical as their more conservative born-again counterparts about claims that America is a Christian beacon to the world. However, if the evangelical Christians tended to see America as a once-Christian nation now swallowed up by secularization and popular culture, the liberal Christians seemed often to believe that the realities of power meant that America was never truly a Christian nation, past or present, but simply one more country among countries, exemplifying the rich oppressing the poor and the powerful oppressing the weak. In a more abstract sense, if there is but a single great religious truth in the world, as the evangelical Christians believed, then America past, present, or future, may conceivably embody that truth. But if there is no single truth, as the liberal Christians verged on saying, then no nation can ever embody truth; because truth is relative, all nations, like all individuals, are in some sense equal in their pursuit of truth. No monopoly on truth, and no judgment of truth, is possible.

No Christian I interviewed completely advocated religious relativism; indeed, if they did – if they no longer professed belief in the particular divinity of Christ – then, arguably, they wouldn't be Christian. Some of the non-Christians I interviewed, however, were religious relativists through and through. Let us now consider the account of one such spiritual searcher, a true explorer of the cultural/spiritual supermarket:

Jill Clemens (34)

I was raised Lutheran, went to church, Sunday school: I just did what I was supposed to do as a kid in our family. Sometimes my dad and I would slip out of the house when I was supposed to be in Sunday school: we'd go get breakfast and go to a bookstore, because my mom would be in church forever, that was her whole life. I remember arguing with my mother when I was a teenager: "How can you tell me that Mormons are a cult and Jehovah's Witnesses are a cult? I have friends in those religions, and that's the way they were raised; they're doing what their parents wanted them to do. Are my friends going to hell because they believe what their parents taught them to believe, just as I'm doing what you taught me to believe?"

In college, I was involved in Campus Crusade for Christ. Later, since I've moved out here, I've tried other churches: I'd go if I wasn't camping or doing something else. . . . I've been an aerobics teacher for the past 12 years; that's my profession. By nature I want to clap, I want to sing, I want to move. So I'd go to some of the Baptist churches: I liked the way they did that. But at the end they say, "Now, if anybody was touched by this sermon, come forward so you can accept Jesus," and then they start playing the organ. I'd almost start laughing, I thought that was so hokey. I really hate the whole, "Hi, what's Jesus doing in your life today?" kind of thing. It's like, "Oh, cut the crap!"

Over the past few years I've begun reading various books about religion and philosophy. I took a class called "Exploring Life's Mysteries," took another class on Buddhism, and went through TM training as well. I have a friend who's really into Gurdjieff, so I'm learning about that. It's really hard for my mom to accept my path. She asks, "What does meditation do for you?" I'm like, "Mom, when was the last time that you ever sat back and looked at how you relate to the world? When you meditate, you can begin to understand your own mind and how it works." Would my mom ever take up meditation? I wonder. She might see how in my life I'm changing in good ways. For now, though, my mother just tells me that she's praying for my salvation. I don't have any problem with her doing her thing religiously, because I really do think that's best for her; but let me do my thing. This is America: that's what freedom is all about. . . .

I got married a few years ago to a man who wasn't religious at all; we're now in the process of divorce. Vic is like, "Well, there might be a God or there might not. I have no idea what's going to happen when I die, so I'm not going to waste my time worrying about it. Let's go fishing." I said to him once, "You know, you don't have to believe what I believe." And he said, "How could I? You don't know what you believe!" In a way he really does know me well. . . .

After all, how do you know what to believe? How do you know if Christianity is right or if Buddhism is right? You just have to go for what has the most resonance for you. At the exercise club where I work, one person says, "I do step class and I love it." The next person says, "I only like riding the exercise bike." We all like different things but we're all getting in shape: we're all reaching our fitness goals in different ways. The same thing is true with a spiritual path. That path might be different in different times of your life. If women have straight hair, they want a perm. If it's permed, they want it straight. Or if it's blond, they want it black. You almost wonder, "Well, since I was born Christian, I know all about that, now let's go try this Buddhist stuff." But do I stop there? Do I need to look at Islam and Judaism? I think that if you could expose a child to everything, teaching them to pray, teaching them to meditate, then you could really let them use whatever is best for them. . . . Sometimes I've thought that there won't be enough time to check everything out, to know what I truly believe in. But it's fun to keep looking!

If Ms. Martin was in conflict over truth vs. taste, a single supreme religious truth vs. pluralism and relativism, for Ms. Clemens taste is all: the cultural supermarket is the spiritual world in which she now lives. Christianity – going to Lutheran Sunday school – was a taken-for-granted part of her early life; but unlike her mother, her father seemed to act as a subversive underminer of this taken-for-granted religiosity, perhaps saying, "Let's not go to Sunday school today but pretend we did." As a teenager, she criticized her mother for asserting that her own taken-for-granted religion was the one true religion, while the religions that others take for granted are merely deluded, no more than cults. As an adult, her spiritual life has been progressively widening in scope, moving farther and farther away from the culturally taken-for-granted religion of her childhood: from Lutheran, to Baptist, to, eventually, meditation, Buddhism, Gurdjieff, to, perhaps, all the world's religions explored in turn.

The realm of *shikata ga nai* seems present in two senses in Ms. Clemens' account, just as it was for Ms. Martin. In one sense, it is the particular spiritual world in which she grew up, her own ineradicable roots, which she no longer takes for granted but which she cannot fully escape. She speaks of how if only a child could be educated in all spiritual traditions, then it could choose among them – as she herself, raised in but one spiritual tradition, and only now exploring others, cannot. The cultural supermarket, her words imply, cannot be freely enjoyed, since one must necessarily experience it from within the bounds of one's own given culture. In another, less abstract sense, *shikata ga nai* is the world of other people, in their criticisms of her spiritual path. To her mother, she is spurning Christ's salvation; to her soon-to-be-ex husband, she is a spiritual dilettante. Both these people are questioning the validity of her cultural supermarket approach to religion, albeit from different angles; but as she seems to realize, given cultural relativity, how could religion be anything but a cultural supermarket? Because she was born within a particular religious tradition, she wasn't exposed to the full panoply of world religions, and so she must explore all those religions, she tells us. But she cannot know, she says, which of these religions is ultimately true. All she can do is pursue a spiritual path not on the basis of truth but of taste, whatever happens to resonate with her life.

One's spiritual path, in her account, becomes analogous to hair coloring which one changes to suit one's mood and taste, or to one's choices of exercise at a fitness club. This may seem like a cheapening of religion; but in fact, if truth is unknowable, then religion can exist only on the basis of personal taste. This, Ms. Clemens says, is what America is all about: the freedom to do your own thing, to follow your own path through the aisles of the cultural supermarket, picking and choosing to suit yourself or the self that you seek to become.

The principles that Ms. Clemens has formulated for herself were held, more or less, by 10 American spiritual seekers I interviewed, most of whom had grown up in Christian or otherwise religious households (Mormon, Seventh-day Adventist), but who had abandoned these religions, in search of spiritual paths that they felt might be more attuned to their own lives' courses; they actively sought to understand the world's religions through books and classes and workshops. Several I interviewed were, like Ms. Clemens, pursuing their paths individually; several more, whom I will now discuss, pursued their spiritual paths within a religious group that seemed explicitly to advocate the principles of the cultural supermarket. "Science of Mind," or "Religious Science" seeks evidence of what it calls Universal Mind in all the world's religions:[32] "Religious Science is an accumulation of principles from every religion in the world," I was told. Thus it seems hardly surprising that a key tenet of Science of Mind is non-judgmentalism: in the published testimony of one adherent, "I had to learn . . . to junk all tendencies to be judgmental. . . . I had to learn to allow everyone to be just whatever they happened to be."[33] The adherents of Science of Mind whom I interviewed – including a real estate agent, a technician, a housewife, and a retired person: ordinary Americans getting on with their lives, often alongside spouses and children who had no interest in their religious beliefs – echoed this view. In one person's words, "We don't allow our . . . ministers . . . to denigrate any religion or philosophy in any way. That's a real no-no. We honor every religious tradition" – as if to say that the only judgment one is allowed to make is against those who make judgments.

Indeed, if one's society and world are but a cultural supermarket open for one's choices, one can hardly pass judgment on another's particular spiritual choices, just as one can hardly criticize another for preferring pumpernickel over rye, Pepsi over Coke. "All religions can serve as a path to truth," I was told; "We are all expressions of Universal Mind. . . . One can be Christian, or Muslim, or Shintoist, or Hindu, or whatever. It's just whatever way opens up their spiritual growth, their spiritual understanding." Of course, these people did believe that Science of Mind offers, by its very inclusivity, the most effective path to spiritual understanding; otherwise, why adhere to it, as opposed to any of a dozen or a thousand other religious paths? But as they defined Science of Mind (and their conceptions seemed a bit more liberal than the written doctrines of that path), it could include anything and everything in the realm of spirit.

In this openness to all the world, Science of Mind as they conceived of it seemed a religious embodiment of the American individual pursuit of happiness within the cultural supermarket. The adherents I interviewed emphasized the individual choice they felt they now had in their lives; in one person's words, "Religious Science means that my life is really my own." They also emphasized the power they had to transcend cultural conditioning in all its limitations: "Science of Mind is based on uncovering our limiting beliefs, to make our lives work better by changing our thinking." This involves the gaining of wealth as well as knowledge: in one person's words, "the universe is abundant, and God intends for us to experience that abundance"; as a Science of Mind "affirmation" has it, "I accept financial prosperity as my divine right."[34]

Indeed, wealth as well as knowledge is the currency of the cultural supermarket, enabling one to have maximum informed choice in shaping oneself and world: "You can choose your behavior. And we can make our choices away from those things that cause pain . . . and align ourself with what we feel is the nature of God or the universe," as one person I interviewed said. This religious teaching enables adherents of Science of Mind to believe that they are masters of their own fate, shapers of their own destiny – to believe that they create the world from which they consume. This is a particularly American gloss on the cultural supermarket: if America is the material consumer's dreamland, as earlier mentioned, so too it is the spiritual consumer's dreamland, with all the world's religious traditions free to be used to justify the primacy and power of the free individual consumer over all else. This is not to denigrate Science of Mind, which, from all I can ascertain, truly helps the people I interviewed to lead fulfilling lives, but only to indicate the remarkable way in which it uses the world cultural supermarket to justify its particularly American vision of the world, as articulated by the people I interviewed. I went to a number of services, and was continually surprised by how the minister's references to tao and karma could sound as American as God and apple pie.

Other spiritual searchers I interviewed also used the very American principles of the cultural supermarket to justify their non-American choices. One woman, a Buddhist, said, "The [Christian] church I used to belong to nurtured a kind of co-dependent behavior, where everyone had to live for the church. With Buddhism, you can live for yourself: people are individuals instead of belonging to institutions." You can pursue your own happiness as an individual consumer, without having to be concerned about the well-being of the group to which you happen to belong, she seems to say, following the time-honored American tradition of emphasizing the individual and denigrating institutions (she also embraces American psychology as a means of justification: "commitment to one's group" becomes, in her words, "co-dependency").

However, the cultural supermarket was not just lauded but also criticized, not just by Christians I interviewed, but by those of other traditions as well. I spoke with a particularly eloquent American Jewish woman who said this:

> Should a person follow the cultural tradition into which he happens to have been born? Absolutely. Because that's his culture. We're back to the Holocaust, because we've been decimated, because we're a tiny people in danger of disappearing from the face of the earth. . . . You have to learn your own culture, because otherwise it isn't deep enough. Of course all religions have something good. So you go to synagogue one day, church the next day, the Buddhist fellowship the next day. And there's no sense of

continuity, rationality, or depth. What you get is an American
version, like processed cheese.

Despite the allure of the cultural supermarket, this woman is saying,
you need your own cultural tradition – without that, everything
becomes Velveeta and Disney World, a superficial melange of world
cultures without real meaning. A joke told in American Buddhist circles
reiterates this point.[35] An elderly New York woman travels to Tibet to
visit a guru. After a long and arduous journey, she arrives at the monas-
tery of the guru high in the Himalayas; she joins a long line of pilgrims,
and is told, "when you meet him, you can only say three words." After
days of waiting, her turn finally comes, and she is ushered into the
guru's presence. She looks at him in silence, and then exclaims,
"Sheldon, come home!" She is, we might imagine, saying to her Jewish
Brooklyn-born son, now a spiritual master in a foreign cultural world,
"Sheldon, don't follow someone else's tradition. Return to your own!"
   The problem with this view we explored in discussing the Japanese
artists of last chapter: in a world without roots, can it be said that any
of us belong to a cultural tradition? Does a person of Jewish ancestry
raised in a wholly secular environment have any more natural affinity
for Judaism than anyone else in the world? If one grows up in a world
of the cultural supermarket, then how can one claim to be rooted in a
particular cultural tradition? Of course, it may well be that some aspects
of traditional Jewish culture and religion will be present in the early
life of a secular American Jew, just as elements of Christianity will be
present in the early environment of those of a Christian background;
but so, in all likelihood, will elements of other traditions as well, sacred
and secular. We may of course choose from the cultural supermarket
the tradition lived by our ancestors; but in an experiential sense, as we
discussed last chapter, this is not our roots but our choice: our cultural
home only as we construct such a home from the cultural supermarket's
shelves.
   This matter of belonging to a cultural tradition was brought up with
some poignancy by a young woman I interviewed who had grown up
in a conventionally Catholic family, but in her twenties found herself
transfixed by Japanese art, and subsequently by Buddhism:

> The beauty of Japanese art, and, later in my life, my study of
> Buddhism, have shown me that I was born in the wrong culture.
> When I began to study Japanese art, I was absolutely captivated:
> all that mattered was Japanese culture and all of a sudden, I had
> no friends anymore because we were talking a completely different

language. . . . I wish I'd been born in Japan. And if there is such a thing as reincarnation, I must have been Japanese in a previous life. I only wish I remembered the language!

'This woman seeks a transfer to her company office on the Pacific coast "so that I can be closer to Japanese culture: first I'll get to San Francisco, and then I'll just have to go to Japan." But she is at least somewhat aware that the Japan she imagines is not the Japan of reality – "My fascination isn't with modern-day Japan. I know that if I went there, I'd feel disappointed." Her cultural and spiritual fixation with Japan are not shared by many Japanese today, as we've seen: her mind's creation of Japan as her cultural home will surely be more effective in the US – where she can study traditional Japanese art, and practice Zen, and imagine Japan to her heart's content – than in Japan, where in the words of an artist quoted last chapter, "'Japanese culture' is preserved only to show tourists and foreigners." This construction of a foreign tradition as one's cultural home is true not just for this woman, but for the final group of American religious seekers that we will examine in this chapter: American adherents of Tibetan Buddhism.

The creation of Buddhist America

At present there are between half a million and a million Buddhists in the United States, with a significant percentage of these being not ethnic Buddhists – Asians who have emigrated to America and taken their Buddhism with them – but rather those who have grown up in this country and its JudeoChristian tradition and have chosen Buddhism as their spiritual path. We saw last chapter how "Japanese jazz" and "Japanese rock" seem, to some extent oxymorons, not yet really existing in Japan (although Japanese schools of contemporary art such as *mono-ha* have indeed existed); but American Buddhism – the meditative traditions of Japan, Korea, Thailand, and Tibet, taking root in the United States with their own emerging American forms – does seem to exist. Kornfield outlines the key features of this new American Buddhism: women play a full role in following the Buddhist path in the United States, unlike in Asia; the Buddhist community takes on more democratic forms in the United States, with teachers not always unquestioningly followed; and in the United States, unlike some Asian societies, there is no clear division between monks and lay people: adherents both meditate, following the monk's path, and work in the world, following the lay path.[36] All of this indicates an emergent American form of Buddhism.

I interviewed 14 American adherents of Buddhism, primarily Tibetan Buddhism, and engaged in meditation sessions and attended Buddhist ceremonies conducted by visiting Tibetan teachers. I chose Tibetan Buddhism as my focus because of all the kinds of Buddhism practiced in America, it has always struck me as most obviously foreign. Tibetan Buddhism, in contrast to the relative simplicity of Zen Buddhism, offers over the many years of its training an array of meditative practices and symbols that seem very far from the conventional patterns of American life. How do American Tibetan Buddhists culturally comprehend themselves as both American and Buddhist? How do they synthesize these different aspects of their cultural identities?

Let me begin with the account of one American Tibetan Buddhist, to see how he explains his path:

Mark Petrovich (40)
I practice Tibetan Buddhist meditation 15 to 20 hours a week; and I go on intensive retreats whenever I can − I hope to go off on retreat for a year pretty soon. It's the most important thing in my life. I'm married; my wife doesn't practice. But she understands how important Buddhism is to me in my life. . . .

I come from a Catholic background; I was the head altar boy, the whole thing. My experience of Catholicism is that it's a dead tradition in our culture; it's only rhetoric − I left it as a teenager. In college, I started exploring different traditions − started shopping around in "the spiritual supermarket" (that's a term I use when I teach meditation classes: I had a credit card in the spiritual supermarket for a number of years!). Later, I had an experience where my mind spontaneously opened: I saw things I still can't express, the oneness of the world. . . . I entered a period of deep introspection, trying to figure out the nature of my existence; I went through three years of distress, thought of suicide. Eventually I discovered Buddhism, and there was tremendous resonance with my own experience − it was a life raft. At first it was slow − my teachers, who were Tibetan, seemed so foreign that I just couldn't connect. But then the power of the practice began to unfold. . . .

In Buddhism, you're given these meditation practices that can fit anybody in any culture − just as there's no difference between the science of a Chinese and a European, there's no difference in the contemplative tradition − it doesn't matter what culture you're coming from. They talk, in our teachings, about, "don't mistake the tea for the cup" – don't mistake the contemplative tradition for its container, the culture. That's the challenge with Tibetan Buddhism: because it's so exotic, so colorful, it's easy to get tripped up. But our own American culture is fiercely independent, it has a cowboy mentality, "don't tell me what to do," and Buddhism fits well with that. You don't have faith – you sit on the cushion and look into your mind. Nobody has a patent on the mechanics of mind: it doesn't matter what tradition you're in – a Christian or Muslim could reach enlightenment. But Tibetan Buddhism has hundreds of meditation practices which allow you to work very specifically with different aspects of the mind. Because of that, I think that Tibetan Buddhism is the most evolved tradition in the world. But this path isn't for everyone – you have to reach a certain level of development (although I don't mean this with any arrogance) to find this path attractive. You have to completely realize the futility of conventional life; you have to truly understand that "all life is suffering". . . .

I'm a dentist by profession; I try to work just four days a week, so that I have time for Buddhist practice. I studied to be a dentist because I knew I had to make a living in society; I'm also a classical violinist, but it's difficult to make a living from that. Contrary to most people's opinions, you don't have to run away and become a monk to practice Buddhism; I become a better dentist, a better violinist because of my Buddhist practice. . . .

I have a shrine room in my house, with various Buddhist symbols. If I simply go to my shrine for two hours to meditate, then maybe I'm just indulging myself. The central challenge is to bring the Buddhist teachings into my life as a whole. I don't talk about Buddhism in my work – it's important not to vomit your teachings on other people; I won't talk about it unless I'm asked very persistently. Still, I can practice my Buddhism without anybody ever knowing. The most effective Buddhists are those you never know about. I deal a lot with pain, with screaming children. My ability to be with the person in pain, to empathize: that's directly related to Buddhism. . . .

I play tennis. If you look at tennis in a competitive way, Buddhism damages that sense of competition. I no longer have the killer instinct. Yes, it does go against the American grain not to be competitive, and that's why it's so hard to be a Buddhist in our culture – everything is designed to pull us away from a contemplative life: everything pulls us back towards ego. Most people in

America only aspire to be wealthy – they're stuck in a realm of ignorance. But look at what the so-called American way is doing to our planet! If that's American, I'm proud to raise the banner of Buddhism as unAmerican! . . .

Mr. Petrovich was raised in a taken-for-granted Catholicism that he later rejected; he wandered the aisles of "the spiritual supermarket" and eventually chose Tibetan Buddhism as his path. In his descriptions of Tibetan Buddhism, he sounds at points like a spiritual salesman, saying (in paraphrase) "it has hundreds of options! . . . it's not for everyone, it's elite!"; indeed, as a teacher of meditation, he is a salesman of his chosen path to prospective consumers. However, this makes Mr. Petrovich's path seem frivolous; like Ms. Martin, his choice from the cultural supermarket was no lighthearted matter of fashion, but a wrenching decision, that by his account saved his life. An underlying question raised by his account is, "Why do this? Why spend so much of your life meditating?" (We might speculate that his wife, left alone, may particularly wonder about this.) His answer is that he is following the most direct path to ultimate truth, a truth beyond the suffering of this world. Most of his fellows are not yet sufficiently evolved to take the meditative path he is on, he maintains; but it is not for him to preach that to them – they must discover for themselves that they are "stuck in a realm of ignorance." In his belief in truth over taste, he differs from Ms. Clemens and resembles Ms. Martin; but of course his truth and hers contradict one another.

Tibetan Buddhism transcends the culture of its origin, to have, like science, a universal validity, Mr. Petrovich argues. The "Tibetanness" of Tibetan Buddhism got in the way at first, he says, but this was transcended by the universality of the method. But culture still matters; by his account American culture is particularly suitable for this method in its "cowboy" mentality, its willingness to test and try, rather than accept on faith; but at the same time, America is the realm of *shikata ga nai* for Mr. Petrovich. America has been seduced by the pursuit of wealth, blinding Americans to the truth of their condition; America makes the contemplative path extraordinarily difficult to follow. America is a land in which he must work as a dentist rather than following his path as a Buddhist, or for that matter, a violinist; America, he says, is the land of ego, and his spiritual path is designed to transcend the false bonds of ego, and thus to become "unAmerican."

Mr. Petrovich teaches meditation; but at work, he tells us, he practices Buddhism in invisible form, empathizing with his patients in pain, and seeking to attract people not through words but through example.

In an America based on self-assertion, competition, ego, perhaps no one will notice such activity; but then, for Mr. Petrovich, it is perhaps better that they not notice – if enough people are like him, practicing their Buddhism unnoticed, then perhaps the meaning of America too will change before anyone notices: perhaps America as a whole will become "unAmerican." One may wonder, from his account, whether his compassion is anything more than his own imagination: if no one notices, then do the subtleties of his meditation make any difference to all the people in pain in the world around him? Just possibly, they do.

Let me now turn to Tibetan Buddhists as a whole. Over half of the 14 people I interviewed had been Tibetan Buddhists for 15 years or more; almost all were white. Professionally, they included graphic designers, doctors, dentists, psychotherapists, lawyers, architects, and accountants, as well as spiritual counselors and acupuncturists. These people are mostly members of America's upper-middle class, in terms of educational and occupational attainment, but in their lives as they described them to me, they are not much pursuing occupational success – the major commitment in their lives is to their spiritual practice. The accountant spoke to me of the holes in his resumé from the years he has spent in meditation retreats; Mr. Petrovich told me that he chose dentistry as a path so that he could have freedom in his career to take time for meditation practice, rather than be tied to a 40-hour work week.

Tibetan Buddhist practice requires, as Mr. Petrovich said, many hours each week. The details of the practice are kept secret, but by all accounts it is extraordinarily demanding: at various points on the spiritual path, 108,000 prostrations before a shrine and 1,080,000 recitations of a guru supplication are required, as well as many additional levels of complex practice.

> Students develop the habit of using every vacation for intensive retreats. . . . Some students will quit their jobs and spend a year just meditating. . . . The most committed and trained students [go on] . . . the Three-Year Retreat . . . and . . . practice day and night for three years, three months, and three days.[37]

The purpose of this intense practice is eventual liberation from the bonds of one's ego, one's "false self." We don't exist as selves, Buddhism holds, but we cling to the illusion of self, and this is the ultimate source of our own and all the world's suffering. A central doctrine of Buddhism is *samsara*, the wheel of birth and death operating lifetime after lifetime; only through spiritual practice can one attain liberation from this cycle of suffering. Most forms of Buddhism hold that liberation may take place over many lifetimes, but Tibetan Buddhism holds that liberation can take place in this lifetime, and martials its array of meditational practices to attain this end. "There are no guarantees," it is often stated – there are no promises that this will succeed; but the people I interviewed were convinced by their own experiences in meditation that this was the path for them.

It is important to remember the cultural milieu within which the people I interviewed adopted Tibetan Buddhism. Almost all grew up in Christian or Jewish households, and rejected, like Mr. Petrovich, the taken-for-granted religion of their youth. Most were also touched by the cultural ferment of the late 1960s, during which American institutions and life in general were called into question. Many of those I interviewed spoke at length about how at an early age they rejected the lifestyle of their parents, and felt alienated from American society. The antitheses of materialist America for such people was the spiritual Orient, and above all, Tibet:

> Mysterious, remote, closer to the heavens perhaps? – the Himalayas have long been a kind of spiritual frontier to the West. Be it earthly paradise, "higher" consciousness or loving heart, we have used the region of the world's highest mountains to tell ourselves hopeful spiritual stories.[38]

As one person told me, "From my early adolescence, I was totally fascinated with Tibet, a society that's essentially developed in total remoteness. . . . One can trust it, because it hasn't been through all the garbage of the rest of the world." This vision of remote Tibet is an illusion, as scholars point out[39] – Tibet was never that remote, nor was it free from the inequities that beset the rest of the world – but the drawing power of the illusion remains unabated today, as the spate of recent Hollywood movies portraying Tibet attests.

The longer-practicing Buddhists I interviewed turned to it because of the teachings of Chögyam Trungpa, who established a center for Tibetan Buddhism in Boulder, Colorado in the early 1970s. Trungpa was by most accounts an extraordinary teacher, a "cultural magician" in bringing the teachings of Tibet to Americans so that Americans could comprehend them. In his early years in America, he worked to destroy all senses of the exoticism of Tibetan teachings, seeing such an attitude as "spiritual materialism"[40] – the ego using spirituality as a source of pride in itself, as if to say, "Look at me! I'm learning Oriental wisdom!" "Trungpa Rinpoche [teacher] drank beer, smoked pot, slept around: he fit in the hippie American culture of that time," I was told – he sought to quash notions of the wise Oriental teacher by behaving like an American and teaching within an American countercultural mold. In later years, however, Trungpa became more strict, bringing back the hierarchy and formality of Tibetan teachings: "Slowly he started tightening the reins, bringing in discipline, which at that point we were ready to accept. Before that, it would have been like a Martian coming off a spaceship."

Trungpa embodied the "crazy wisdom" tradition of Tibetan Buddhism, whereby the teacher will do anything to enable students to attain liberation from the bonds of ego. There is a long Tibetan tradition of teachers asking students to do outrageous things – jumping off cliffs, cutting off their limbs, and so on – and Trungpa continued that, albeit in less physically dangerous form. Many people I interviewed told me stories like this: "You'd be talking with him, asking him your earnest and so profound questions, and he'd look out the window and yawn. Gestures like that would make you feel disenfranchised on the spot." "Sometimes I wouldn't have seen him for a couple of months, when he was traveling," said another person, a woman who worked closely with him (and who had a sexual relationship with him, as did a number of his female students),

> and he'd look at me like he didn't know who I was. I'd really be wanting to be recognized and said hello to, and his ignoring me was a strong lesson. He could just annihilate your ego in a second. . . . I mean, you might be crying, but somewhere inside yourself you're relieved that someone actually understood.

By normal standards of behavior, these examples depict boorishness; but the people I interviewed believed that such behavior showed how their teacher was using every possible means to try to wake them up from the dream of self.

Chögyam Trungpa died at the age of 46, of alcoholism. His taste for alcohol, as well as for women, was something he never hid, and most of the people I interviewed insisted that his teachings shone through the alcohol, and that his sexual behavior was a form of teaching. Few said the same about Osel Tendzin, an American designated by Trungpa as his dharma heir. Tendzin, it was revealed in the early 1990s, had had sex with several male students, knowing that he had the HIV virus, and had transmitted AIDS to one. This split the Tibetan Buddhist community, and left wounds still healing even now. Buddhist journals in the last few years have had frequent articles asking, "How does one balance one's own critical intelligence and integrity with a need to surrender to the teacher to some degree?"[41]

Most often, the given answer is that one must not abandon one's critical intelligence in dealing with one's teacher. But this is problematic; as a person I interviewed said, "Yes, you have to use your critical intelligence, but who knows if it's not just your preconceptions," preconceptions that the Buddhist path is attempting to transcend. One's own judgment, after all, is necessarily an ego-based judgment; one's teacher, who as a Buddhist master is presumably egoless, is the only one who can help the student to transcend ego. Ego achieving spirituality on its own is, in Trungpa's words, "like wanting to witness your own funeral:"[42] "Devotion to teacher in the vajrayana [the advanced level of Tibetan Buddhist teachings] demands the total surrender of ego, the complete renunciation of all clinging to self."[43] But is the teacher truly egoless? Is enlightenment real, or is it just as chimerical as the mythical Himalayan kingdom of Shangri-la? Is there any such thing as spiritual truth through this path, or is this merely one more form of exoticism? In his book *The Double Mirror: A Skeptical Journey into the Buddhist Tantra*, Stephen Butterfield writes, "The robed and suited people on thrones to whom I had bowed and prostrated, and helped support year after year, were they any more enlightened than anyone else, or were they just skillful at putting on a good show?"[44] He is unable conclusively to answer this question.

This brings us to the matter of truth vs. taste. If Tibetan Buddhism is seen as a way of making one's life in this world a better one, then it is a matter of taste – different people have different ways of pursuing happiness, however bizarre and exotic they may seem to others; if Tibetan Buddhism happens to work for you, then by all means pursue it. But if there is indeed a cosmology of reincarnation and eventual liberation from the cycle of birth and death, then Buddhism is not a matter of taste but of truth: this is the way the world is, whether one recognizes it or not. Is Buddhism a this-world therapy, or a cosmology transcending this world? If it is therapy, then it fits well within the American cultural supermarket. If it is cosmology, then it cannot avoid making a judgment about comparative realities: "they're wrong, but this is right"; it is, in effect, an alternative to Christianity in its truth claims, and in its claims for America.

Trungpa in his books discusses reincarnation strictly in psychological terms; as a person I interviewed said, echoing Trungpa, "Every instant we're dying and being reborn. You're not the same person you were two seconds ago, let alone two minutes or three years ago." Some other Tibetan teachers, however, scorn the psychologizing of Buddhist cosmology. Another person recounted a teacher saying: "You know, you Americans seem to think that the six realms [of reincarnated beings, central to Tibetan teachings] are psychological states. You need to understand that these are actual states that you could be reborn into. Be careful!" I went to a ceremony performed by a distinguished Tibetan Buddhist teacher, speaking in Tibetan as translated by an American student. He said:

> We're lucky to be born as humans, because we have consciousness and can choose; but if we don't live right, we'll be reborn as less than human. It's entirely possible to be liberated in this lifetime; but if we don't follow the dharma, then we remain in this cycle of birth and death indefinitely. Liberation may take place in this lifetime, or it may take place after seven or sixteen life cycles. . . . If you say this prayer I now offer you, you can be cured of heart disease and mental illness.

As this teacher spoke, I could see his American audience – consisting, it seemed, of some committed Buddhists, but many more curiosity seekers who had seen a poster advertising the event – shift restlessly in their seats. This teacher was no doubt accustomed to a Tibetan or Indian audience, for whom enumeration of life cycles before liberation and promises of miracle cures are standard rhetorical devices. But for many Americans, even those seduced by "the wisdom of the East," this might seem too much. One person I interviewed said, "We cringe a little when people like him talk, and go, 'Gosh, I wish we didn't publicize this one quite so much.'"

As for Buddhism's claims beyond this world, some I interviewed were wholly agnostic: "I don't know what happens after I take my last breath." "A friend of mine who was dying said, 'I'm looking forward to this, because I'll find out whether these teachings have any validity.' I thought that was pretty good." Others felt that one's choices in this world may shape worlds beyond this one: "The mind is a powerful thing, and it wouldn't surprise me if people create the world in which they find themselves after death"; "Yes, I believe that Christians may go to heaven or hell, just as Buddhists may be reincarnated, to eventual liberation." What these people are saying is that the world of taste transcends this world, to shape one's world beyond: one's choices from the cultural supermarket are matters not just of one's this-world tastes but of one's subjective ultimate truth as well. Still others were more absolute in their truth claims. In one person's words: "For most people who've been on this path a long time, reincarnation is a non-issue; it's a given. Pretty much everyone I know believes in it." This person, like Mr. Petrovich, as we saw, sought to transcend relativism, to claim a higher validity for Buddhism: "Yes, this path is true, I believe, for everyone. But most people aren't at a stage of development to realize this yet."

Concepts of ultimate truth have been argued extensively in Buddhist publications; one featured a debate between a scholar who maintains that belief in reincarnation is an absolute necessity in Buddhism and another who claims that agnosticism is the most appropriate Buddhist attitude: the former position being that of Buddhism as ultimate truth, the latter that of Buddhism as this-world taste.[45] These different concepts relate directly to concepts of America: Is Buddhism one more choice in the cultural supermarket that is the essence of America? Or is Buddhism an emergent alternative American truth, to replace an outmoded and unsustainable American Christian truth?

To some Tibetan Buddhists, being American was no more than a happenstance of their lives:

> I was born here, I have a social security number, I pay my taxes. Being American is just a technicality: I happen to live here. . . . But then, I guess that's part of being American: America allows that kind of multiplicity. You can be almost anything, as long as you're not harming other people. You're free to think pretty much whatever you want to.

This man realizes that the fact that he doesn't need to feel particularly American is itself American. America, he is implying, is the land of the cultural supermarket, where you can pursue happiness in whatever way you please, including being a Tibetan Buddhist. This view was echoed, in various words, by the majority of the Tibetan Buddhists I interviewed.

Earlier in this chapter, we discussed the dilemma faced by evangelical Christians between the demands of their faith that they proselytize to non-believers and the demand of their social world that they leave other people alone, to believe whatever they want. The Tibetan Buddhists did not suffer from this split nearly as much as the Christians did – their religious path seems, if anything, to discourage proselytizing, and the people around them within the liberal social environment of Boulder seem generally to accept their spiritual path as one more choice from the cultural supermarket. The people I interviewed did on occasion speak of a family member who was a Christian being disturbed that they had rejected God's word; but more typical were words such as these: "My mother's a practicing Catholic, but when I told her that I was thinking of becoming a Buddhist, she said, 'Well, if it makes you happy, I'm all for it.'" These Buddhists had, if they were married, often married other Buddhists, and if they hadn't, their spiritual paths tended to be viewed by their spouses as time-consuming pastimes rather than alternative versions of ultimate truth (although this too could often create considerable marital tension). One of the few people I interviewed who did face a conflict over different religious beliefs was a man who worked as a spiritual counselor in a hospice:

> Sometimes, staff who aren't in pastoral care will get a little pushy. They'll say things to non-believers like, "Are you sure you don't believe in God?" When someone is on their deathbed, and highly vulnerable, that's pure spiritual aggression. . . . At case conferences, I say, "There's some missionary activity happening here, and that's not appropriate." I am not bashful about reminding people that if they can't do spiritual care properly, they should stay out of it.

He seems to win these battles, with the chastened guilty parties agreeing to try to mend their ways. Taste thus wins out over truth, with "missionary activity" – the proclamation that one truth fits all, and that you'd thus better believe – being a sin to be confessed and expunged. America as the land of the cultural supermarket means that anything you happen to believe about the ultimate is worthy, and should not be challenged.

It was interesting, however, that while parents and employers would only rarely dispute the spiritual choices of the people I interviewed as against other spiritual choices, they would dispute those choices in terms of what they meant occupationally. To take just one example, a former computer programmer who left that occupation for one more attuned to his Buddhist practice recalled a dinner with his father: "He said 'When are you going to get off this Buddhist kick, and get serious about your career?' The computer programming was what was real and important to him, not my Buddhism." In an America defined by the cultural supermarket, one's particular choices are not to be condemned; but what may still be criticized is one's less than wholehearted pursuit of occupational success. This may be in part because such success is what enables one to have maximum freedom to consume in the economic and cultural supermarkets.

If many Tibetan Buddhists, in keeping with the social world around them, see the United States as the land of the cultural supermarket, others have a darker view. In one woman's words, "There are so many lost souls in this country; the norm is for people to be depressed, feeling like they're not getting their piece of the pie. Our culture is so materialistic that it has destroyed people's spirits." A number of people, echoing Mr. Petrovich, said that the gap between Tibetan Buddhism and contemporary America was not simply a matter of East versus West; more, it was a matter of a spiritual path whose purpose is the transcendence of ego being transplanted to a land that in its wealth and arrogance is the quintessence of ego.

And yet, it was, for several of these people, the very darkness of contemporary America that could lead Buddhism to flourish there:

> We've hit bottom in America, in the unending pursuit of entertainment, going out to buy shit to make you feel better every day. Buddhism is emerging because people are coming to see the limits of all that, that it's not enough. And after that, there's nowhere to go but in, to look inside yourself – that's what people are beginning to realize.

I interviewed the editor of a book entitled *Buddhist America* who said, "At the time I did the book, the Christian right was saying very insistently that America is a Christian country. I beg to differ. It's a pluralist country." But as he spoke, it became apparent that he dreamed of a future America that was not simply a cultural supermarket, but more, an America where a vast range of people meditate – not just a pluralist America, but one becoming a Buddhist America. The scholar of Tibetan Buddhism Robert Thurman has spoken in utopian terms about his American dream:

> A Buddhist political perspective reinforces the best of Jeffersonian democracy. . . . Buddhist insight provides powerful support for secular humanism and enlightened individualism. . . . The Buddha really could have dreamed America . . . because the ideal of a democratic country . . . is definitely the dream of every Buddhist adept. . . . America can express something about . . . generosity. . . . That's our role and that's our goal. We're to be a beacon to other nations.[46]

Thurman here sounds remarkably like the Buddhist equivalent of an evangelical Christian preacher, albeit without their pessimism. His vision of Buddhism mirrors his vision of an ideal America, which, suitably Buddhist, can apparently Americanize the world.

Several people I interviewed expressed reservations about Thurman's equation of Buddhism with American liberal ideals; but whatever the validity of his depiction of Buddhism, the words cited above are highly significant. We saw last chapter how some Japanese rock musicians and visual artists are using the imported forms they have chosen from the cultural supermarket to attempt to create a new sense of a Japanese cultural home. These American Buddhists are attempting a parallel creation: Thurman's equation of Buddhism with Jeffersonian democracy is saying that "this Buddhism we follow is not something foreign; it fits perfectly our own Americanness." Indeed, *American* Buddhism may seem more convincing than *Japanese* jazz or rock or visual art, because Americans tend to be so comfortable with seeing the cultural supermarket as the essence of America. But this may be the problem: Can Tibetan Buddhism survive its immersion into America's cultural supermarket?

There are huge cultural barriers that Americans may face in following the Tibetan Buddhist path. Having to prostrate oneself to one's teacher and lineage ("I won't bow down to anyone" being an oft-expressed American attitude), having to hold utter devotion to one's teacher (who is, after all, no more than a fellow human being, no better than oneself according to oft-held American beliefs), having to visualize various Tibetan deities and chant to them for one's protection (even if these deities are sometimes explained as representing aspects of mind rather than actual beings), and having to some degree to accept a cosmology of reincarnation – all of these may involve significant cultural clash and cognitive dissonance for many American followers of Tibetan Buddhism.

There are other, more deepseated cultural gaps as well. Future Tibetan spiritual leaders are selected as young children (including today some non-Tibetans) thought to be reincarnations of recently deceased leaders, and then raised within Tibetan Buddhist monasteries. From a secular point of view, this situation is not that different from one of monarchy, with a particularly fortunate young child selected to be a future "king." As said one long-time practitioner of Tibetan Buddhism, "We have these American ideas about democracy. And frankly, I think that if you have democracy, you're going to lose the transmission," lose the ability to find the teachers that enable Tibetan Buddhism's ongoing survival. In Tibet, women are not full participants in Tibetan Buddhism, and are not even allowed onto monastic grounds; as this practitioner said.

One woman here has done a three-year retreat. Because she has done that, she has the title of lama. Now, to ask a traditional Tibetan to call an American woman a lama is so offensive to their sensibilities, it's just . . . it's impossible.

In the face of cultural obstacles such as these, some Tibetan teachers are deeply skeptical about whether Americans can ever really enter into Tibetan Buddhism. As one teacher recently wrote:

Tibetan lamas . . . [may] adopt the attitude that Westerners are merely . . . window-shopping, telling the younger lamas like myself, "See, we told you! They are not here for the dharma [teachings]. For them, we are a mere curiosity". . . . The Western shopping mentality . . . regards the dharma as merchandise and our [students'] own involvement as an investment. . . . It is easy to forget that such supposedly universal notions as "ego," "freedom," "equality," "power," and the implications of "gender" . . . are all constructions that are culture-specific and differ radically when seen through different perspectives. . . . Ideas such as democracy and capitalism, as well as equality and human rights, can be seen to have failed miserably in the West, and to be nothing but new dogmas. [47]

For all their rhetorical overkill, the above words are important: perhaps, in its transplantation to the glittering cultural supermarket that is America, Tibetan Buddhism risks losing itself, for (despite the words of Thurman that we examined above) it seems not to be based on the values of capitalism, equality, and individualism that form the underlying assumptions of the cultural supermarket. Perhaps in order to fight off the inroads of the West and its subverting powers, Tibetan Buddhism still has empowered few Western teachers. [48] Indeed, it may be the case that Tibetan Buddhism can preserve itself on American soil by keeping itself as unAmerican, as unsupermarketed, as possible.

The Americanness of Tibetan Buddhism, and of meditative Buddhism in general in the United States, is in one sense quite limited: its adherents are overwhelmingly affluent, educated white people. "In the ongoing discussion about the meaning of an emergent 'American Buddhism,' it is mainly white Buddhists who are busy doing the defining." [49] Some I interviewed explained this whiteness as follows: "Only when you have education can you see how meaningless acquisition is, and seek to transcend it: that's why students of Tibetan

Buddhism tend to be white and middle class." An African-American Buddhist writer offers a harsher interpretation:

> We cannot separate the will of so many white comrades to journey in search of spiritual nourishment to the "third world" from the history of cultural imperialism and colonialism that has created a context where such journeying is seen as appropriate [and] acceptable, an expression of freedom and right.[50]

These words touch upon how the cultural supermarket's shelves are slanted, shaped by global power inequities; it indeed remains disproportionately the province of the Europeans and Americans who colonized the world, and now enjoy its cultural fruits: rich white people going cultural shopping. I discussed these issues with an African-American Tibetan Buddhist, a man acutely aware of America's legacy of racial injustice: "Being American means, for me, living with blatant contradictions every day. I mean, this is a country that claims to be about freedom and equality! America is a land of cowards." He felt uneasy about engaging in his Buddhist studies in an almost totally white environment:

> I have a deep drive to pursue the Buddhist path, and the way to do that in this country, unfortunately, is to hang out with white people. . . . Yes, I'm benefitting from the legacy of white colonialism, in the fact that there's Buddhism in this country, and that I have an avenue of practice here. That troubles me a bit.

But he also maintained that his personal path was not reducible to issues of race: "One's motivation has everything to do with it. . . . There's nothing about Buddhism that inherently separates me from black people. I can be a Buddhist and still be black." Nonetheless, his uncertainty clearly remained.

This is one sense in which the emergence of an ideal Buddhist America seems questionable; but an even deeper reason involves the very nature of the cultural supermarket in its American manifestation. Horkheimer and Adorno[51] wrote 50 years ago about how American capitalism tends to subvert all cultural forms, swallowing everything in its path to make all the stuff of commerce; this can be seen, for example, in how the countercultural music of the 1960s became in later decades the background music for soft drink and sports shoe ads. What is true of the economic supermarket may be true of the cultural supermarket as well: all that is consumed within the cultural supermarket in America may more or less lose its original character, to become ineradicably

American – and this may be no less true of Tibetan Buddhism than of the tacos one consumes at Taco Bell. Can American Buddhism survive as Buddhism rather than an American distortion? One Buddhist writer thinks not. He describes being at a week-long Zen retreat at the end of which the Chinese participants spoke of how, through meditating, they realized how selfish they had been in their lives, while the American participants felt they had gotten in touch with themselves, and made progress toward self-realization. This opposite reaction leads him to reflect upon the transformation of Buddhism in America:

> Americans turn to a foreign religion like Buddhism only insofar as that religion affirms American values. During the sixties, Buddhism experienced a boom . . . because so many people saw Buddhist practice as a way of affirming the American values of individual commitment and self-reliance. . . . Just as pouring a little sweet-and-sour sauce over Western food does not make it Chinese, so also flourishing Buddhist terminology over Western concepts of self, society, and consciousness does not make them "essentials of Buddhism." We are not Westernizing Buddhism so much as Orientalizing Westernism.[52]

This writer's claim is that Buddhist America is more American than Buddhist: taken-for-granted American values such as individualism are interpolated into Buddhism by Americans unwittingly recreating Americanness wherever they go. Beyond this, I argue that in today's United States, values such as individualism are taken for granted largely because they are the values of the cultural supermarket; "the individual pursuit of happiness" is transmuted into the singleminded principle of the economic and cultural supermarkets, where the consumer is king. Can Buddhist America escape this? Chögyam Trungpa often stated, as echoed by many I interviewed, that "Buddhism can fit many containers"; "don't mistake the tea for the cup." But perhaps the container does alter the liquid therein: maybe the tea is indeed the cup, at least in the United States.

We saw last chapter how some Japanese artists and musicians working in imported forms struggle to invent a Japanese home from the cultural supermarket's shelves, but may have trouble doing so because those forms continue to seem so foreign. The American Buddhists seem to have an opposite problem: they struggle to achieve wisdom and perhaps create an alternative Americanness within an imported spiritual tradition, only to find that the taken-for-granted Americanness they already have is so powerful that it subverts any alternative to itself. If, for Japanese artists, materials from the cultural super-market must somehow be transformed into home, for American reli-gious seekers, the cultural supermarket already is America's home, and perhaps cannot be escaped: for them, foreignness is perhaps not inevita-ble but impossible.

But then, the Buddhist ideal is not to recreate home but to transcend home; as the American teacher of Tibetan Buddhism Pema Chodron has said, "Becoming a Buddhist is about becoming homeless":[53] having no particular place, culture, nation as home, but rather all the cosmos, nowhere, and everywhere. Whether Buddhism can enable its American adherents to transcend all sense of home, or rather will merely confirm that all the cultural supermarket is affluent America's home, is perhaps the key question facing "Buddhist America" today.

Conclusion

There are broad parallels between the different groups of Japanese artists examined in Chapter 2, and the different groups of American religious seekers examined in this chapter. Japanese traditional artists may see Japaneseness as the essence of their arts, but an essence now forgotten by most of their fellow Japanese; American evangelical Christians may see America as a once-Christian nation now Christian no longer. Some Japanese contemporary artists see Japan as a cultural obstacle blocking their pursuit of their universal arts; some American liberal Christians see their Christianity as a path given them because of their culture, but only one of many paths to universal truth. Some Japanese artists see themselves as world citizens pursuing their arts within the global cultural supermarket; some American spiritual seekers seek wisdom through their choices as consumers from the global "spiritual supermarket." Some Japanese contemporary artists seek to reinvent Japaneseness from their imported art forms; some American Buddhists seek to reinvent Americanness, a new "Buddhist America."

This parallel is remarkable, I think; but it masks a fundamental difference between Japanese artists and American religious seekers, in their conception and use of the cultural supermarket. For Japanese artists, the cultural supermarket, whether seen as eroding Japaneseness or as providing materials for the reconstruction of Japaneseness, tends to be thought of as other than Japanese; it is foreign, or, as more typically put, "Western." For some American Christians, the cultural supermarket may be seen as bringing strange "Eastern" religions to America's shores, subverting Christian values, but more typically, the global cultural supermarket is seen as American, embodying the pursuit of happiness that is thought to be every American's birthright. To a degree anyway, Japanese artists' consumption from the global cultural supermarket is a threat to their Japaneseness; American religious seekers' consumption from the global cultural supermarket is a confirmation of their Americanness. A Japanese anthropologist friend has said that when he eats a peanut-butter-and-jelly sandwich, he is criticized by some Japanese for having become "Westernized," but when his friends in America eat sushi, they are simply enjoying one more taste that is part of contemporary America.[54] Indeed: Japan is ever under threat from the foreign, but America simply swallows the foreign. This is not only because the principles of consumption from the cultural supermarket are the American cultural principles of free individual choice and the pursuit of happiness; it is also because of America's global power in shaping cultural images and cultural consumption. East Asia may in recent decades have come to rival the United States in economic power; but the United States and (to a lesser extent) Western Europe continue to wield dominant cultural power. Thus, while Japanese may still fear "Westernization," few Americans fear "Easternization": rather, "the East" is rendered one more kind of Americanness.

In the course of American religious history, as paralleled by the different groups of religious seekers depicted in this chapter, we see the ongoing expansion of the cultural supermarket: from a largely Christian America, to an America with a multiplicity of homegrown creeds, to an America open to all the world's religions. One result of this, as this chapter has discussed, is the shift from truth to taste as the dominant marker of religion in America: When there are so many different religious paths to choose from, when so many people have so many different spiritual choices, who is to say what is true and what is not? For this reason, a "Buddhist America" is no more likely in America's future than is the resurgence of a Christian America: America will only be the cultural consumer's dreamland, the pursuit of happiness through the shelves of the cultural supermarket. This, for better or for worse, is the American home.

4   What in the world is Chinese?

On the cultural identities of Hong Kong intellectuals in the shadow and wake of 1 July 1997

On 1 July 1997, political control over Hong Kong was passed from Great Britain to China. Some observers in Hong Kong, in China, and overseas have interpreted this as Hong Kong's return to its home and motherland after 150 years of colonial rule by a foreign usurper. But many in Hong Kong have not felt this way. They have believed that they are Hongkongese more than Chinese, and have felt uneasy about returning to a national home that they do not sense is theirs. Chinese control over Hong Kong signifies to these people less a return home than a loss of home. But this also fills many of these people with ambivalence: for are they not, after all, Chinese? But what, in Hong Kong, does it mean to be Chinese?

This chapter explores how Hong Kong intellectuals before and after the handover formulate their identities as Chinese and as Hongkongese between the claims of state and market, and between belonging to a particular culture and belonging to the global cultural supermarket. In the previous two chapters, we saw how Japanese artists and American religious seekers use art or religion as a means of constructing their senses of national cultural identity; we saw how once rooted senses of identity have been shaken loose, some artists and religious seekers struggle to reinvent their cultural identities from within the cultural supermarket's shelves. In this chapter, we examine what might be thought of as the reverse of this process: Hong Kong intellectuals who have not had a sense of national cultural identity are now, after 1 July 1997, asked to assume that identity, an assumption that some embrace and others resist. This chapter differs from our earlier chapters in that it is framed by a particular historical event, Hong Kong's return to China; we are not dealing with art or religion but with politics, and the political shaping of cultural identity at a pivotal historical juncture. Despite this difference, however, the people in this chapter speak with voices remarkably similar to those of our earlier chapters. They ask, as we will see, "Where, beneath the claims of governments, is my cultural home?"; and they ask, "Can I make a true cultural home from the cultural supermarket's shelves?"

Two histories of Hong Kong's cultural identity

Who are the people of Hong Kong? Most people in Japan feel themselves to be "naturally" Japanese; most people in the United States take for granted, in at least some contexts, their Americanness. But in Hong Kong in recent decades, national identity has been even at the most mundane level a matter of ambiguity and confusion. For the past five years – years covering the last years of British rule, the handover, and the first years of Chinese rule – I have taught anthropology at the Chinese University of Hong Kong, and have had frequent opportunity to question students as to who they are, culturally, as well as interview a range of Hong Kong people. The responses I receive to my questions are various and ambiguous, even down to the seemingly obvious question of nationality. As one young Hong Kong woman told me,

> Every time I travel to another country, I have to write down my nationality. Because I have a British National Overseas passport, I guess I'm supposed to write "British," even though I have no right to live in Britain. . . . I have to ask the stewardess, "What should I write: 'British,' 'British Hong Kong,' 'Hong Kong,' or 'Chinese'?" For a long time, I didn't know how to properly fill out the forms; I didn't know what country I was supposed to belong to.

Politically the national identity of this woman has become clear after 1 July 1997, and will become clearer once her passport expires and she obtains a new passport identifying her as a citizen of the Hong Kong Special Administrative Region of China. Culturally, however, the issue of Hong Kong identity remains murky. Over the past 15 years, as Hong Kong's return to China loomed, there has been an extraordinary degree of questioning as to "who we Hong Kong people really are." The fundamental terms of this debate seem implicitly to be "Hong Kong as a part of China" versus "Hong Kong as apart from China": Hong Kong as Chinese versus Hong Kong as different from China. Whenever I ask the students in my classes about cultural identity, I get a chorus of conflicting replies: "I'm Hongkongese!"; "Not me, I'm Chinese!" These replies tend to be related less to the objective circumstances of students' lives (most were born in Hong Kong but some emigrated from China at an early age with their families) than to their particular choices as to how they want to culturally construct and present themselves, between, as I will argue, belonging to a particular national home and belonging to the global cultural supermarket.

Scholars echo my students' assertions. "Hong Kong is Chinese in many ways. . . . Yet it is also evident that Hong Kong . . . has developed its unique identity and culture," writes one; "Hong Kong is not a Chinese city, although more than ninety-seven percent of its population are ethnic Chinese," writes another; "Hong Kong is a *very* Chinese city," exclaims a third; "Unlike any Chinese city on the mainland or perhaps anywhere else, Hong Kong is that seeming contradiction: a Chinese cosmopolitan city," exclaims a fourth.[1] This ambiguity is also expressed in the numerous public opinion surveys asking about cultural identity in Hong Kong in recent years, which typically show a large minority of people claiming to be "Hongkongese," and a somewhat smaller group claiming to be "Chinese." These surveys show a remarkable discordance over cultural identity in Hong Kong; Hong Kong people in recent decades have had no common cultural label for who they are.

This has not, apparently, been true through most of Hong Kong's history. Up until World War II, the border between Hong Kong and China was open, and people went back and forth at will, perhaps indicating a similar fluidity of identity: most Hong Kong people apparently felt themselves to be Chinese. One writer asserts that "until recent years, perhaps as late as the 1960s, most Hong Kong Chinese residents considered the mainland to be their 'motherland.' They belonged to it. Hong Kong was only their transitional home."[2] However, it is not easy to assess the history of Hong Kong's identity, largely because the issue of Hong Kong's past has been in recent years so politicized. Historical depictions of Hong Kong clearly fit into two camps, the Chinese camp and the British or Western camp, with their depictions sometimes so different as to hardly be describing the same place; and Hong Kong historians themselves seem unable to detach themselves from this divide. (As one recent book has it, "There is not yet a Hong Kong history book which is able to use both Chinese and Western materials in giving a complete history of Hong Kong's political, social, and economic changes from different perspectives."[3]) Let us now examine these very different depictions.

Lord Palmerston, the British Foreign Secretary in 1842, described Hong Kong island, just ceded to Great Britain by China, as "a barren island, which will never be a mart of trade." As the historian Chan Kai-cheung notes, "every British official and semi-official narration of Hong Kong history in the past century and a half has repeated one or

another version of the 'barren island' remark."[4] Recent archaeological
and historical research, however, has led to the presentation of a very
different picture of Hong Kong's precolonial history: Hong Kong,
writes Chan, "for most of the past 6,000 years with the exception of
recent centuries [has] been a busy crossroads of world trade and cultural
intercourse," taking part in the mainstream of Chinese history.[5] Some
scholars go further: "The ancient residents of Hong Kong already had
a strong ethnic consciousness, and a tradition of protecting the family
and defending the country."[6]

   This reconstruction of history is due in part to the discovery of new
empirical evidence over the past few years, archeological findings that
illuminate Hong Kong's past in a new way; but it is very much inter-
woven with the politics of Hong Kong's shift in sovereignty. "The
British pretend they created Hong Kong's prosperity from scratch.
They say it is all their own work. . . . It is the same in every colony.
They want people to forget their history, to forget themselves,"
comments one archaeologist.[7] This may be true, but on the other
hand, there is a particular kind of remembering sought by the advocates of China, that may or may not accord with the reality of Hong
Kong's past. Did Hong Kong's ancient residents really have "a strong
nationalist consciousness"? Who today could ever know?

   I interviewed an archeological curator at a Hong Kong museum who
mulled over the boundaries of fact and interpretation in her work:

> I think we should believe in the scientific methods of excavation;
> but on the other hand, archeologists of Hong Kong each interpret
> things in their own way; it's impossible to decide who's right. . . .
> Yes, maybe it's all political. But it's taboo to think about these
> things; as a museum, we try to be neutral. We can't give a wrong
> interpretation to the public; we just try to present what's real.

And, then, with a wry laugh, she finished her thought: "And what's real
depends on me!"

   If Hong Kong's precolonial history is open to fundamental dispute as
to Hong Kong's Chineseness, so too is its colonial history. The Anglo-
Chinese War that led to British control over Hong Kong is otherwise
known as the Opium War. A number of Western or Western-influenced
historians stress that opium was a minor issue: "the war would not be
fought over opium; it would be fought over trade, the urgent desire of
a capitalist, industrial, progressive country to force a Confucian,
agricultural and stagnant one to trade with it."[8] Mainland Chinese or
Chinese-influenced historians, on the other hand, emphasize that the

issue was not trade but the British effort to enslave the Chinese people to opium and subjugate them to colonialism; as one historian writes:

> The real reason for the Opium War was that Britain had been selling opium to China on a large scale, and this was forbidden by China, setting off the war. During the war, the Chinese government banned all British merchants from trading in China . . . and this became the excuse for the British to twist the truth and claim that the war was a "trade war." However, without a doubt the real nature of the Opium War was the invasion of China by British colonialism. The truth of this part of history should not be changed.[9]

I asked a number of the people I interviewed to recall their schooling, and found that they too are divided in their views. Students in Hong Kong secondary schools in the decades before the handover studied world history and almost all other subjects using English-language textbooks; only Chinese history was studied in Chinese. Thus the English-language and Chinese-language instruction they received concerning the war sometimes greatly differed, depending on the textbooks schools chose to use. One man waxed indignant over what he saw as the colonial effort to avoid teaching the truth of Hong Kong's founding: "When I studied history in middle school, my emotions were aroused. The Opium War: English history textbooks call it a 'trade war' – that's not true! I felt a great resentment at the British for that." But as another person said,

> When I was in secondary school, I thought, "Was the Opium War really bad?" In history classes, we were taught that the British were very bad. But then I thought that without the Opium War, Hong Kong wouldn't be what it is today!

Others held that the distinction between English- and Chinese-language textbooks was not so clear; but it does seem that these very different interpretations of Hong Kong's founding have been regularly reproduced in the Hong Kong school system. The above two statements imply two different senses of Hong Kong people's identity: of Hongkongese as Chinese deprived of their Chinese culture by colonialism, and of Hongkongese as people rescued from Chinese culture by colonialism. These in turn may imply Hong Kong people belonging primarily to a particular Chinese culture, as opposed to Hong Kong people belonging primarily to no particular culture, but to the global cultural supermarket.

Western and Chinese views of Hong Kong's 150 years of colonial history also portray a dichotomy. Recent histories of Hong Kong by British writers portray the cavalcades of British governors and merchants, with Chinese serving as a hazy, all-but-forgettable background. As Jan Morris comments in seeming embarrassment about Hong Kong of the 1920s (as well as, perhaps, about the absence of much Chinese presence in her own book):

> For like it or not – ignore it if you could – all around the 4,500 Britons of Hong Kong lived 725,000 Chinese. . . . Very few Chinese names appeared in the history books, because very few Chinese had played public parts in the development of Hong Kong; and the mass of the Chinese population seemed to most observers oblivious to public events, intent only on making a living.[10]

In these books, Hong Kong Chinese appear most often as mute victims. Welsh reports Isabella Bird's nineteenth-century comment that "you cannot be two minutes in Hong Kong without seeing Europeans striking coolies with their canes or umbrellas"; Morris says that "when I first went to Hong Kong in the 1950s, I noticed that Britons habitually spoke to Chinese in a hectoring or domineering tone of voice."[11] While sympathetically portrayed, Hong Kong Chinese nonetheless appear in these books with no voices of their own.

Recent mainland Chinese and Chinese-influenced histories of Hong Kong have similarly emphasized the brutality of the British treatment of Chinese in Hong Kong's history; but the large-scale backdrop of these books, missing from their British counterparts, is the sense of historical humiliation of China by Britain and other colonial powers, finally to be rectified. These books stress the close relationship between Hong Kong and south China throughout Hong Kong's history; chapters in one book covering such topics as "The activities of the Chinese Communist Party and other democratic parties in Hong Kong during the Liberation War Era" minimize all distinctions between Hong Kong and China, thereby shaping a sense of common history and common identity.[12] Great Britain appears in these volumes as a shadowy usurper, robbing China of its territory; British figures and policies, with just a few exceptions, appear in their pages only to be vilified. But as with their British counterparts, in these books Hong Kong Chinese do not appear as actors. Hong Kong's people merely respond to China, supporting political and social movements on the mainland: this is the lone historical role they are allowed.

Where, then, are Hong Kong's people to be found? Great Britain was indeed seen as an interloper and usurper by at least some of Hong Kong's people throughout its history, as can be seen in the acts of resistance to British rule that have intermittently taken place, from the poisoned bread case of 1857 (in which a baker spiked his loaves with arsenic for his British customers), to the military struggle of New Territories' indigenous residents against their British occupiers in 1899, to the General Strike in 1925, to the 1967 riots, which saw "Red Guards in [Hong Kong's] . . . streets, and the *People's Daily* exhorting . . . protesters to 'organize a courageous struggle against the British and be ready to respond to the call of the Motherland for smashing the reactionary rule of the British oppressors.'"[13] It is certainly true that, as the Chinese-oriented historians have indicated, Hong Kong and China have been closely linked throughout Hong Kong's history, with events in China acutely affecting Hong Kong's people, as well as, to a far lesser degree, vice versa.[14] But Morris, as quoted above, may also be correct in her speculation that most Hong Kong Chinese were concerned more with making a living than with overthrowing the chains of colonialism; and the reputation of Hong Kong people as being "apolitical" has continued up until recent decades.[15]

By the late 1960s and 1970s, however, something completely new in Hong Kong history took place. A postwar generation reached adulthood that had only known Hong Kong as home – a Hong Kong beginning to emerge from poverty into middle-class affluence – and that felt cut off from China, immersed in ideological strife and closed to the world outside. It was from this generation that a sense of Hongkongese as an autonomous cultural identity began to emerge: for the first time, "Hongkongese" became distinct from "Chinese." The 1967 riots, inspired by the Cultural Revolution and directed against British rule, showed the strong ideological influence communist China held over some of Hong Kong's people; but the Cultural Revolution, in all its chaos, seemed for many in Hong Kong less an inspiration than a threat. One person I interviewed said this:

> I went to China in 1974, before the Cultural Revolution was over. I still remember the horrifying experience. There were lots of songs everyone had to sing together; everyone was dressed in either grey or blue. I felt I was a Hong Kong Chinese; I had to get out from that place.

These words reflect a newly emergent Hong Kong identity of affluent choice, confronting a communitarian world next door and finding it foreign. And while some critics describe this new sense of Hong Kong identity as one cynically engineered by the colonial government, it seems clear that it was also the fruit of a genuinely new sense of Hong Kong cultural autonomy.

In the decade that followed, Mao Zedong's Cultural Revolution gave way to Deng Xiaoping's economic reforms; the strangeness of the Cultural Revolution to Hong Kong's people gave way to familiarity, as China began to open its doors to the capitalist world that Hong Kong represented. In 1982, negotiations began for the return of Hong Kong to China – Great Britain had a 99-year lease on the New Territories, the northern land area of Hong Kong, due to expire in 1997, and without the New Territories, Hong Kong could not survive. The Sino-British Agreement of 1984 guaranteed that, although Hong Kong would indeed be returned to China, "the economic, legal and social system in Hong Kong and its citizens' way of life will remain in force for fifty years after 1997" – there will be "one country, two systems." For several years in Hong Kong, optimism about the future prevailed; but the Tiananmen Square massacre, on 4 June 1989, dashed Hong Kong dreams of a benevolent China. A million people in Hong Kong protested, close to 20 percent of Hong Kong's population: the first time in Hong Kong's history that Hong Kong people have demonstrated en masse against the Chinese government.

The last British governor of Hong Kong, Chris Patten, proposed in 1992 electoral reforms, bringing to Hong Kong in the last five years of British rule at least a measure of the democracy that Great Britain had denied to Hong Kong over the initial 150 years of its rule; China furiously denounced all such reforms, heaping obloquy on Patten. There was the widespread sense among Hong Kong's people over the years before the handover of having been cast aside to fend for themselves by Great Britain, just as there was widespread apprehension about China and its intentions.[16]

The handover itself, 1 July 1997, was fervently celebrated in China, and among some pro-China advocates in Hong Kong; but many more Hong Kong people seemed to greet the handover with mixed feelings. One report several months after the handover proclaimed that "Since the establishment of the new government and the resumption of Chinese sovereignty, the people have now been awoken by a sense of nationalism and patriotism never seen during the colonial days";[17] but such sentiments seemed not to have been widely shared in Hong Kong. A newspaper column reports on a Hong Kong person's encounter in China with a mainland PLA soldier just before the handover: "He asked me if I was happy [about] . . . Hong Kong's return to China and I didn't know what to say. So I just kept smiling and pretending that I did not understand his Putonghua [Mandarin Chinese, the official language of mainland China; Hong Kong people speak the Cantonese dialect instead]."[18] As said one person I interviewed, "Sometimes I ask myself, 'Shouldn't I feel pride over the handover?' Maybe I should feel pride, but I don't" – a sentiment shared by many Hong Kong Chinese, according to media reports and opinion polls,[19] and reflected in my interviews since the handover.

Despite the fears of many, the coming of Chinese sovereignty over Hong Kong meant little immediate transformation of Hong Kong life. In the years before 1 July 1997, many in Hong Kong wondered if dissidents and democratic politicians would be rounded up and jailed, and if radio broadcasts critical of China would be jammed, and newspapers closed down. These things have not happened. There have, to be sure, been worrying developments. Under the rule of Tung Chee-hwa, the first chief executive of Hong Kong's post-handover era, there is the popular perception that the government has become more secretive, less transparent. The rule of law appears to have been endangered in several high-profile cases in which people with connections to Chinese and Hong Kong leaders have not been charged for criminal acts they are alleged to have committed. The Hong Kong government in May 1999 asked the Chinese National People's Congress to override a decision by the Hong Kong Court of Final Appeals, rendering that court no longer final, and rendering law the servant of political expediency. The Legislative Council has been rigged so that even though the Democratic Party and its allies won a majority of popular votes in Hong Kong in the 1998 elections, they occupy only a small minority of seats.[20]

Nonetheless, it can be argued that this is no more than a return to the old colonial status quo, albeit with a different colonial master.[21] Most people in Hong Kong over the past two years have been concerned less with Hong Kong's political transition than with its stumbling economy, as a result of the East Asian economic crisis. Unemployment is at a record high, and property prices have collapsed: "To Hong Kong's 6.5 million people, used to continuous economic expansion and unfettered growth in prosperity, the present recession is a major disaster that has plunged many into despair."[22]

Practical matters such as the economic downturn may seem to render debates over cultural identity a luxury; however, debates over Hong Kong's economic policy as well as over its political relation to China in the years since the handover are very directly debates over cultural identity, as we will discuss. Tung Chee-hwa has often spoken since the handover about Hong Kong's Chineseness: "We in Hong Kong take tremendous pride in our Chinese identity," he has said;[23] but many in Hong Kong continue to stoutly resist such "Chineseness," and government attempts to inculcate Chineseness are often mocked. This may indicate that many of Hong Kong's people continue to suffer from what used to be called in mainland Chinese rhetoric, "colonization of the mind": they are Chinese, but having been colonized, they have forgotten who they truly are. But this reluctance to accept China and Chineseness may be interpreted in other ways as well. It perhaps reveals Hong Kong's 6,700,000 affluent residents being unwilling to accept oneness with the far poorer 1,200,000,000 people to the north. It perhaps reveals Hong Kong people's unwillingness to accept the Chineseness proffered by a communist government they see as illegitimate. And perhaps too, it reveals how some Hong Kong people, immersed in the world of the market and the cultural supermarket, are unwilling to accept belonging to a state, any state, and the national identity it proffers.

As earlier noted, I teach at the Chinese University of Hong Kong, a key site for contestation over Hong Kong's identity as an institution specifically created to encourage Chinese learning. It is the only university in Hong Kong (of seven) officially to allow instruction not just in English, but in Cantonese and Mandarin. Thus, the issue of Hong Kong's cultural identity is one that I encounter, at least indirectly, every day. I have also conducted interviews with 36 Hong Kong people, and have had my students conduct interviews with some 60 more, on the question of cultural identity before and after the handover.

My students and I have interviewed a wide range of people, of different ages and social classes. However, in this chapter I have focused most particularly on 42 people among the above total who are university-educated and hold occupations such as journalist, social worker, solicitor (lawyer), university professor, and government administrator, as well as businessperson, secondary-school teacher, and graduate student. I call these people "intellectuals," which they are in the broad Chinese sense of the term, although not necessarily in the more narrow American or English sense: they are educated people playing a variety of roles in society, who through their education reflect upon their society.

These people are not atypical of Hong Kong people as a whole in their views, as I can tell from comparing their views to those indicated by a range of Hong Kong public opinion surveys. It is important to remember that, although the popular image of Hong Kong's people that some in the world still hold is one of street hawkers, the per capita income of Hong Kong is close to 90 percent that of the United States – the typical Hong Kong person is an analyst at her computer rather than a laborer. I emphasize intellectuals in this chapter not because their education or occupation makes them more worthy of study than other people, but rather because these are the people for whom the contradiction between market and state, particular national culture and global cultural supermarket, seems most readily apparent. These people, more than members of many other social groups in Hong Kong, are those who are most fully comfortable in the global cultural supermarket: this is the world in which they were raised, within which they were educated, within which they choose aspects of their identities. It is these people for whom the newly imposed identity of belonging to the Chinese state may seem most fully and poignantly problematic.[24]

Let me turn first to the account of one such man, a professor of literature at Chinese University. His description of his life reflects the last four decades of Hong Kong – and, as he discusses, the past emergence and possible future eclipse of Hong Kong's autonomous cultural identity.

Wong Fok-kwong (44)
Every one of us, when I was small, was afraid of white foreigners: because of their size, because they belonged to the ruling class, because they spoke a language we didn't understand. I still remember one of my greatest shocks. I was in a lesson in primary school, and a British inspector came in. He asked me a question, and I answered yes. He asked, "yes what?" I didn't know how to answer. He struck me on my head, very hard. Do you know what I should have said? "Yes, sir"! After this, I had a traumatic fear of foreigners. Why did I study overseas, get my Ph.D. in European literature? Maybe my experience of being hit by a foreigner formed an inferiority complex. Maybe, to compensate, I learned their language, studied what they have done. But then, a lot of us think that Western thought is a means for us to reintegrate our own culture. That's why I'm trying to be bicultural. . . .

You have to understand that when I was in school in Hong Kong, it was the essence of colonial education. We had to forget our past, forget our culture, forget what being Chinese means to us. In secondary school, except for Chinese lessons, all lessons were conducted by teachers speaking English. We were trained in an English environment; to loved ones we wrote "I love you" in

English. On the other hand, in our everyday life we were Chinese, in a traditional sense. We lived in a very schizophrenic way. It was paradoxical, but also taken for granted; we didn't question it. I did eventually come to feel great ambivalence toward my colonial education; I felt that toward China as well. But there's a big difference: China didn't exist abstractly. England, America were far away; but we still sent, when we could, rice and oil to relatives back home in China. . . .

At that time, the communist Chinese government was a terrifying regime. Especially the Cultural Revolution: I still remember seeing the dead bodies floating down from China into Hong Kong waters. I still remember how they stank. It's difficult to imagine it now, with the border so open, but prior to the 1980s, China was cut off: a tourist spot in Hong Kong was Lok Ma Chau, a mountain from which you could peek through the iron curtain into China. At that time there were so many people risking their lives to escape to Hong Kong, so many sad stories. A couple was found tied together – they didn't want to be separated in their attempt to swim to Hong Kong from China – the woman was alive but the man had been eaten by sharks. But today's generation never sees this; they only see a more open, more prosperous China. . . .

The Hong Kong identity problem came about in my generation, born after 1949 [when China became a communist state], and educated in Hong Kong. My family was a typical poor, Hong Kong family. My parents didn't give a damn about Hong Kong identity: they just lived as Chinese in Hong Kong. But we, the so-called middle class, are different. We realized that Hong Kong was colonized by England and belongs to China; but Hong Kong has its own separate sense of identity. Hong Kong Chinese – that identity is very practical, without any idea of absolute truth. It's full of eclecticism, pragmatism. We can accommodate everything. . . .

When I heard the Joint Declaration being signed in 1984 [whereby Hong Kong was to be returned to China], I was happy. National integrity should be respected. But the problem, I came to realize, is that the last 30 years might be the only years when Chinese people are really free, prosperous, able to do what we want in the whole three thousand years of Chinese history. Hong Kong in the last 30 years is the most prosperous and free society that China has ever known. Compared with my father's generation, we are really in heaven. We didn't go through war. We never felt hunger. And we witnessed all the change. This is not shared by my children, and by my students. They have been brought up as if prosperity is simply a given. . . .

With all this in mind, to stay on after 1997 is our only choice and responsibility. Nationality isn't just something you can buy, like a passport to different countries if you're rich enough! But Hong Kong people are practical. If one day we find we can't say what we want to say, we'll leave. Hong Kong people are leftovers, left over by the West, by China, used as an instrument by all owners; we must try to survive as leftovers. We can't fantasize ourselves as revolutionary, trying to transform China; all we can do is try to survive in a politically neutral Hong Kong. We are now entering a second era of colonialism; this is the crisis we have to face. . . .

Mr. Wong tells us that his early shock at being struck in school by an Englishman might, ironically, have propelled him to study European literature and try to become bicultural. But it seems from his words that he has already been bicultural for most of his life. His secondary-school education, conducted almost entirely in English – for him as for almost all Hong Kong students in recent decades – seems to have been his real immersion into biculturalism, or in his terms, "schizophrenia": a schizophrenia that through much of his early life, he took for granted as the natural state of his life. At home he was Chinese, in a traditional sense, he says, but at school, he learned to write even love letters in the colonizer's tongue. As a youth, China remained more real for him than the abstractions of Europe or America, he tells us; but China, the home of his relatives, was also the source of the stinking corpses washing up in Hong Kong, and the desperate fleeing couple attacked by sharks; that China was foreign, bizarre, "terrifying." The taken-for-granted world of Mr. Wong's youth thus consisted not of a single cultural home, but of two, neither of which seemed truly home.

From this schizophrenic state – of having two ill-fitting cultural homes, and thus no home – a new cultural home emerged, Mr. Wong tells us. As his generation entered adulthood, a separate Hong Kong identity developed that was unknown to his parents, who saw them-selves simply as Chinese in Hong Kong. This new Hong Kong identity Mr. Wong characterizes as practical, pragmatic, eclectic, accommodat-ing, with no absolute truth. This identity seems born of Hong Kong's status as, in his word, "leftover," on the margin of both China and the West, unable to confront either, but rather bending with the political wind. But it also seems born of Hong Kong's cosmopolitan character: those on two cultures' periphery are bicultural, able eclectically to construct themselves from either culture – and indeed, Hong Kong identity, as he describes it, seems very much to mirror the values of the cultural supermarket.

However, this identity may turn out to be fleeting, occupying no more than a blink in the long passage of Chinese history, as the *shikata ga nai* imperative of Hong Kong's return to China becomes reality. Mr. Wong was initially happy, he tells us, at the news of Hong Kong's return to China; but he eventually realized that this may spell the end of Hong Kong's prosperity and freedom, the ability of Hong Kong people to do and be what they want. He is proud to be of Chinese nationality, it seems – nationality isn't just something that can be bought and sold, he tells us – but he also realizes that Hong Kong's return to China may usher in a "second colonialism," under a new master who may not preserve the affluence, peace, and freedom that Hong Kong has briefly enjoyed. Mr. Wong sees his generation as unique, in experiencing the emergence of a Hong Kong identity unknown to his parents, and perhaps to his children as well, who may only see a taken-for-granted affluence and freedom fade away as Hong Kong identity is gradually extinguished by the Chinese state.

The meanings of Chinese in the Hong Kong cultural supermarket

One of the more unusual features of Hong Kong life in recent years has been the prevalence of public opinion surveys asking people who they think they are, culturally. In 1986, one such survey found that 59 percent of respondents thought of themselves as "Hongkongese" and 36 percent as "Chinese." A 1996 survey showed that 35 percent of Hong Kong residents consider themselves Hongkongese, 30 percent Chinese, and 28 percent Hong Kong Chinese. A post-handover survey comparing Hong Kong attitudes with those of mainland China found that while 88 percent of Beijing respondents and 82 percent of Guangzhou respondents felt that Hong Kong people were Chinese, only 43 percent of Hong Kong respondents felt any inclination toward a Chinese identity.[25] One recent survey I've come across has indicated that, as of October 1998, 40 percent of Hong Kong people saw themselves as "Hong Kong people," 23 percent as "Hong Kong people in China," 16 percent as "Chinese in Hong Kong," and 21 percent as "Chinese" – findings that led one Hong Kong newspaper, clearly disappointed that more Hong Kong people don't yet identify themselves as Chinese, to proclaim in an editorial that "'Hong Kong' identity is really a non-issue."[26] Senses of cultural identity in Hong Kong have been found to vary with gender, education, social class, and generation, with somewhat more women than men, more educated than less educated, and younger than elder people feeling a sense of distance from China, and a sense of separate Hong Kong identity.[27]

These surveys are interesting in that they show how the percentages of people claiming a Hong Kong identity and the percentages of people claiming a Chinese identity have remained fairly consistent over the past decade and a half, with perhaps a slight turn in recent years toward more people identifying themselves as Chinese than as Hong-kongese. They are also interesting in that they show that many people seek to split the difference, identifying themselves neither as Hong-kongese nor as Chinese, but in the middle categories of "Hong Kong people in China" or "Chinese in Hong Kong." This implies that Chinese and Hongkongese, *jùnggwokyàhn* and *hèunggóngyàhn*, are not mutually exclusive categories; rather, as we will see, "Hongkongese" may include but also transcend "Chinese" identity. However, the surveys are limiting in that they don't indicate what these identities mean to those who adhere to them. This is why interviews are so important: only through extended conversations with people and close analysis of what they say can we understand the complexities of who, culturally, they feel they are.

The people we interviewed often told us that their senses of cultural identity shifted in different contexts. As a graduate student said, "If I went to Europe I might say to people that I'm Chinese. But in China, I definitely say that I'm Hongkongese – unless I'm trying to pay cheaper Chinese prices, and I have to pretend to be Chinese." They also often maintained that "Chineseness" and "Hongkongness" came into play in different aspects of their lives. As a social worker said, "When you talk about food, then of course I'm Chinese. But when you talk about communism, then I feel that I'm Hongkongese, not Chinese." (Indeed, the interview itself – the fact that many of these interviews were conducted in English with a white foreigner – "expatriate" in the news-papers' term; *gwáilóu*, "white devil," in popular Cantonese parlance – may have had significant impact on what people said, although those I interviewed stoutly denied this: and indeed, there is not much difference between what people said in my interviews and what was said in my students' interviews in Cantonese.)

However, although these people's senses of identity may be situa-tional, they are hardly situational alone. The people we interviewed did not see themselves as chameleons, merely shifting to fit whatever social world they might happen to be in; rather, cultural identity was something that most of them had thought about deeply; it was something that really mattered to most of them. As said one person, a Hong Kong Chinese businesswoman who had lived abroad for a number of years (as have a surprising number of people in Hong Kong), "Most of the time, questions of identity don't bother me. But every now and then, I feel like I've fallen through the cracks and don't belong anywhere. Who am I? Where do I belong?" Many of the people we interviewed echoed these sentiments: cultural identity was neither taken for granted nor foregone; rather, it was something they pondered, wondered about, or longed for in their lives.

Most of those we interviewed – 27 of the 42 people – held that their primary sense of identity was Hongkongese, but almost all also acknowledged that they were Chinese: the majority of people we spoke with said that they held both identities. Chineseness was expressed at a number of different levels: as one's ethnicity, and the culture of one's daily life; as one's ancestral background and its civilization, history, and heritage; and as the nationality and state to which one now belongs.

First, let us examine Chineseness as ethnic identity: "What does it mean to be Chinese? Race: the race factor is first. It's something that you cannot change, cannot transform. If you're born Chinese, you're always Chinese," said an engineering professor. "Yes, maybe some American-born Chinese deny that they're Chinese; maybe some Hong Kong Chinese deny it too. But they're culturally conquered!" His views were more pointed than most; much more typical were the words of a journalist, speaking of the taken-for-granted Chineseness of his daily life: "Of course I'm Chinese. I'm physically Chinese, I speak Cantonese, a Chinese language; the newspapers I read and television programs I watch are often in Chinese, the food I eat is mostly Chinese."

This underlying sense of Chineseness may seem at first glance to be common sense – of course people who are ethnically Chinese and speak a Chinese language are Chinese. Indeed, the large majority of the people we interviewed spoke of their Chineseness in exactly this sense. But this sense becomes problematic upon closer examination. Chineseness may be thought of as "race," but one who claims such a thing must account for the fact that, for example, Chinese and Japanese are often physically indistinguishable. (The engineering professor quoted above claims that he can always distinguish Japanese from Chinese in Hong Kong; but my wife, who is Japanese, is invariably mistaken in Hong Kong for a Hong Kong Chinese.) Chineseness may be thought of as language, but Cantonese and Mandarin are as spoken languages mutually unintelligible: many Hong Kong people can't speak the language spoken by Chinese people to the north. (The head of Chinese University recently attempted to give a speech welcoming a group of mainland students to the campus, but upon seeing that they couldn't make any sense of his Mandarin, he gave up and completed his speech in English.[28]) Chineseness may be thought of as the culture of one's daily life, and this may be accurate in large part for many in their lives. However, in a place as cosmopolitan as Hong Kong, life is far from Chinese alone. As James Watson has written:

> Hong Kong in the late 1990s constitutes one of the world's most heterogeneous cultural environments. Younger people, in particular, are fully conversant in transnational idioms, which include language, music, sports, clothing, satellite television, cybercommunications, global travel, and . . . cuisine. It is no longer possible to distinguish what is local and what is not. In Hong Kong . . . the transnational *is* the local.[29]

Extrapolating from these words, we may say that daily life in Hong Kong, for the cosmopolitan people I interviewed, is not simply Chinese; rather it is the global cultural supermarket, one predominant choice from which may be designated Chinese.

Chineseness was held by some we interviewed to consist of what was thought of as Chinese tradition: Chinese philosophy, poetry, art, and history. "I am Chinese because of the cultural tradition I belong to: Confucianism, Taoism, Buddhism, as well as thousands of years of literature – all that has shaped who I am," said a history professor. "Confucius and his teachings constitute a key part of Chineseness. That's something we've culturally inherited from our ancestors." This was phrased by some we interviewed as "traditional Chinese values": belief in the importance of social harmony and commitment to family and respect for hierarchy. "What is Chinese? Being obedient. Being submissive to your parents," said one young researcher, who had long chafed under parental restrictions, but who now, after her father's death, felt considerable guilt. As a journalist said, "Chinese means having respect for people who are older than you; it means not asserting yourself and your views. I don't necessarily like those values, but that's what Chinese means."

These values are, however, hardly unique to Chinese, but are also held by American conservative Christians[30] among others in the world; such traditional Chinese thinkers as the Taoist sage Chuang Tzu seemed to delight in spurning such values. Thus, what makes these values Chinese seems open to question. Beyond this, there is the fact that "traditional Chineseness" – Chinese customs and religious practices, for example – has been obliterated in mainland China by communism over the past 50 years, just as it has been eroded in Hong Kong by colonialism. Cultural inheritance – just as it was for some of the Japanese artists of Chapter 2 – seems problematic.

A few of the people we spoke with recognized the difficulty of formulating "Chineseness"; as one person, a civil servant, said, "I don't know what 'Chineseness' is – there are many different cultures in China"; as another, a social scientist, said, "I only use 'Chinese' in quotation marks." This is occasionally echoed in mass media. An article in the newspaper *Ming Pao* asks "How many Chinas are there?," answering "not just the PRC and the Republic of China . . . but also the poems of the Tang and Sung dynasties. . . . There are different images of China in different people's minds."[31] Who can sum up in a single label four thousand years of history and a billion people? But the majority of the people we interviewed, whether because of or despite their higher education,[32] claimed an underlying Chineseness that they took for granted as a natural part of themselves. This was a Chineseness that some felt to encompass ethnicity and tradition, and to transcend today's borders: "The people in Macau, China, Hong Kong and Taiwan, we're all Chinese. Yes, China and Taiwan have different political structures, but we are the same, we are one race and one culture," a student political activist told me.

However, some of those we spoke with framed the question of Chineseness in terms of China today, and were reluctant to think of themselves as Chinese. While people we interviewed after the handover acknowledged that they now belonged, at least indirectly, to the Chinese state, this did not necessarily mean that they were culturally Chinese. A bank employee mused as follows:

> I've wondered sometimes if I may be Chinese. But I find that it is just impossible to think this way, because I grew up in Hong Kong, a different environment, in which Chinese and Western cultures are mixed; I have too many differences with mainland Chinese to think that I'm Chinese.

A woman who works for an NGO expressed her longing for a China that she wants to be her home but feels cannot be home:

> Even though I'm ignorant about China, I feel like an abandoned child. I don't know who my mom is, but there's the longing to return to her. No, my country's not China – it's a dictatorship; I don't belong to that – but there is that dream. . . . What do I belong to? I don't know; I don't know where home is.

Linguistically, many of these people expressed a distinction between Chineseness of ethnicity and tradition and China today: many said that they were *jùnggwokyàhn* (Chinese) but cringed at being thought of as *daaihluhkyàhn* ("mainlanders": mainland Chinese, a derogatory label in Hong Kong in recent years). They were ethnically Chinese, perhaps bearers of cultural Chineseness, but, they felt, certainly not Chinese like their Chinese neighbors north of the border.

For some, this disdain for China is rooted in economics: "Chinese, for me, connotes something dirty, disorderly, backward. . . . Hong Kong is rich and sophisticated, but China is poor and unsophisticated," said a businessperson; "basically, Hong Kong is first-world but China is still third-world," said a graduate student. Although China has been economically growing at an extraordinary pace in recent years, Hong Kong's per capita income (in adjusted terms to reflect actual purchasing power) remains today a little less than seven times that of China;[33] economically, the two societies remain in different worlds.

For others, this disdain for today's China is political, reflecting their distrust of the Chinese government and the Communist Party: "If being Chinese means supporting the Chinese government, then I don't want to be Chinese," said a social worker and political activist, echoing many of his less politically active fellows. Many in Hong Kong were refugees from China, fleeing the communist takeover in 1949, or later, the Cultural Revolution. The Tiananmen Square massacre solidified for many Hong Kong people a fundamental distrust of the Chinese government, a distrust that, despite Tung Chee-hwa's entreaties that Hong Kong people put aside the baggage of 4 June 1989, has for many in Hong Kong yet to dissipate. Mr. Wong's comment that "Hong Kong in the last 30 years is the most prosperous and free society that China has ever known," sums up the attitude of many we interviewed, that Hong Kong may be Chinese, but still it is transcendent of China, at least of China today: it is economically affluent and politically open, as China is not.

There are people in Hong Kong who do identify themselves as Chinese, as defined by the Chinese government, a Chineseness that is synonymous with support for the Chinese Communist Party; judging from voting patterns and opinion surveys, perhaps as many as 10 percent of people in Hong Kong can be so identified. Surveys indicate that such people tend to be older, and of lower educational and socioeconomic status.[34] Business tycoons in Hong Kong are also often said to be pro-China, but since many were once fervent supporters of the British colonial government, this is thought to be indicative more of their pragmatic desire to make money than to any committed sense of underlying identity; the same is true for some appointed political figures in Hong Kong, whose pro-China views are often viewed as being less a matter of their convictions than of their desire to get ahead. My students and I have diligently sought out people who define themselves as Chinese in line with the Chinese government's conception of Chineseness, but have had little success; in our interviews, the people we targeted as holding such beliefs expressed great hope for China in the future, but backed away from identifying themselves with the Chinese government at present, despite the apparent comparative benignity of its current leaders.

However, I have met a number of people who claim their Chineseness on very different grounds: a Chineseness that is distinctly opposed to the Chinese government at present. I earlier noted that the demonstrations in Hong Kong following the Tiananmen Square massacre drew some 20 percent of Hong Kong's population to the streets to make their views known. With these demonstrations, one commentator has noted, "Hong Kong people suddenly discovered a new identity: they were also Chinese!":[35] an identification forged through their sense of identification with the protesting students. This process of identification may be ongoing; in the years I have attended the Tiananmen Square memorial demonstrations in Hong Kong, I have observed a subtle difference in tone. Before the handover, the message of some speakers seemed to be, "Let us work to preserve Hong Kong's freedoms after the Chinese government controls Hong Kong." In the years after the handover, the rhetoric seems to have shifted. In the demonstration of 4 June 1998, attended by some fifty thousand people braving a torrential downpour, the dominant tone was, "We are all Chinese. Let us work together to create a better China, a China that respects freedom and human rights and democracy." The rhetoric has become not that of Hong Kong as apart from China, but Hong Kong as a part of China – but a different, alternative China. It is, I think, remarkable that China allows these demonstrations to take place in post-handover Hong Kong, now Chinese territory, but take place they do: some of the people I observed at the last demonstration had tears streaming down their faces along with the rain, tears of grief for China of the recent past, but perhaps too of hope for China of the future.

Let us now consider the words of one such man, a regular at the 4 June demonstrations, dreaming, as a Chinese nationalist, of a free China tomorrow as opposed to communist China today.

Leung Ji-lai (30)
I work as a solicitor. A lot of the litigation my firm does is for free, to
help people who are oppressed by the government in Hong Kong,
or by rich people. Since the handover, I've been concerned about
how the rule of law in Hong Kong is being undermined by China.
Still, I'm more optimistic than I was before the handover. The
Chinese government hasn't sought control overnight; they'll gain
control over a number of years – they've been more clever than I
thought they'd be!

I am Chinese, and am proud to be Chinese. Being Chinese means
knowing traditional Chinese culture and knowing Chinese history;
and it's a matter of holding Chinese values: respect for knowledge,
harmony between people, and a sense of responsibility to family
and country. Being Chinese doesn't contradict democracy: individual rights and rule of law can definitely be a part of Chinese
culture. But these values are very different from those of communist
China: communist China doesn't respect intellectuals, doesn't
respect knowledge, doesn't respect harmony! Chineseness is the
land and the people and their traditional philosophy and history;
it's not the government. If you respect and obey the Constitution
of the People's Republic of China, does it mean you consent to be a
Chinese? I don't think so: Chineseness is much bigger than that. In
modern China, there's not much to like – it's a tragedy. . . .

Where did I learn to feel such pride in being Chinese? It wasn't
from home, although my father would to some extent agree with
my views. It's more the influence of my teachers in secondary
school (it was a typical school in Hong Kong; I was just lucky to
have such teachers) – they taught me about the goodness of traditional Chinese culture. I talk about Chineseness sometimes with
my close friends and my girlfriend, but not so much with other
people. Many people in Hong Kong don't share these values –
today, in the university, many students don't like traditional
Chinese culture – they say they're Hongkongese rather than
Chinese. That's sad. Hong Kong people, I believe, have much
more in common with Chinese people on the mainland than with
Europeans or Americans. Our particular socialization may be different, but we're all Chinese. I can understand what the Chinese
leaders today will think or say, however much I hate them, because
we belong to a common culture. . . .

Chinese culture is flexible. There's nothing wrong with a Chinese
person being, for example, a Western classical musician, because
Chinese culture does not oppose outside things. People in Hong

Kong eat Western food; they use many English words in their daily conversation. But they remain Chinese. . . . I know many people whose work life or life as a student is filled with English, but their family life is Chinese. So it's very complicated. . . . The identity of Chinese isn't a matter of ethnicity, but of culture: people can choose. If people in Hong Kong don't see themselves as Chinese, that's their personal choice. If a person wants to emigrate, I respect that too; many people, after they emigrate to Canada or America, become more aware of their Chinese identity. If a person totally loses Chineseness? Well, I feel that it's a big loss for them. If they could learn about Chinese culture, they would benefit from it. Yes, you too could be Chinese. Chinese isn't the color of your eyes and hair: it's a matter of what you know, what you believe, how you live. . . .

I think it's easier to be a Chinese in Hong Kong than in China because traditional values are so affected by the government there. In China, they interpret traditional values by one approach, the party's approach; and so young people can't understand traditional values as much as they can in Hong Kong, where the government doesn't interfere. But China is changing: the Chinese government doesn't suppress traditional Chinese culture as they did 20 years ago. People in China are becoming more like Hong Kong people. I go into China every week, and I really enjoy talking with people, even though my Mandarin isn't good. . . . But yes, basically I am deeply disappointed in China today. I want China to change, to get better! I want China to keep its traditional culture, so that Chinese people know their history and identity; but I also want China to have democracy, to have human rights, to have rule of law. I have great expectations for China in the future!

Mr. Leung's words echo and make more complex many of the themes we have seen in the past few pages concerning the meanings of Chineseness in Hong Kong. He is proud of his Chineseness, he tells us, which he conceives of in terms of traditional Chinese culture and values; but this Chineseness is the opposite of the values upheld by the Chinese government today – indeed, it is easier to be Chinese in Hong Kong than in China, he maintains. However, in Hong Kong, most people don't fully recognize their Chineseness. He thus talks of his Chineseness only with those he knows most intimately – others, seeing themselves as Hongkongese, might not understand, he seems to say.

Mr. Leung portrays Chineseness as the taken-for-granted basis of life – he says that for all his dislike for the Chinese leaders, he can understand them because he and they share a common culture, a culture not shared by Americans or Europeans. This – like the Japanese-ness proclaimed by the some of the artists of Chapter 2, or the lost Christian America lamented by some of the evangelical Christians of Chapter 3 – corresponds to culture as "the way of life of a people." In another sense, however, he thinks of Chineseness as a personal choice from the cultural supermarket: even I, with blue eyes and brown hair and American background, could become Chinese if I chose, and if I devoted myself to that choice, he maintained. Mr. Leung's meaning seems to be this: people living in China and Hong Kong have an under-lying Chineseness that is distorted in China and often denied in Hong Kong – the *shikata ga nai* of contemporary history, the devastating effects of communism and colonialism – but that remains as the way of life of Chinese people, even if it is not recognized by some. Mr. Leung himself recognizes his Chinese identity only because of the good fortune of encountering certain teachers who taught him who he was, a good fortune never experienced by most of his fellow Hong Kong residents. At the same time, outsiders too can adapt a Chinese identity if they learn about Chinese history and tradition; and Chinese culture can adopt democracy and human rights and rule of law.[36]

Chineseness in Mr. Leung's view thus seems to consist of particular cultural values, but it is also highly flexible and malleable; Chineseness consists of the land and people of China and its cultural tradition, but is also something that anybody in the world can enjoy and become. Chineseness, in his view, is thus both particular and universalistic, both the identity of a particular people and also of worldwide choice from the cultural supermarket. But can it be both of these? Mr. Leung's hope, that China can keep its traditional culture and also become demo-cratic and have human rights and rule of law, is a noble one. But ques-tions remain, as we earlier discussed. What, given the extraordinary diversity of China in its history, is Chinese culture? Where, after all the depredations of communism and colonialism and capitalism, is Chinese culture to be found? Are there Chinese roots, or is this but a contempor-ary dream of roots? Is there a Chinese home, or is this too to be one more construction from the cultural supermarket?

The meanings of Hongkongese in the Hong Kong cultural supermarket

Mr. Leung was, in his beliefs, in the minority among those we inter-viewed. The substantial majority held that their primary identity was Hongkongese rather than Chinese. Some we interviewed felt no tension between these identities; in one person's words, "I'm both Hongkongese and Chinese: I'm a Chinese in Hong Kong. There's no contradiction between these two. Just as a person can be Shanghaiese and Chinese, a person can be Hongkongese and Chinese." For most, however, there was indeed felt to be a tension; in another's words, "I'm Chinese, but more than that, I'm Hongkongese. No, they're not the same at all." On the basis of the people we interviewed, I characterize this sense of Hong Kong likeness to yet difference from China as what I term "Chineseness plus."

Most typically, this "Chineseness plus" seemed to be thought of in geographic terms by the people we interviewed: Hong Kong is "Chineseness plus internationalness," or "Chineseness plus Westernness." This is what the tourist brochures often glibly proclaim, but this is also what many of the people we interviewed seemed very much to believe, and how they tended to formulate their separate Hong Kong identities. "Hong Kong is different from the mainland because it's open to the world," said a graduate student. "Hong Kong is an international place, not just because there are many foreigners, but because many Hong Kong people have traveled and lived in places around the world, unlike mainland Chinese." Indeed, there are people from all over the world in Hong Kong life – from Filipina maids to Canadian financiers – as is not the case in Chinese cities; and middle-class Hong Kong people have very often themselves lived overseas for many years, often in Canada or Australia. The top Hong Kong universities hire almost no one with a Ph.D. from Hong Kong or mainland China; the Hong Kong Chinese they employ, along with the foreigners they employ, have acquired their doctorates in Europe, the United States, Australia, or Japan. This internationalization is also apparent in mass media: "We can watch news from all over the world in Hong Kong, and buy magazines from anywhere. People in China can't do that," as a bank employee we interviewed said, echoing many others. On my TV in Hong Kong I can watch the nightly news from Hong Kong, mainland China, Taiwan and the United States, and on cable, Japan, Australia, and Great Britain as well; in mainland China, outside of tourist hotels and southern Guangdong Province, which can pick up Hong Kong stations, all news is strictly Chinese.

"Chineseness plus Westernness" often seemed, in the words of the people we interviewed, to be more or less synonymous with "Chineseness plus internationalness": as if Westernness was the only kind of internationalness that really mattered. Filipinos and Indians are sometimes scorned in Hong Kong, and are often victims of racial discrimination, as a number of recent reports attest.[37] In this sense, Hong Kong's openness to the world seems to refer to the West as well as to Japan, seen, in its affluence and cultural influence, as a sort of honorary member of the West. Other people may enter Hong Kong to do the dirty work, but in terms of the cultural portrayal of Hong Kong given by the people I interviewed, in a very real sense they unfortunately don't count.

Hong Kong as "Chineseness plus Westernness" often seemed to refer to Hong Kong's modernity as opposed to China's perceived lack of modernity, as earlier noted. In one businessman's words, "When I go back to the mainland [China], I can feel what the tourist brochures mean when they say that 'Hong Kong is a mixture of China and the West.' We are really different from those mainlanders." "Westernness" also refers to the values of individualism and self-assertion: "Being Western means speaking up, doing what you yourself want to do, without worrying about what other people think," said a social worker. This was not always viewed positively by the people we interviewed. As a researcher said, damning Westernness with faint praise,

> People in the West have more alternatives, more freedom in doing what they want to do. Even the violence in American movies – people admire that because it shows individuality. Violence is a form of personal expression that's tolerated in the West.

As we saw with "Chineseness," the conflation of a particular value with a region of the world is problematic. With all the diversity of "the West," all the variegated strands of history, are there really any common "Western" values? Of course not, just as there are no common "Chinese" values. But what I initially saw as the cultural naivete of the people we interviewed, I later realized was more complicated. I came to see that when people refer to Hong Kong as "Chineseness plus Westernness," they don't mean a confluence of real cultural places. "Chinese" and Western" refer less to actual regions of the globe than to different ways in which one might behave and believe – different aisle signs over sections of the cultural supermarket.

One window into the meanings of "Chineseness" and "Westernness" in Hong Kong today is provided by the names that people use. Older people in Hong Kong tend to go by Chinese names, but younger people often go by both their Chinese name – or names: many have nicknames – and a Western name as well. (The majority of people we interviewed used Western names, although I won't discuss them here, in order not to compromise their anonymity: I discuss students' names instead.) My initial assumption, upon coming to Chinese University, was that students were using Western names for my benefit, as a foreigner, and indeed, that was what I was told by students; but I soon realized that those were the names they used with one another – students speak with one another in Cantonese, yet address one another by their Western names. Often these names are more or less mundane – Shirley, Edith, Sally, Derrick, Jack, Ronald – but sometimes they are of considerable flair: Jocasta, Saville, Anthia, Lavinia, Plato, Pillow, Almond, Apple, Money, Myth, and Freedom, among many others I've heard. I call these names Western because almost all are; but I know of several people who gave themselves Japanese-sounding names – for example, Suki and Saya – Japanese goods and perhaps identities too remaining highly fashionable in Hong Kong today.

Most people first assume Western names in secondary school: typically, they are required by their English classes to choose names for themselves. Sometimes these chosen names are close in pronunciation to one's given Chinese name – Ka-man may become Carmen, for example; Wai-ki may become Viki – but often they bear no relation to those names. The woman who calls herself Jocasta chose it from her readings of Greek mythology. Another calls herself Kelly because of her admiration for Grace Kelly. Another calls himself Hoffmann: after the opera *Tales of Hoffmann*, he claimed, although I wonder if he didn't follow Dustin instead. Although students report that they were required to choose their Western names, it is remarkable that so many keep those names. I was Pablo in my high school Spanish class, but never outside the classroom door; some Japanese students report being given American names in their English classes, but would not dream of using those names within their lives at large. Many of these Hong Kong students make their Western names a part of themselves, sometimes registering them, at age 18, on their Hong Kong identity cards, and probably using them in university and in their future workplace. Students estimate that anywhere from 50 to 90 percent of their friends go by Western rather than Chinese given names.

There are practical reasons for using Western names. The use of full Chinese names connotes formality; the use of given Chinese names may connote intimacy, "like a parent talking to her children": and indeed, most students who go by Chinese names are addressed by nicknames that seem sociologically equivalent to Western names, having neither the formality of full Chinese names nor the intimacy of given Chinese names. Most of the people I've spoken with, however, don't discuss such reasons, but simply say that Chinese names are "old-fashioned." Chinese names are used at home – students have told me that when their friends call them at home, asking for them by their Western name, their fathers may hang up the phone in confusion, assuming a wrong number – and are specifically the province of family. Often the nicknames used for family members – *mùihmúi*, "little sister," *b-néuih* "baby girl," *"daaih-yi"*/*"sai-yi*," "big yi" and "little yi," referring to two brothers with "yi" as a part of their given names – refer specifically to one's position within one's family. Western names, on the other hand, are for use in the world of school and work. One student tells me that when she addresses her friends in the university by their Chinese names, she is quickly corrected by some of them, and told to use their Western names instead – as if to indicate that the use of Chinese names in this sophisticated public context is inappropriate. There are, of course, many exceptions to this – there is wide individual variation, and many young people in Hong Kong do adhere to their Chinese names in public, just as some go by Western names within their families – but the above patterning seems broadly accurate.

In my teaching I've sometimes tried to bring students to question their use of Western names – "Why do you need a Western name? Aren't you Chinese?" – but I rarely get very far in these provocations. When, on the other hand, I ask students who use Chinese names why they decided not to use a Western name, the most typical response is that "I couldn't find a Western name that fit me" – larger cultural and political factors seem irrelevant to them. A graduate student told me of how she and several friends had gone to meet a well-known American scholar, and had introduced themselves by their Western names. The American was taken aback: were they all victims of colonialism? The Hong Kong Chinese were in turn taken aback by the American's vehement reaction:

> At first I thought that maybe that American woman was right. But later, when I reflected upon it, I realized that I'd been living with my Western name most of my life; why should I reject it? If my Chinese name is part of my identity, so is my Western name. Why should I give that up?

She knows well the history of British colonialism in Hong Kong and the impact of American cultural imperialism on the world. But she sees her Western name not as her submission to that history, but as an authentic part of herself, no less real a part of herself than her Chinese name.

And this is the way that most of the Hong Kong Chinese I interviewed saw their given and chosen names: as separate, legitimate parts of themselves. Chinese names seem, for most, to connote one's family, and the intimacy and hierarchy that family entails. Western names seem for most to connote one's individual freedom, and one's egalitarian relations to others within a wider, public world. More broadly, Chinese names seem to signify the particular personal and cultural world to which one belongs; Western names seem to signify the cultural super- market from which one may choose oneself.

The foregoing analysis of names illustrates "Chineseness plus Westernness" within Hong Kong identity: many Hong Kong people seem to use these names as if specifically to label different parts of them- selves as "Chinese" and "Western." However, the "Chineseness plus" of Hong Kong identity is apparent not just in mock-geographical terms, but in descriptive terms as well. One meaning given by many of the people I interviewed to Hong Kong's "Chineseness plus" was that of wealth: Hong Kong is "Chineseness plus affluence/capitalism/ cosmopolitanism." As one businesswoman said, "The best thing about Hong Kong is we can make lots of money here. Money is important in that it gives you choices as to how to live: with money you can do any- thing you want." Money enables you to buy anything you desire from the material supermarket, and so too, more indirectly, from the cultural supermarket.

Of course China itself has become immersed in the market; in a city like Guangzhou, the large city in China several hours north of Hong Kong, few pay any attention any more to the state's exhortatory posters; instead people flock to the newest stores in all their glitter, their offer of international goods and potential identities. But the people we interviewed asserted a great difference between China and Hong Kong. Some have relatives over the border in China, in Guangdong Province, that they regularly visit; several reported on Guangdong acquaintances or relatives saying to them, at certain awkward moments in their conversations, "We're not inferior to you!"; but they themselves continued to insist on their superiority over their "mainland cousins." "Hong Kong TV in Guangdong Province may lead Guangdong people to think that they're like Hong Kong people, but *we* don't think they're like Hong Kong people," a graduate student told me, echoing a common Hong Kong line: "We're not like them: we're rich and sophisticated."

One aspect of the disdain that Hongkongese feel for Chinese revolves around immigration. Many people in Hong Kong, having come to Hong Kong themselves from China in years past, want to see the door slammed shut on later would-be immigrants, who, they fear, will take away jobs and strain already overburdened government agencies. "Ah Chan" was the name given in a 1979 Hong Kong TV drama to a Chinese country bumpkin in flip flop sandals and undershirt, who immigrated to Hong Kong and suffered many travails. The name became widely used in Hong Kong to disparage mainland immigrants: those "who spat in public and jumped queues [or who dressed in an old-fashioned way] would immediately be spotted by Hong Kong people, who whispered among themselves, 'Here's an [Ah Chan].'"[38] This attitude continues as a way in which Hong Kong people can distinguish themselves from mainlanders. Hong Kong students in my own department doing research on mainland immigrants have sometimes hardly been able to contain themselves when they describe their fieldwork. To paraphrase one's words, "And then – I couldn't believe it – she bought an old-style fisherman's cap, and walked down the middle of the sidewalk with it on! I almost died! No Hong Kong person would *ever* do that!" Surveys confirm this attitude; one, conducted several months before the handover, found that most Hong Kong people "consider new migrants from China to be ignorant, impolite, dirty and greedy, and believe they are introducing evils from the mainland."[39]

Many mainlanders in Hong Kong in recent years are affluent; a more recently heard Hong Kong line is not that mainlanders are poor and dirty, but rather that they have no sense of sophistication. As one pre-handover report had it, "If you see women in the streets wearing Chanel from head to toe, chances are they're from the mainland. They know the brands, but do not have real taste or style."[40] My students tell me that mainlanders "overdress": they "try too hard to be fashionable, but they don't know how"; "you'll almost never see a mainlander wearing blue jeans!" "Mainlanders," this claim holds, "may sometimes have as much money as we do, but we have a cosmopolitanism that they can't possibly match." Unlike Hong Kong people, this claim has it, they are far from being sophisticated consumers in the cultural supermarket.

This is one substantive element of Hong Kong's "Chineseness plus": that of affluence and sophistication. Another is that of "Chineseness plus English/colonial education/colonialism." "What makes Hong Kong different from China is its heritage of colonialism," it is widely acknowledged.[41] For a few we interviewed, the "Chineseness plus" of colonialism and colonial education seemed more a "Chineseness minus," as we have seen; in one journalist's words, "We in Hong Kong have had our Chinese identity stolen from us: because we have been a colony of Great Britain, we no longer know who we are." Colonial education, as we saw from Mr. Wong's account, seemed designed to diminish any sense of national identity in Hong Kong, whether British or Chinese: "In school, we didn't study anything about national identity, citizenship, civics," said a secondary school teacher. "That's why Hong Kong people are rootless." But this was viewed by many other people we interviewed as a plus rather than a minus: "It is only because of colonialism that Hong Kong was able to develop as it has. I wish Great Britain were ruling Hong Kong today," said a business-woman, who cautioned that her words should never reach print in this book if ever her identity could be discovered.

One aspect of this colonialism has been the English language. English has been the dominant language of schooling (at least in textbooks, if not necessarily in classes themselves) in Hong Kong until recently; but when I challenge students as to why they are willing to speak the language of "the colonial oppressors," I am told that English has nothing to do with colonialism and everything to do with business, international commerce: good jobs go to those who are most fluent in English. In today's Hong Kong, Mandarin has also become important – Mandarin language tutors have apparently been making very good money in Hong Kong's downtown offices over the past several years – but it remains the language of China (albeit the divided China of the mainland and Taiwan). English, on the other hand, tends not to be seen primarily as the language of Great Britain or of the United States, but rather of the world: it is seen as the language of the market, and as well – as exemplified by the Internet, in a largely English-language format – the global cultural supermarket.

A third element of Hong Kong's "Chineseness plus" identity is that of "Chineseness plus freedom/ democracy/ human rights /the rule of law" – attributes that are legacies of the last years and decades of British rule, but that are now seen by many of the people we interviewed as universal attributes of development. As said a political activist, echoing many others we spoke with, "Human rights and rule of law don't just belong to a particular culture; they're universal. But China doesn't yet recognize their universal meanings." To give just one example of China's lack as depicted in Hong Kong media, the *South China Morning Post* reports on how "New migrants [to Hong Kong] are being taught not to offer bribes to prospective employers while looking for jobs":

> One student in the course [for new immigrants] said it was common in her hometown of Guangzhou for job applicants to offer potential employers a bribe in the hope of being offered a preference in their applications. "I always understood that corruption was to do with those who accepted a bribe. I'd never heard that the person who gave it was just as guilty". . . . The 33-year-old mother hoped the course would help her to stay out of trouble while she looked for a job.[42]

She is being taught in her course the "universal" rule of law which China is said to lack but that Hong Kong purportedly possesses.

It seems clear that the rule of law is valued in large part because it enables the conduct of business not according to particular connections – connections [*guanxi*] thought to characterize business in mainland China – but to rules that apply indiscriminately to everyone. Human rights represent in part the right to choose one's identity as one sees fit from the cultural and economic marketplace, regardless of what the state may advocate. Democracy too is thought by many of those we interviewed to be a universal good, that was being at least temporarily eclipsed in Hong Kong by China's and now Hong Kong's own backward government. In its contemporary form democracy, as we discussed in Chapter 1, involves one's conditioned choice of leaders as depicted in the mass media, just as the economic and cultural markets involve one's conditioned choice of goods and identities. It is in a sense the reflection in politics of contemporary capitalism: the market.

We see in all of these attributes of Hong Kong identity a positive valuation given to the global cultural supermarket over any particular cultural tradition: Hong Kong identity, by these formulations, is particular Chineseness plus the global cultural supermarket, with the latter clearly given precedence over the former. A minority of people we interviewed did not think this way: Mr. Leung's views of the glories of Chineseness, although not the Chinese state at present, were not his views alone. But several people who more or less shared his views did so with a sort of mournfulness: as if, from within the cultural supermarket, they long to return to "China" but feel that they cannot. Consider this young man's words, a particularly brilliant (and highly unusual) Chinese University student, now a reluctant businessman in the global market:

> If I could have chosen to be born anywhere, it would have been in a small traditional village in China 500 years ago, where I'd know nothing about the outside world. Yes, I'd prefer to be ignorant. I'm corrupted by Western education, individualism. If I hadn't been exposed to these values, I'd be more traditional, more trusting – my life would have turned out differently – but those values have shaped my mind.

For this man, the fact that he has received a "Western" education means, in a sense, that he has been stolen from his Chinese roots, his home, and cannot ever return: he has no choice but to be cosmopolitan, knowing the world and choosing, creating himself culturally from that knowledge. If "Westernness," in his terms, is thought to signify the cultural supermarket, and "Chineseness" a particular cultural tradition, the former will inevitably precede the latter: even if you choose "Chineseness" from the cultural supermarket, you still remain within the cultural supermarket's confines. You can't go home again.

But while this man lamented his loss of home, many of the people we interviewed were quite happy to be homeless wanderers within the cultural supermarket's aisles. Consider the following account, from a discerning consumer from the cultural supermarket who is also, paradoxically, a Hong Kong civil servant working to educate Hong Kong people as to their cultural identity:

> Chan Pui-shan, Angelita (30)
> I'm a civil servant, working in education. Some people say that we should teach young people in Hong Kong about our mother country, China, but others say, no, we should teach them to think independently. I'm not interested in patriotism – I don't particularly care about loving China – but that's no problem in my work. I'm an administrator, that's all. There are so many people with so many different views in society; our job is to find a way to satisfy the most people in the community. I don't feel political pressure from Beijing in this job; I only feel pressure from the Hong Kong public, in all their different views. . . .
>
> Some people in Hong Kong now seek the government to have more control over society by legislating on this and legislating on that, but that's not the trend. It's very difficult for civil servants now, because people have more information. You can learn a lot about the government on the Internet, and from all kinds of publications. This makes my workload increase – whatever I do, I have to be ready to explain it; people have all kinds of questions, and I have to be able to respond quickly. I'm lucky if just a few days a week, I don't have to stay in my office until eleven at night. Still, I like what I do. In the private sector, your goal would be helping your boss to earn more money. At least now I can say that I'm trying to do something for the public.
>
> I've traveled in China and overseas; I went to the United States for high school. In China I tried to dress like local people, so that I could get cheaper rates than those charged to foreigners. I had been told so many bad things about China – it wasn't as bad as I'd imagined; I was cheated, but nothing big. The parts of China I visited felt much more strange to me than the US. When I go

shopping in the US, I'm familiar with all the brand names. But in China, if I shop, it's not the style I need. . . . My father says that I should feel closer to China; he was born on the mainland. I don't talk to him much, because I already know what he's going to say; he thinks I'm immoral. He knows that he can't control me. So he just says, "Do what you want to do." My mom, on the other hand, is very open-minded; she's always encouraged me to be independent, and has really influenced me in my life. She and my father fight a lot. . . .

Am I Chinese? I don't think so. I'm not Hongkongese either. I'm human. There is only one race in the world, and that's the human race! Maybe I know more about Chinese culture than about some other culture, say, Indian culture. But that doesn't make me Chinese. Yeah, I like Chinese food, but it's just a matter of habit. In my daily life I speak Cantonese more than English, but so what? If I worked in America, I'd speak English – does language really matter in shaping your identity? I live here in Hong Kong, but it's not really home. It's more convenient because I know the place well. But if I stayed five years overseas, then I'd be more familiar with that place than with this one. My parents don't make this place home. I still live at home, but I don't see them that much; I didn't miss them much when I was in the States. I have relatives living all over the world – some in Australia, some in Taiwan, some in Canada, Malaysia, the Philippines, Singapore. Probably that's why it's easy for me to think that I'm not Chinese. When I was a kid, already my relatives were all over the world – they talked about this country and that, and they brought me stuff from all over the world. . . .

The night of the handover I watched TV for maybe a couple of hours. When I saw the British flag go down and the Chinese flag go up, I didn't have any feelings. It's just flags – I can't draw either one! I don't know what will happen to Hong Kong in coming years, but I'm ready for whatever may come, for better or worse – nothing ever remains unchanged; no place can be safe and prosperous forever. I hope I won't be living in Hong Kong 15 years from now; I'd rather live in some other places. Yeah, I guess I'm homeless. That's a very sad thing, isn't it? [Laughs loudly]

Ms. Chan works in education yet disavows any sense of patriotism, any sense of "loving her country." By viewing her work strictly in administrative terms, as a matter of satisfying the different groups she serves, and by stressing "Western" values such as human rights and gender equality as well as the contemporary "Chinese" value of "learning about the Motherland," she can avoid having to be patriotic; she simply does her job, and struggles not to be engulfed by its demands. (Indeed, it may be that her avowed lack of any feeling for her country is a direct reaction against her job of formulating Hong Kong's new education policy of "loving China"; but she denied it when I brought up this possibility.)

Her own cultural identity appears to be closer to the United States than to China: China, in her visits, was not as bad as she had been warned, but in the United States, she knows the brand names – that society seems closer to her home. Underlying this is a cultural identity based, it seems, wholly on the cultural supermarket. If her father apparently sought to instill in her a sense of Chinese values, her mother instilled in her a sense of her own independence; and the presents from her far-flung relatives across the globe when she was a child confirmed this to her, giving her a taken-for-granted membership in the global cultural supermarket. This continues today: more than anyone else we interviewed in Hong Kong, she denied any membership in any particular culture. Any grounding she has in Hong Kong is only a matter of habit, she tells us – language, food, all of the markers of cultural identity in a particular place she could easily enough discard, she says; were she to live in some other worldwide city, that city would become home to her in a scant few years, just as Hong Kong is her home now.

The *shikata ga nai* realm for her is immediately one of work, and the exhausting hours she must put in; more, it is also perhaps a matter of having to belong to any particular place, rather than the globe as a whole – like the spiritual shopper Ms. Clemens last chapter, seeking to immerse herself in all the world's religions – and it is one of Hong Kong's inevitable transformations. She has no allegiance to any state, and can't even remember their flags; rather, the essence of her identity, she says, is the entire globe. When, at the close of our interview, she laughed about being homeless, I sought a touch of yearning beneath her words, but I heard none. Perhaps, despite the civic role she plays in her work, she truly is a member of the global cultural supermarket, finding home in no place but the globe as a whole. In this very lack of commitment to Hong Kong, she may be in some sense a quintessential Hong Kong middle-class person, rooted in no place but seeking the main chance anywhere in the world it may be found.

State and market in the shaping of Hong Kong's new Chinese identity

In the previous section, we explored how the "Chineseness plus" of Hong Kong identity seems to indicate that internationalness – or at least "Westernness" – is valued over Chineseness, and the global cultural supermarket is valued over any particular culture in many formulations of Hong Kong identity. A fundamental transformation has of course taken place that continues to affect these views: from 1 July 1997, Hong Kong became a Special Administrative Region of China. But while politically, Hong Kong is part of the Chinese state – although the untested waters of "one country, two systems" generates continuing debate as to how much Hong Kong is to be part of the Chinese state – culturally, this remains unclear. In the first 18 months after the handover, an intense battle has been conducted in the words of Hong Kong public figures and in Hong Kong mass media: a battle between Chineseness and internationalness, and between the forces of state and market, particular culture and cultural supermarket, to win the hearts and minds of Hong Kong's people. This battle is reflected in the words of the people we interviewed.

The legacy of the handover, 1 July 1997, remains relatively muted in Hong Kong at present, as noted in the first part of this chapter; life in Hong Kong has been most affected by the legacy not of 1 July but of 2 July 1997, the day the Thai baht fell, triggering the East Asian economic crisis, a crisis inescapable in Hong Kong in lost jobs and diminished expectations. The legacy of these two dates seems quite different on the surface. As *Time* Magazine put it, "a year after the handover, the territory realizes that the enemy wasn't communism. It was capitalism"[43] – the enemy, for the time being, is less Chinese state control over Hong Kong, than the buffeting of Hong Kong by the global market. However, these different legacies are explained and disputed in Hong Kong through the basic rhetorical division discussed throughout this chapter. Conflicts in Hong Kong over politics and economics remain inseparable from an underlying conflict over cultural identity.

Immediately after the handover came a barrage of news coverage in Hong Kong about the glories of returning to the motherland; but after the initial euphoria, the reality of many Hong Kong people's continuing sense of alienation from the Chinese state set in. Pro-China newspaper accounts thus increasingly emphasized not Hong Kong people's innate love for China, but rather the need to re-educate Hong Kong people so that they will feel that love. One newspaper columnist wrote that "Under colonial rule, our education into nationalism and ethnicity was deprived. With the [Hong Kong] mass media's one-sided reporting, Hong Kong people . . . misunderstand China. Their ethnic emotion is thus shallow. . . . Patriotic education can strengthen young people's identity as Chinese." But as another, more skeptical columnist wrote, "If patriotic education means telling locals that . . . the mainland system is great and the Chinese leadership is superb . . . it is more likely to backfire than instill a sense of national pride and dignity among local citizens."[44]

The Hong Kong government moved in the autumn after the hand-over to restore mother-tongue education in Hong Kong: it was decreed that, unlike previous years, in which almost all secondary school education was at least theoretically in English, only the top quarter of secondary schools in Hong Kong would now be permitted to educate students primarily in English. This issue is practical – presumably, students learn better when taught in their own native language – but also highly symbolic: "mother-tongue education" is linked to one's "motherland"; English is the language of the repudiated colonizer. The government's move was met with howls of dismay by parents worried about their children's future employment prospects: "Three out of four parents are willing to go to great lengths to get their children into the 114 English-medium secondary schools, a survey has found. Just 4 percent of parents said they would opt to send their children to Chinese [Cantonese]-medium schools."[45] The Hong Kong government seems to have felt it only natural that once Hong Kong's colonization had ended, Hong Kong education should be returned to Hong Kong's native language; but parents, thinking practically, saw English not as a colonial but as a world language: if their children failed to become proficient in English, they would fail to enter the global market and would be hindered in their pursuit of worldwide success.

In autumn 1997, there was much controversy in Hong Kong over the proposed playing of the Chinese national anthem before movie show-ings: "Films are for enjoying leisure, not for listening to the national anthem," read a headline in Hong Kong's *Apple Daily*;[46] several of those we interviewed claimed that they would be spending time in the restroom at the start of movies. Eventually it was decided that only movies from the mainland would have the Chinese national anthem played at their start. This controversy did not simply show "residents' deep-seated sense of alienation from the mainland," as one columnist put it,[47] but more, an alienation from the very idea of belonging to a state. When I tell my Hong Kong students that the American national anthem is played before sporting events, some are shocked: "In America, you do that? That's just like the Chinese!" While a few we interviewed expressed a degree of patriotic feeling upon hearing the Chinese national anthem – "When I heard it recently," a secondary school teacher said, "I thought of all the suffering of Chinese people at the hands of the Japanese in World War II" – others expressed only puzzlement: "When I hear it, I don't feel anything. I can't really imagine what I'm supposed to feel," said a businessman.

Some may suppress such feeling because of social pressure; a university student is reported in one newspaper article as saying that she wanted to love her country, but didn't dare do so,[48] apparently due to the scorn she might receive from her fellow students. But others look upon those who express such patriotic feeling as being bizarre, akin to religious zealots. As one newspaper columnist wrote, "I once was at an event where everyone stood at reverence before the rising [Chinese] national flag and sang the national anthem. It was even more embarrassing than being at church . . . when everyone else is praying."[49] A graduate student I interviewed went to Guangzhou as an exchange student and was amazed by what she heard: "Those students there – they feel proud of their country! Students like me, from Hong Kong, had never thought about that before."

As earlier noted, Tung Chee-hwa often proclaims Hong Kong's fundamental Chinese identity, linking that identity to such values as obedience to authority. Anson Chan, Tung's chief secretary and head of Hong Kong's civil service, has spoken of how Hong Kong's "real transition is about identity, not sovereignty. . . . For the first time I [have begun] . . . to appreciate the spiritual propriety of Hong Kong's return to the mainland."[50] But statements such as these have been greeted with skepticism in Hong Kong:

> Beijing clearly expects the chief executive to be someone who is proud of Hong Kong's reunification with China. That explains why Mr. Tung continually harks on about this, even when he knows it makes him look slightly ridiculous in the eyes of many in Hong Kong. It also explains why Mrs. Chan has now begun echoing the same theme.[51]

It seems necessary for Hong Kong's leaders to proclaim their Chineseness whether they believe in such Chineseness or not: since Beijing has ultimate political control over Hong Kong, the leaders of Hong Kong's government cannot afford not to proclaim their undying love toward China. But there remains widespread skepticism toward those who proclaim Chineseness. Chris Patten, Hong Kong's last British governor, caused a furore but also much agreement when he said that many rich businessmen in Hong Kong who sing the praises of China are in fact carrying foreign passports in their back pockets. Patriotism, one newspaper article states, should be viewed not as a civic duty to the state but as a personal choice from the market: "Nationality is like clothing. You can change it whenever you like."[52] As another article maintains, "Hong Kong people are citizens of the globe; only after that are they Chinese."[53] The people we interviewed often echoed these words, Ms. Chan, as we saw, most vociferously: "Am I Chinese? I don't think so. . . . There is only one race in the world, and that's the human race!"

In May 1998, a new program of patriotism toward China was launched by the Department of Education in Hong Kong, seeking to "inculcate students with a sense of their Chinese identity"; "Schools were encouraged to raise the five-star flag of the People's Republic of China and sing the national anthem. . . . The response so far in the former British colony can be politely described as lacklustre," with school principals largely ignoring the advice.[54] Perhaps realizing that younger children might be easier to inculcate with patriotism, the Committee on the Promotion of Civic Education issued in September 1998 a booklet aimed at 4–6-year-olds entitled "I am Chinese," seeking "to understand our own country and introduce Hong Kong as an inseparable part of China"; "With the guidance of parents and teachers, it is hoped that . . . children could have a better understanding of their national identity and . . . develop a stronger sense of belonging to China."[55]

A pivotal date in the effort to shape hearts and minds in Hong Kong to believe in the Chinese nation is 1 October, the Chinese National Day; the outpouring of media effusions on that day clearly reflect the pattern of state versus market, and national culture versus the global cultural supermarket, as the dominant competing discourses seeking to shape Hong Kong hearts and minds. One pro-China newspaper quotes a high school student as proclaiming "Born a Chinese, die a Chinese. These are the words inside my heart that I dedicate to my mother country"; another quotes, without attribution, "a famous old saying": "Ask not what your country can do for you, but what you can do for your country"[56] – one's duty is to be dedicated to one's country. *Apple Daily*, on the other hand – a highly popular newspaper in Hong Kong, and an exemplar of the cultural supermarket in all its forms, both the tawdry and lurid and the high-minded and democratic – affirms not duty but choice; its editorial on the first National Day after the hand-over was headlined, "You celebrate, he doesn't celebrate: National Day with Hong Kong characteristics."[57] A survey after the 1997

National Day showed that 71 percent of respondents felt "indifferent" toward the holiday – for them, it held no patriotic meaning, but was just a day off from work.[58] Some of the people we interviewed reflected this: in a world of high stress, where one's occupation demands almost all of one's attention, a day off was for them a day of rest and relaxation, not a day of patriotic duty. "To be honest, I was too tired to pay attention to National Day. I wanted to sleep, and be with my family," said a businessman. Others were more politically pointed: "I would never celebrate National Day. . . . I hate the Chinese government," said a social worker.

The 1998 National Day was rendered particularly surreal by the craze for Snoopy dolls that engulfed Hong Kong. McDonald's restaurants held a month-long promotion in Hong Kong, featuring Snoopy dolls garbed in different national costumes, peaking on National Day, when a Chinese doll was on offer. As newspaper stories breathlessly asserted, "Tens of thousands joined queues which formed before dawn outside many of the McDonald's 147 outlets [in Hong Kong] as Snoopy hysteria reached fever pitch on National Day"; "Police reinforcements are being called in to guard McDonald's outlets today after the stampede for Snoopy toys triggered violence."[59] This is a wonderful irony: the quintessence of American taste marketed world-wide capitalizes on Hong Kong's new Chinese national identity by devising a marketing gimmick that drives consumers wild – thereby the market subverts and satirizes the earnest efforts of the state to mold its new citizens' identity. "In this age, of McDonald's hamburgers, what can National Day mean to us? Is it no more than an extra holiday, to line up to buy Chinese-style Snoopy dolls?" asks one lamenting news-paper columnist.[60] Apparently so in Hong Kong today. Some of my students sheepishly admitted their desire for Snoopy dolls, but it is rare to find any student, or anyone we interviewed, who admits to feeling patriotic on National Day.

This conflict between Chineseness and internationalness, and between state and market, is the case not just in terms of politics, but also economics. One of the key aspects of Hong Kong's cultural identity for many of the people we interviewed involves, as we have seen, Hong Kong's wealth, enabling Hong Kong's middle-class people to enjoy a cosmopolitan life. If Hong Kong people can no longer enjoy their cosmopolitan lifestyle, then they become "just like the Chinese" and Hong Kong becomes "just another Chinese city" – something that many of the Hong Kong people we spoke with desperately deny might happen, as we saw.

It is sometimes assumed outside of Hong Kong that the effect of the handover was to open the gates of Hong Kong to all Chinese. In fact, it is now as difficult as it ever was for most mainland Chinese to enter Hong Kong, with visa policy and border controls remaining stringent; but some more affluent and sophisticated mainland Chinese are indeed able to come to Hong Kong. We saw earlier how mainland Chinese in Hong Kong may be mocked as "Ah Chan," unsophisticated country bumpkins; but the tables may be turning. It is now said that sophisticated mainlanders in Hong Kong have taken to calling their Hong Kong compatriots "Kong Chan," Hong Kong bumpkins.[61] Indeed, with the economic downturn, China, for many in Hong Kong's middle class, no longer represents unsophistication; to laugh at Chinese as naive countryfolk is becoming increasingly untenable. "Hong Kong Chinese still think the [mainland] Chinese are the stupidest bumpkins on earth. But the elite in China know what they're doing these days – and they don't need the middleman," says one noted Hong Kong investment manager.[62] One corporate employee we interviewed said this:

> It's more dangerous to make fun of mainlanders now; you have to be careful. Now a lot of Chinese from the mainland are very rich and have a lot of power. In the business world, people learn Mandarin to communicate with them – I'm taking Mandarin lessons now. If a mainlander were to feel you were making light of him, that you didn't respect him – you'd lose his business.

The sophistication of some mainland Chinese is also apparent at my university, which has long accepted a few Chinese graduate students. In the past, in the social sciences anyway, these have often been students who speak little English or Cantonese, and who lack the intellectual background of their Hong Kong counterparts; but in the past two years, to my own surprise, I have encountered mainland students from top Chinese universities who are more knowledgeable, sophisticated, and fluent in English than Hong Kong students. It is wondrous to behold the initial shock of Hong Kong students upon hearing mainland students knowingly expound upon the latest trendy Western academic theories of which the Hong Kong students may know little. As a newspaper article puts it,

> Hong Kong students still think of themselves as being better than their mainland fellows, in their level of English, their inter-nationalism, and their flexibility. They don't realize that the

English standard of top mainland high school students is far better than that of Hong Kong law-degree holders.[63]

This change can be exaggerated: there are many different kinds of Chinese immigrants coming into Hong Kong today, from the illegal immigrants who on occasion break into the mansions of the rich in Hong Kong, to the mainland laborers still scorned in Hong Kong for their habit of spitting in public,[64] to the young mainland women who have married working-class Hong Kong men unable to find Hong Kong wives, to the elite businessmen and students described above. Recently, however, this latter group has expanded, leading to the beginnings of a change in the image of China in Hong Kong: as if to confirm the claim that "we Chinese aren't just ignorant bumpkins/puppets of the Chinese state. We're as sophisticated and worldly as you are."

This sea change in views toward China is dramatically linked to the current economic crisis afflicting Hong Kong. Before the handover and the economic downturn, many in Hong Kong's business community were worried that the Chinese state would intrude upon the free workings of the market; but according to some, the Chinese state has instead acted as a salvation from the market, in pledging the might of its currency reserves to protect Hong Kong against the vicissitudes of the market. As one newspaper in Hong Kong put it, "Hong Kong was strongly attacked in the Asian economic crisis . . . but the Mother Country has immediately reached out to help Hong Kong. The central government has repeatedly said that it will support Hong Kong at any price"; as another newspaper later stated, "Facing the severe blow of the Asian economic crisis, if we hadn't had the strong backing of the Motherland, it is hard to imagine what Hong Kong's economy and financial situation would be like today."[65]

But this is only one side of the discursive conflict; just as in politics, as we've seen, some voices in the economic arena proclaim oneness with the Chinese state, but others proclaim fealty to the international market. After having withstood several waves of speculators trying to break the Hong Kong's dollar's linkage to the US dollar, the Hong Kong government in August 1998 abandoned its *laissez-faire* policies and intervened in its stock market, buying US$15 billion of Hong Kong stocks. This move, seeming to signify a departure from the free-market principles upon which Hong Kong had long been based, was widely criticized as indicating a turn away from international economic transparency to Chinese-style opacity. Hong Kong's intervention meant "The End of a Free Market," *Asian Business News* lamented.[66] "Hong Kong in the old days – what did it stand for? A free and

unfettered market through competition. But now with this massive
intervention, the picture is blurred and raises the question, if Hong
Kong doesn't stand for free markets, what does it stand for?" said
Nobel laureate economist Morton Miller as reported prominently in
the Hong Kong press.[67] Some of the people we interviewed directly
linked this intervention to the influence of the Chinese state upon Hong
Kong. As a Hong Kong politician said to me, "Of course China intervenes in Hong Kong's market. It's all very subtle; China doesn't have
to intervene directly. It is obvious that China uses its own factors to
influence everything the Hong Kong government does." A bank
worker asserted that, "The Chinese government holds all power and
all secrets, never letting things work beyond its control, and now the
Hong Kong government is acting in exactly the same way."

How much the Chinese government in fact intervenes in Hong
Kong's economy is unclear; but these people believed that Hong Kong
as a symbol of the market was giving way before Hong Kong as a pawn
of the state. Indeed, the intervention into the Hong Kong stock market
came to be described in militaristic terms, as a matter of China fighting
off the evil machinations of the world beyond, or, alternately, the
world struggling to help reform a backward China. "The stance of
the financial jingoists is that this is war: war between the valiant SAR
government and unnamed 'international speculators.'"[68] Hong Kong
people "have started to lose confidence in Hong Kong dollars,
exchanging Hong Kong dollars for US dollars; this indirectly assists
international currency speculators to continue invading our economy.
Unconsciously we have become economic traitors to China," claims
the *Hong Kong Economic Times*[69] – one who follows the logic of the
market is an enemy of the Chinese state, this argument holds. On the
other side of the discursive trenches, the Hong Kong scholar Lau Siu-kai
argues: "Hong Kong is a symbol of a free capitalist market economy. . . .
[But now] sentiments of economic xenophobia have grown. . . . We
should not give an impression that we become 'more and more
Chinese' after the handover."[70] As Martin Lee, perhaps Hong Kong's
foremost government critic, has asked, is Hong Kong becoming an
"international finance centre with Chinese characteristics"?, an "international" center that is not international?[71] As said a financial analyst
we spoke with, "Maybe Hong Kong's market intervention was a good
thing, in the short term. But in the long term, to the extent that Hong
Kong becomes closed to the market, it is no longer Hong Kong, but a
Chinese city. Then Hong Kong will lose what makes it special."

What all of the above demonstrates, I think, is that the discursive war
of state vs. market – a conflict also phrased in terms of Chineseness vs.

internationalness, and particular cultural identity vs. the global cultural supermarket – continues unabated in Hong Kong; and indeed, as I write and revise these words, new events take place every week that add further wrinkles to the conflict. In fact, the division of the world into Chinese state versus international market that we've examined masks a more complex intermingling of the two forces: market and state are not the black-and-white alternatives that the rhetoric seems to presuppose. But on the level of discourse, of how mass media and the people we interviewed describe Hong Kong since the handover, this is what we see. Those who support China in Hong Kong tend to believe that the state should take precedence over the market as the central underlying principle of Hong Kong cultural identity; those who are distrustful of China tend to believe that the international market should remain the basis of Hong Kong's cultural identity.

This struggle is Hong Kong's particular variant of what we have seen in our earlier ethnographic chapters: the tension between belonging to a particular national culture and the global cultural supermarket. In this case, however, the debate is in an immediate and urgent frame: now that the Chinese state has ultimate political control over Hong Kong, how, in these years following 1 July 1997, is Hong Kong to define itself between national state and global cultural supermarket? Those who advocate the different positions we have examined will continue competing to sway the hearts and minds of Hong Kong people. And which of these groups "wins" will determine, in part, the future of Hong Kong.

It appears, as we discussed in Chapter 1, that in China and throughout the world, the market, along with its analogue, the cultural supermarket, is eroding away at the claims of the state, in the power of its discursive arguments and the force of its mass-mediated technologies. But in Hong Kong, as in few other places in the world, the opposite is taking place, as the state attempts to supplant the market, and particular national culture attempts to supplant the global cultural supermarket in Hong Kong people's minds. Perhaps the state will not succeed; perhaps Hong Kong's middle class, ensconced in the market as they are, will not accept this molding (at least not before China itself bursts the bounds of national identity before the forces of the market); perhaps Hong Kong people, and particularly the more educated, affluent people we have discussed in this chapter, are sufficiently immersed in the market and in the cultural supermarket to make the acquisition of national consciousness at this late date all but impossible. As a businesswoman we interviewed said, "A handover alone can't change an international cosmopolitan city into a mainland city" – Hong Kong people won't leave the market to believe in the state: they are too cosmopolitan for that.

Or perhaps, on the other hand, the Chinese state, with its ultimate control over education and perhaps, in the future, over mass media as well, will succeed in shaping a new national identity in Hong Kong, and the coming generation of Hongkongese will be Chinese in a way that many of their parents never were. As a social worker said, "I don't know whether nationalist education is right or wrong, but kids will gradually come to think that the motherland is better: Hong Kong will inevitably become more and more Chinese." Or perhaps both of these are true. Perhaps Hong Kong intellectuals and people as a whole will learn to live, in coming decades, with the same contradiction that many of the rest of us live within: the contradiction between state and market that we take for granted as the natural order of things.

Conclusion: what in the world is Chinese? What in the world is Hongkongese?

In this chapter, we've examined the varieties of cultural identity among Hong Kong intellectuals in the wake of Hong Kong's return to Chinese sovereignty. We've seen how some adhere to a Hong Kong identity, but one that may now gradually fade away, as Hong Kong becomes Chinese; we've seen how others assert an underlying Chinese identity that may conflict with the identity proffered by the Chinese government; and we've seen how still others may insist on no particular cultural identity, but rather an identity rooted in the world as a whole in all its cultural choices. Underlying these different portraits, we've analyzed Hong Kong senses of cultural identity as a matter of state vs. market, of belonging to a particular culture vs. belonging to the global cultural supermarket. Hong Kong's cultural identity, among many of the intellectuals whose voices we've heard in this chapter, is based upon the worldwide market, and upon its parallel, the cultural supermarket. What happens to this identity as the Chinese state politically and culturally intrudes upon Hong Kong is the huge question that Hong Kong now faces.

In Chapter 2, we saw how some Japanese traditional artists felt themselves wholly rooted in Japaneseness; some contemporary artists sought to define themselves within the cultural supermarket, while other contemporary artists sought a return to Japanese roots which they now had somehow to reinvent. In Chapter 3, we saw how some American Christians saw their faith as their American truth; others, seeing religion as a matter of taste rather than truth, explored the cultural supermarket for the religion that might happen to suit them, and still others tried to assert Buddhism as a new American truth, a truth that might somehow transcend America's cultural supermarket. In this chapter, we've seen a parallel disagreement over home and roots, with several differences. First, this disagreement has taken place within an extraordinary political transition, and second, there is no taken-for-granted cultural home in Hong Kong. Is Hong Kong Hong Kong's cultural home, or is such a place too fragile and transient to serve as home? Is China Hong Kong's cultural home, or has Chineseness been too eroded by communism, too manipulated by political leaders, to serve as a real home for Hong Kong? Is Hong Kong returning home in the wake of its handover, or has home already become lost, to be reinvented only through state propaganda that some may believe but that many more will only snicker at or sigh before? For the culturally supermarketed Hong Kong lived in by the people whose voices we have heard in this chapter, is a home created by the state believable? Or does the cultural supermarket, once consumed from, become all that can ever be imagined?

These questions are fundamental to Hong Kong's future, but they also transcend Hong Kong. Let us now, in this book's final chapter, turn from the ethnographic particulars of our past three chapters to a larger examination of the issues these particulars raise. What, in today's world, can be the meaning of home?

5 Searching for home in the cultural supermarket

We have looked at Japanese artists, American religious seekers, and Hong Kong intellectuals over the past three chapters; but in their various formulations of cultural identity, these groups transcend their particular social and historical worlds, I argue, to speak to us all. In this chapter I compare these three groups, focusing on the nine people whose accounts we examined at length, to consider where they fit in the spectrum between having a particular cultural identity and belonging to the global cultural supermarket. I then place the findings into a larger perspective, examining recent theorizing on globalization, postmodernism, and nationalism, and find that they do indeed reflect larger currents in the world today – to some extent, anyway, their struggles over identity can be seen in the developed world as a whole, as it rushes toward globalization while its inhabitants may cling to a sense of home. This leads us to consider the nature and meaning of anthropology today: What is the significance of anthropology in a world of roots uprooted? And this leads to a final question: What, in today's world, is the meaning of home?

Japanese artists, American religious seekers, and Hong Kong intellectuals in comparison

The three groups we have examined in the preceding chapters are quite distinctive in the particular ways in which cultural identity is struggled over within each of their arenas: the realms of art and artistic roots, of religion and truth, and of cultural identity in the shadow and wake of political transformation.

For traditional Japanese artists, their arts may be proclaimed as representing the cultural essence of Japanese, though it is a Japaneseness that most Japanese today have forgotten; they may market their arts as Japanese roots, though their arts are perhaps but choices from the cultural supermarket. Some contemporary artists see Japaneseness not as roots but as chains, hindering them from excelling at the foreign art forms to which they aspire. Other contemporary artists disregard Japaneseness, seeing their artistic paths as matters of choice from the global cultural supermarket. Still others, working within contemporary global forms, seek to recreate Japaneseness, seeking, through all of their Western training, their Japanese roots. For these artists, we see the ongoing loss and reconstruction of Japaneseness, through the intervention of the cultural supermarket.

For some American born-again Christians, their religion may be seen as the original basis of the United States, which Americans today have forgotten; but more, their religion is the truth, a truth which many of their fellow Americans, lost in relativism, ignore. For some American liberal Christians, this truth is but one path to truth of many potential paths to truth; for some American spiritual searchers, truth becomes unknowable and taste is all: the global cultural supermarket, their birthright as Americans, may be trolled for whatever paths toward personal happiness it may reveal. For some American Buddhists, religious truth again reasserts itself, an alternative religious truth, as does too the possibility of an alternative Buddhist America; but America as the cultural supermarket may serve less to make America Buddhist than to make Buddhism American, one more flavor within the Americanized cultural supermarket.

For many Hong Kong intellectuals, their cultural identity is as Hongkongese, an identity that transcends its Chinese cultural basis in its affluence, its rule of law, and its immersion in the global cultural supermarket – but an identity that has very recently emerged, only to now be endangered with Hong Kong's return to the Chinese state. Others see their identity as Chinese, but a Chineseness that is opposed to that proffered by the Chinese government: their Chineseness is based on a traditional Chinese culture, Chinese cultural roots that may or may not any longer exist, and indeed, may evaporate when looked at too closely. Still others assert no particular cultural identity, but proudly proclaim themselves homeless members of the global cultural supermarket. All of this takes place within a Hong Kong that is now engaged in an intense discursive battle between Chineseness and internationalness, state and market, particular culture and cultural supermarket, in the shaping of Hong Kong's economic, political, and cultural future.

These groups are highly particular, but they share broad themes that make them comparable. If the Japanese artists in my narrative sequence follow the pattern of proclaiming Japanese roots, to chafing at the chains of Japan, to pursuing choices from the cultural supermarket, to returning to Japanese roots, then the American religious seekers follow a parallel pattern of believing in ultimate truth, to pursuing one's own taste within the cultural supermarket, to believing in an alternative ultimate truth. Both roots and truth, in these two cases, seem in opposition to the cultural supermarket: as if to say, "We have our own roots/ our own truth/our own home. All isn't just choice, taste, flux." In both cases, one group – Japanese traditional artists and some American Christians – seems, in effect, pre-cultural supermarket, asserting roots or truth from a "pure" culture prior to the cultural supermarket's depredations, and another group – some Japanese contemporary artists, and American Buddhists – seems post-cultural supermarket, in asserting roots or truth on the basis of selections from the cultural supermarket, and asserting these in opposition to the cultural supermarket. The Hong Kong intellectuals are in a more complex situation, living in one cultural home that now may be vanishing, and engulfed by another that for many doesn't seem like home; some embrace the cultural supermarket, and others long for a home that may ever be absent. Thus, with just a few exceptions, they could not wholeheartedly say that "we have our own roots and home"; more than their Japanese and American counterparts, many seem truly uprooted, and yet many of them too seek roots.

The spectrum between belonging to a particular national culture and belonging to the global cultural supermarket within our three groups can perhaps be seen most clearly by considering again the nine people whose accounts we examined at length in our earlier chapters.

Ms. Ōkubo, the Japanese teacher of traditional dance, and Mr. Leung, the Hong Kong exponent of Chineseness, both believe strongly in what they see as their cultural traditions as Japanese and Chinese, and draw their senses of identity from those traditions; but both also indicate that those traditions are at odds with the contemporary worlds in which they live. Ms. Ōkubo gets stared at on the trolley because of her Japanese dress, and teaches Japanese dance to young women who seem to resist the strictures of her teaching; Mr. Leung keeps his sense of Chineseness to himself and his close friends, believing that most Hong Kong people would not understand his sentiments. Both to some degree accept the cultural supermarket – Ms. Ōkubo tells us that Western music and ballet can be linked to Japanese dance, and that the freedom brought by "Americanization" is in part a good thing; Mr. Leung maintains that Chinese culture can accept everything from the world beyond and remain Chinese – perhaps because they have little choice, given the contemporary world; but the essence of their identities, they maintain, is the particular cultural tradition to which they belong. That this tradition may be invented, or too vague to define distinctly, is beside the point; the point is that it enables them to have a sense of home cultural identity, as if an anchor to their lives.

Mr. Kobayashi, the Japanese painter of avant-garde dance, to some extent resembles Ms. Ōkubo and Mr. Leung in his sense of cultural identity. From within his Westernized artistic training, his cosmopolitan knowledge of world art, his awareness that Japanese artistic culture is in one sense dead, kept embalmed as a marketing device "for tourists and foreigners," he nonetheless beholds in his art what he sees as his underlying Japanese roots, the accretion of two thousand years of Japanese history. Unlike Mr. Leung and Ms. Ōkubo, he seems not really a cultural patriot – he is, he seems to feel, a Japanese *artist* more than a *Japanese* artist – but he seems rooted in his Japaneseness all the same, not, he sees it, as a choice from the cultural supermarket but as his cultural home.

Mr. Wong, the Hong Kong professor, resembles Mr. Kobayashi in having a clear sense of a home cultural identity, that of being Hong Kong Chinese; but Mr. Wong's home, unlike Mr. Kobayashi's home, is the product not of what he sees as thousands of years of history but only of the last few decades, and now it faces possible extinction. Mr. Wong's Hong Kong cultural identity is particular, being rooted in the unique cultural characteristics of Hong Kong, but it also, in his description, resembles the cultural supermarket – left over by the West and by China, Hong Kong's identity partakes of them both, he tells us – but as Hong Kong becomes politically and culturally part of China, it may lose its status as a hub of the cultural supermarket. Ms. Martin, the American born-again Christian, refers to an America that has moved in the opposite direction from Mr. Wong's Hong Kong, a more typical direction in the world as a whole today. Instead of moving from identity as defined by the cultural supermarket to identity as defined by a particular state and cultural heritage, America, as she discusses it, may once have been the home of Christian truth, but it is no more. She struggles against both self-righteous American Christians – as if emblems of a particular American cultural identity – and Americans who see religion as no more than a lifestyle choice, America as the cultural supermarket.

Mr. Petrovich, the American Buddhist, and Mr. Sasaki, the Japanese frustrated artist, both base their lives in their choices from the cultural supermarket in the realms of religion and of art, but they feel more (Mr. Sasaki) or less (Mr. Petrovich) opposed by their home societies and cultures in their choices. Mr. Sasaki dreams of creating great works within imported Western forms of art and music, but feels blocked from such creation by his Japaneseness: Japanese can only imitate, he tells us, because their Japaneseness gets in the way; the cultural supermarket is not theirs but foreign, he believes. Mr. Petrovich, on the other hand, indeed believes that he can progress on the Tibetan Buddhist path, for that path belongs to no particular culture, but is universal, like science. However, American culture, in its materialism and its competitiveness, prevents Americans from comprehending the importance of that path; Mr. Petrovich is proud to think of Buddhism as "unAmerican," he tells us.

The two people who portray themselves as most purely consumers in the cultural supermarket are Ms. Clemens, the American spiritual shopper, and Ms. Chan, the Hong Kong civil servant: they seem to bear no particular allegiance to, and indeed, have no strong feelings for or against the societies and cultural traditions in which they were born. Ms. Clemens sees America as a land that enables her to follow any religious path from any of the world's traditions. She seeks to explore them all, she tells us: just as one can choose hair coloring or workout regimens, so too one can choose whatever religion from all the globe's choices that may make one happy. Ms. Chan goes farthest of all in her explicit denial of any particular cultural identity, of needing any cultural home: she is not Chinese but human, she tells us. Anywhere can be home, she says: indeed, who needs any cultural home when the cultural supermarket in all its splendors beckons? The complete freedom of choice these women envision is no doubt largely illusory; but their claim, if not the reality of their lives, is of the freedom to make all the world one's home as one chooses.

We thus see in these nine people a spectrum of identity formulations, from a firm sense of belonging to a particular cultural home, to an equally firm sense of belonging to no cultural home, but to the global cultural supermarket. This spectrum reveals the different ways in which these nine people try to resolve the tension and contradiction between one's cultural home and the cultural supermarket: a tension and contradiction present throughout the developed mass-mediated world today, but that these nine people's accounts reveal with particular acuity. The crux of the matter is that once you're within the cultural supermarket, you can't go home again, but only strive to imagine home from within the cultural supermarket's aisles. All nine of these people, whether they assert a firm cultural home or proclaim no such cultural home, are in their own ways attempting to deal with this inescapable contemporary fact of life.

The cultural supermarket is experienced by none of these nine people, including Ms. Clemens and Ms. Chan despite their occasional words otherwise, as a place where consumers merrily choose identities as they might choose suits of clothes or flavors of ice cream: the degree of social pressure these women face from the people around them in their lives is evidence of the gravity of their choices. The term "cultural super-market" may seem to connote frivolity: "pull up your shopping cart and grab what you please!" But there is nothing frivolous about these people's choices and paths of identity in their accounts. Rather, these people are all struggling mightily in different ways to formulate them-selves, in pursuit of or in flight from home. Their lives depend upon their choices, as their accounts, describing their often difficult and some-times harrowing personal journeys of identity, well attest.

We discussed in Chapter 1 the different levels of the cultural shaping of self; what we have seen consistently from these nine people's accounts is that all that can be taken for granted by these people within their worlds of Japanese art, American religion, and Hong Kong cultural identity is the sanctity of choice, or at least the appearance of free choice, from the cultural supermarket. Roots can only be chosen from the cultural supermarket and then subsequently claimed as roots that go deeper than the cultural supermarket. This goes against the assertions, or at least implications, of Ms. Ōkubo, Mr. Kobayashi, and Mr. Leung, but seems difficult to deny, as our ethnographic chapters have shown.

But this realm of putative choice is for all these people complicated by the constraints of *shikata ga nai*. *Shikata ga nai* is variously designated in their accounts: if for Mr. Sasaki it is the misfortune of belonging to a particular society and ethnicity blocking his art, for Ms. Clemens, it is the misfortune of belonging to any particular society and culture block-ing her spiritual pursuit, as for Mr. Wong it is the unstoppable course of history, creating and then perhaps taking away the particular cul-tural identity to which he adheres. But beyond the different particulars of *shikata ga nai*, for all of these people *shikata ga nai* is the world of other people, the social arena within which their choices from the cultural supermarket are played out. All nine of these people are waging an ongoing struggle to convince others of the validity of their particular cultural path.

Ms. Ōkubo advertises through her dress her unusual cultural path; her kimono is in one sense an implicit rebuke to the people around her, as if to say, "I'm Japanese, and so I wear Japanese dress. Aren't *you* Japanese?" Mr. Sasaki more discreetly shows his artistic tastes through the picture of John Coltrane on his desk; his disdain as an artist for contemporary Japanese society he keeps hidden, he told me, when meeting his business clients, or else he might have no clients left. Mr. Petrovich teaches meditation, but keeps silent about his religious path during his work as a dentist, choosing instead to invisibly empathize with those in pain. Ms. Martin carries her Bible with her but seems disinclined to talk about it with others for fear of offending them; Mr. Leung too keeps quiet about his sense of Chineseness except to his close friends. Ms. Chan and Ms. Clemens are criticized by parents – followers of Chinese and Christian cultural particularism, respectively – for being "immoral" and unsaved in their paths down the cultural supermarket's aisles; Ms. Clemens is mocked, from a different angle, by her soon-to-be-ex husband. Mr. Kobayashi is questioned by his son for his refusal to exhibit his polished Western-style paintings but only his unpolished Japanese ones; and Mr. Wong's sense of hard-earned Hong Kong Chinese identity was apparently understood neither by his parents nor, now, his children.

The complex processes of social negotiation apparent from these accounts exist because of the cultural supermarket: if art or religion or cultural identity were held in common in a given society, such complex negotiations could hardly exist. Whether such commonality has ever truly existed in the history of human societies is open to question, but certainly it does not exist today. The people whose accounts we've looked at seem to experience their choices from the cultural supermarket as inevitably requiring extensive ongoing social negotiation and validation. They may hide aspects of themselves, in some social contexts, to avoid having to engage in such negotiations; or they may have to show these aspects of themselves to the people around them, and face criticism, as their accounts so often reveal – this is particularly the case *vis-à-vis* intimates, who may claim that it is very definitely their business how one chooses to live one's life.

However, because their societies are to at least some degree immersed in the cultural supermarket, these criticisms often only have limited force. The cultural supermarket has as its basic premise the notion that anyone may do or believe anything one desires, so long as it does not directly hurt others; thus, self-conscious consumers in the cultural supermarket like Ms. Clemens and Ms. Chan may find painful the criticisms of family members, but finally seem to shrug those criticisms off. On the other hand, those who claim roots or truth that transcend the cultural supermarket – Ms. Ōkubo, Mr. Kobayashi, and Mr. Leung, and also Ms. Martin and Mr. Petrovich – seem to do so in a reticent way *vis-à-vis* the society around them; otherwise they run the risk of being seen as arrogant or eccentric in their implicit claim to know what is true or best beyond themselves alone. It certainly seems true, looking at the world at large, that one response to the cultural supermarket is to stridently defend one's choices, and to castigate those who choose otherwise: some of the born-again Christians of Chapter 3 fit this pattern. But these five people all seem remarkably tolerant in their claims, despite the implicit absolutism of those claims: they live in a world of others making different claims, holding different ideas as to how one should live and think, and so to some extent they are compelled to be tolerant.

The social negotiation of these people's senses of cultural identity clearly is conditioned by their particular pursuits, as well as by their society's particular circumstances. Our three Japanese artists pursue their arts in a contemporary Japanese society that they feel is hostile to art; our three Americans pursue their religious paths within the contemporary American "culture war" of truth versus taste; and our three Hong Kong intellectuals conceive of their cultural identities against the backdrop of Hong Kong's return to China. But underlying this difference, there is a common pattern in all of these people, of seeking, in some sense, to elevate their particular paths and choices within a social stock market of identity. If Ms. Ōkubo explicitly seeks to restore in her students a sense of pride in Japaneseness, if Mr. Petrovich seeks to spread the Buddhist path through his teaching of meditation, if Mr. Leung seeks to have Hong Kong and Chinese people return to a true sense of Chineseness, so too, in a less direct way, Mr. Sasaki seeks to leave room for the identity of creative artist in what he sees as a hostile and conformist Japanese society, and Ms. Clemens seeks respect for her culturally supermarketed spiritual path from Christians and agnostics alike.

All nine of these people pursue their senses of cultural identity within social worlds that push and pull them in various directions, and within which they explicitly or implicitly seek to elevate the value of the cultural identities that they construct and maintain for themselves. Even the five people who claim roots or truth that transcend the cultural supermarket nonetheless seek to establish maximum value for their paths within the cultural supermarket, as reflected by the social worlds in which they live.

This leaves to one side the question of why these people choose the identities they choose. Why did Ms. Martin become a born-again Christian while Mr. Petrovich, from an equally religious Christian background, became a Buddhist? Why does Mr. Sasaki shun all thought of Japanese roots in his art, while Mr. Kobayashi seeks out such roots?

Why does Mr. Leung find his deepest identity in Chineseness while Ms. Chan, from a somewhat similar background, explicitly denies her Chineseness? Why does one person yearn for a cultural home while another is perfectly happy having no such home? The accounts of these people provide some hints (and the longer transcripts upon which these accounts are based provide many more hints); but finally we cannot know. I believe that freedom of choice in the cultural supermarket is in large part an illusion: we are culturally and personally shaped in ways that very much shape how we ourselves attempt to shape our lives; we are careful performers within the strict limits of our very exacting social worlds; and the cultural supermarket itself is structured in accordance with the balance of political and economic power in the world, heavily conditioning the choices we make. All the same, however, even if choice is objectively hardly free, we nonetheless tend to experience it as free; when I speak of choice in these pages, it is this perception of freedom of choice, rather than the underlying reality of choice or its lack – which I cannot finally judge – that I am referring to. The nine people whose accounts we have examined tend to believe that they themselves have chosen and shaped their cultural identities; and for all I can know, perhaps to a degree they have.

The themes discussed above in terms of nine particular people are reflected in our ethnographic chapters as a whole. Different constructions of national culture are in today's world more or less items of the cultural supermarket; but Japanese traditional art, American Christianity, and Hong Kong's Chinese identity have especially become so due to the nature of the state's public schooling in all three societies. Japanese public schools, as we saw, have not until very recently taught their students anything about traditional Japanese artistic culture; the traditional Japanese artists have had to sell their arts in the cultural supermarket of Japan, proclaiming their arts as Japanese roots as a selling point. The separation of church and state in the United States has meant that Christianity too is not taught in the public schools as a heritage held in common, but rather is in the cultural supermarket as one more choice to be advertised: *Selling God: American Religion in the Marketplace of Culture*, as one book discussed in Chapter 3 has it.[1] Hong Kong may be subject to increasing Chinese national training in its schools, but this has not begun to happen until very recently, and at present there is great resistance – Chineseness, it seems, cannot be taken-for-granted roots, but only a self-consciously chosen identity, among others that might be chosen. The cultural supermarket in these realms has triumphed. One may try to reinvent roots, as, in different ways, some Japanese contemporary artists, American Buddhists, and

Hong Kong advocates of Chineseness are attempting to do; but as long as these roots are chosen by some and not by others, then they're not really roots: roots, by definition, cannot be chosen but only sensed as given. Some of the people in our three chapters do not recognize this, seeing others in their society as blind to roots and truth, deluded as they themselves are not; but in a socially pluralistic world, this view may be difficult to sustain.

There are other areas of life in these three societies where roots seem indeed real, in the sense of being a given part of one's life, the "way of life of one's people." The Japanese language marks Japanese roots: a Japanese person can choose how to speak – how politely to speak; how many foreign terms to use – but hardly whether or not to speak Japanese in his or her life in Japan; and this speech linguistically embodies Japaneseness and Japanese identity. American civil religion and patriotism serve as a marker of American roots: in the United States you may choose how deeply to feel about your country, and whether to support or oppose your country's policies, but you can't choose the country's flag to which you want to say the pledge of allegiance in school or sing the national anthem at baseball games. The family life of many Hong Kong Chinese – the respect shown to parents; the daily familial interactions – reflects a rootedness in what are sensed as "Chinese values" that for many Hong Kong Chinese may be beyond choice: this is simply the way one is to live. Indeed, to some extent, anyway – with the exception of Hong Kong and nationality – all three of the areas of taken-for-grantedness described above apply to all three societies in common. However, in the three realms we've examined in the preceding chapters, the cultural supermarket is indeed paramount.

The cultural supermarket cannot be objectively apprehended; rather, it looks different from different vantage points, as reflected through the lenses of different national cultures. For Japanese artists, the cultural supermarket is seen to represent foreign – Western – art, with Japanese art identified by many not as one's choice but as one's roots and home, being eroded away by the cultural supermarket's depredations. Some artists, as we saw, lament this erosion while others welcome it, but for almost all, the cultural supermarket seems to represent something from beyond Japan's shores, invading and perhaps swallowing Japan's cultural particularity. For most American religious seekers, on the other hand – except for those few who maintain that America is a Christian nation – the cultural supermarket is not from beyond America's shores, but is itself American: the American belief in the sanctity of the individual pursuit of happiness means that any path down which one may pursue happiness thereby becomes American.

This is how tao and karma, as well as belief in reincarnation, prostrations to one's Tibetan teacher, and recitations of deity chants become, in my earlier words, "as American as God and apple pie." Hong Kong intellectuals' cultural supermarket fundamentally differs from the American cultural supermarket. Hong Kong is not at the center, able to encompass and engulf the supermarket's offerings, but rather at the periphery – at the periphery of two major nodes of the cultural supermarket, bearing the labels of "Western" and "Chinese." Many of those we interviewed seemed to see the Western node as overcoming the Chinese node; they saw Westernness as embodying cosmopolitan choice and the Chinese node as a culturally particular givenness – but because they know too much, they cannot return to that givenness. It remains to be seen whether their children, in an increasingly Chinese Hong Kong, will continue to see the global cultural supermarket, as opposed to Chinese cultural specificity, as their deepest birthright.

The foregoing is linked to different views of East and West, as reflected in our three chapters. For most of the Japanese artists, the world outside Japan was never mentioned except as the West: *mukō* ("over there": the United States, the West) was the comparative basis against which Japan and Japanese art were seen. For some, Westernness and Americanness were serving to destroy Japanese culture; for others, Western arts were the standard against which Japanese arts were seen and seen as falling short; for still others, Westernness and Western art forms were the basis upon which a new Japaneseness could perhaps be constructed. For some American Christians, Buddhism and "the Orient" connoted the unsaved; for others it signified a rebuke to America in its imperializing. For some American Buddhists, on the other hand, "the Orient" – the Himalayas and its Shangri-la – was seen as a realm uncorrupted by the West, and thus a realm of spiritual truth that, unlike anything to be found within their own Western shores, could be trusted. For such people, "the West" seemed to represent modernity, but not a modernity they embraced, rather one that they sought spiritual refuge from. For Hong Kong intellectuals, "Chineseness" and "Westernness" represented different aspects of themselves, signifying what they thought of as tradition and modernity, particular culture and the global cultural supermarket. As all this shows, the West is the cultural supermarket in these people's formulations, and the East is cultural particularity; and, having been exposed to the cultural supermarket, you can't return to cultural particularity. You can't return to a culturally given home, but only to a culturally chosen home.

National culture/global culture

In the preceding pages and chapters, we have looked at the interplay between particular culture and the global cultural supermarket in three settings, examining the words of a few dozen people within each of those settings. The ideas these people express, as I will now show, are very much at play in the world at large today.

Theorists of globalization and global culture have often noted that the world now resembles a shopping mall, a merchandise mart, a supermarket; but different thinkers give different emotional resonance to this development. The advocate of global marketing Theodore Levitt seems to see it as a wondrous new advance:

> Everywhere there is Chinese food, pitta bread, country and Western music, pizza and jazz. The global pervasiveness of ethnic forms represents the cosmopolitanisation of speciality. . . . Globalization does not mean the end of segments. It means, instead, their expansion to worldwide proportions.[2]

The marketing of "ethnic forms" means that they cease being a taken-for-granted given of one's particular culture, to become instead a culturally supermarketed choice of people throughout the world: and this, it seems, can only mean more sales and profits.

Those who discuss not products but people tend to be more uncertain. Theodore Von Laue describes the cultural supermarket as "the human condition at the end of the twentieth century":

> In the global confluence of all cultures, religions, and historic experiences evolved over millennia, all of humanity's cultural heritage has now come into full view. . . . In the great metropolitan centers . . . the world's great religions vie with each other; lifestyles from different parts of the world are on display. The world has become a shopping mart crammed full with humanity's riches. . . . The present generation is born to shop – or at least window-shop – in the world's supermarket, challenged but also bewildered by the choices offered. . . . [3]

In a similar vein, Walter Truett Anderson writes, "What gives so many people a feeling of permission to tinker with the hallowed symbolic heritage of societies – mixing rituals and traditions like greens in a salad, inventing new personal identities . . . picking and choosing what to believe and what not to believe?"[4]

What gives them permission is the fact that roots are uprooted, as we have seen throughout this book. In today's world, as Anthony Giddens writes, "we have no choice but to choose"[5] – choice is not a matter of permission but of necessity, not a matter of liberation but, for many, of *shikata ga nai*. Remember the lament last chapter of the young Hong Kong Chinese man who wishes he had been born in a traditional village: "I'd prefer to be ignorant. I'm corrupted by Western education, individualism." He is corrupted, ultimately, by the cultural supermarket, his knowledge that he has in a taken-for-granted sense no given culture, but must choose who he is. Everyone in this book is so "corrupted," although most would not use that term to describe it; and this, Giddens tells us, is the general state of our age. As Joel Kahn writes in his book *Culture, Multiculture, Postculture,* today culture no longer exists except as a cultural construction[6]: culture can no longer be a taken-for-granted way of life for people living within the capitalistic, mass-mediated world, but instead is a set of self-conscious choices.

It is true, as we saw earlier, that many elements of the taken for granted do remain in most people's lives, such as in language and patterns of familial interaction. Ethnicity also remains, as do social class and gender: these are hardly chosen, as billions of oppressed peoples in societies across the globe can tell us. And yet to a degree, anyway, these too may be chosen, at least by those who have the affluence and leeway in life to be able to do so. Both Mr. Leung and Ms. Chan are "physically Chinese," but he chooses to make his Chineseness the core of his identity, while she chooses to disregard hers.

A number of thinkers label this contemporary situation, of choice without roots, flux without foundation, as "postmodern." Postmodernity is a complex term, with many different definitions,[7] but one prominent formulation is that of Jean François Lyotard, who defines the postmodern as "incredulity toward metanarratives"[8] – inability to believe in any larger story about the meaning of human existence, whether that story is one of scientific progress, religion, or – to stretch Lyotard's conception a little – the dream of national cultural roots, the dream that everyone has a particular cultural home that they naturally belong to. The postmodern condition may be thought of as the state of living within the cultural supermarket, with no truth or roots to guide one, but only one's own tastes, as shaped by the market. As David Lyon has written,

> The postmodern is . . . associated with a society where consumer lifestyles and mass consumption dominate the waking lives of its members. . . . Will the postmodern condition leave us in a

permanent flux of relativity, where all is subject only to the arbi-
trary machinations of the marketplace? . . . Shall 'we' henceforth
discover our identity and integration in the marketplace alone?[9]

The answer, he implies, is clearly yes: all is market-mediated choice.
This freedom of choice, to emphasize once again, is not open to everyone. Zygmunt Bauman has discussed how, while some people in our
globalizing world have the freedom to choose, many more do not:
"Universally adored in the persons of the rich is their wondrous ability
to pick and choose the contents of their lives. . . . Being local in a globa-
lized world is a sign of social deprivation and degradation,"[10] a local
state that continues to characterize the majority of people in the world.
Nonetheless, in the cosmopolitan realm inhabited by the people
described in this book, and by I who write this book and probably you
who read it, this world of choice as to who we are and who we might
become is in large part what we experience today.

Many of the analysts cited above emphasize the unprecedented
nature of this shift from a world of roots to a world of choice, but others
are more skeptical. As Ulf Hannerz comments on recent theories of
globalization, there is a "tendency to resort to hyperbole . . . to tell a
story of dramatic shifts between 'before' and 'after'":[11] there is a
tendency – that the ethnographic snapshots of this book may contribute
to – to think that people once lived in a world of roots and now,
suddenly, have them no longer. Roland Robertson notes that global
culture, in the sense of the idea of humankind, has existed at least since
Karl Jaspers' Axial Age,[12] with the emergence of universal religions
such as Buddhism and Christianity – many people in eras long before
this one had a sense of humankind beyond their own society's particular
way of life. Jonathan Friedman argues that "the global is the true state
of affairs, and the only adequate framework for the analysis of any part
of the world, at least since the rise of the first commercial civilizations"
several thousand years ago; Fernand Braudel has depicted in broad
sweep the global interlinkages of societies throughout human history.[13]
It may be that the spectrum of positions depicted in this book, of some
people claiming cultural roots and others lionizing choice within the
cultural supermarket, has existed for thousands of years: one merchant
in ancient Rome becomes a Christian, declaring the brotherhood of all
believers, while another stoutly insists upon the particular truth of the
Roman gods; one wealthy trader in ancient China decorates his house
with goods from the Silk Road and further afield, while another insists
on the pure Chineseness of his home and his life. Maybe, for at least a
tiny, privileged elite of people throughout history, roots always have

been a matter of the chosen as much as the given – and thus not really roots.[14]

But it also seems true that there really is something wholly new about our era, in the way that the mass media, mass transportation, and capitalism have transformed the way in which culture is experienced. "The media now make us all rather like anthropologists, in our own living rooms, surveying the world of all those 'Others' who are represented to us on the screen," write Morley and Robins.[15] It may be that the very fact that something is on the TV screen renders it not "other" but "self": the Mbuti pygmies and Sufi mystics on the Discovery channel are domesticated by their presence within the screen's confines and by the narrator's mediation. But there seems little doubt that television and other mass media enormously expand our linkage to and choices from the world at large. The cultural supermarket enjoyed by all the people in this book is largely transmitted through mass media: the Japanese artists who can experience the world's arts and musics through the televisions, computers, CD players, and books in their living rooms, the American religious seekers who browse the Buddhist and Christian bookstores for the books and videos explicating their spiritual paths, the Hong Kong intellectuals whose senses of cultural identity are subtly shaped by the reports about Hong Kong in Chinese and world media on television and in magazines and newspapers day after day, week after week. These three groups, in their spectrum of cultural identities, could hardly have existed in an earlier era, without the plethora of ideas and identities offered in contemporary mass media.

Developments in mass media bring more and more of the world to one's living room; developments in travel enable one to ever more easily leave one's living room for the world. Through contemporary travel, Paul Ricoeur writes,

> the whole of mankind becomes an imaginary museum: where shall we go this weekend – visit the Angkor ruins or take a stroll in the Tivoli of Copenhagen? We can very easily imagine a time when any fairly well-to-do person will be able to leave his country indefinitely in order to taste his own national death in an interminable aimless voyage.[16]

Few people are quite so footloose in today's world; but many of the people who appear in this book, from the Japanese musician casually hauling out his aboriginal friend's didgeridoo at dance parties, to the American Buddhist adepts making quick journeys to northern India or to Tibet itself to learn more about Tibetan culture, to the Hong Kong people who have spent years overseas, returning to Hong Kong to wonder where in the world they truly belong, do seem to wander the globe with remarkable ease. Just as cable channels and web sites expand the flavors of the cultural supermarket, so too does the expanding list of worldwide destinations accessible within a day from one's doorstep: one may take home from these destinations not just photographs and souvenirs but aspects of one's identity as well.

But perhaps the most fundamental underlying factor shaping the cultural supermarket as something different from that of the past, a factor underlying both mass media and mass transportation, is contemporary capitalism. Several influential writers on postmodernism/postmodernity interpret this state as a cultural reflection of underlying economic transformations. Fredric Jameson notes how contemporary capitalism may involve "a new and historically original penetration and colonization of Nature and the Unconscious,"[17] as capital enters and subverts all realms of contemporary life, creating the contemporary cultural condition of postmodernism. One may choose one's spouse by her resemblance to a movie actress; one may journey to distant coral reefs, only to be disappointed at how they don't appear as bright and fresh as those that can be seen on television: the commodified world thus becomes the unwitting standard for all of our judgments. "Postmodernism . . . signals nothing more than a logical extension of the power of the market over the whole range of cultural production," writes David Harvey. "Precisely because capitalism is expansionary and imperialistic, cultural life in more and more areas gets brought within the grasp of the cash nexus and the logic of capital circulation."[18] It has long been noted that the free flow of capital erodes all senses of fixed identity: in Marx's words, 150 years ago, through capitalism "all fixed, fast-frozen relations . . . are swept away. . . . In place of the old local and national seclusion and self-sufficiency, we have intercourse in every direction, universal inter-dependence of nations."[19] But by Harvey's analysis, it is capitalism's shift over the past three decades, from Fordism to flexible accumulation, from a rigid mode of capitalism involving mass production and consumption to a new kind of capitalism characterized by maximum flexibility of labor markets and capital, which has been most responsible for creating the postmodern cultural condition. As goes the market, so in its wake, the cultural supermarket; just as in the market there is no standard of judgment other than money, so too in the cultural supermarket there is no judgment other than one's choice and taste – in both, one is no more and no less than a pure consumer by this view.

In a phenomenological sense, the linkage between the two markets is not apparent. The cultural supermarket seems to transcend the economic market in the choices and identities of the people we looked at; their accounts reveal them as striving, struggling, complex beings, rather than supermarket shoppers consuming identity like soup or soap. Yet, in a larger, global sense, the link does seem indisputable: the fact that the world's wealthiest societies seem to be the most fecund sources of the cultural supermarket is hardly a coincidence.

This leads to the question explored in our ethnographic chapters: is the cultural supermarket Western? This is how, as we've seen, the people I interviewed tended to feel. Many of the thinkers cited above reflect this view; Von Laue, for example, whose discussion of the world as supermarket I earlier quoted, arrives at that discussion after a booklength argument concerning "the world revolution of Westernization."[20] While later scholars have been somewhat less forthright about equating global capitalism with Westernization, some offer the same basic view:

> For all that it has projected itself as transhistorical and transnational . . . global capitalism has in reality been about Westernization – the export of Western commodities, values, priorities, ways of life. . . . The category "West" has always signified the positional superiority of Europe, and then also of the United States, in relation to the "East" or "Orient". . . . Historically the West has provided the universal point of reference in relation to which Others have been defined as particular.[21]

One problem with this view is that "Western" is hardly a monolithic category, but encompasses many different societies, ideas, values: are there really any such things as "Western values," "Western ways of life"? Even if the idea of "Western" is used narrowly to describe only the United States, how much cultural power does it really have? As Appadurai has written, "the crucial point . . . is that the United States is no longer the puppeteer of a world system of images but is only one node of a complex transnational construction of imaginary landscapes."[22] However, many people outside the United States do indeed see "the West" as a universal point of reference, and the United States as a cultural puppeteer. I earlier quoted Jameson's comment concerning capitalism's penetration of the unconscious; as a character in a Wim Wenders film said, "The Americans have colonized our subconscious."[23] The French Foreign Minister recently spoke of the American worldwide dominance of "attitudes, concepts, language, and modes of life";[24] the top-grossing movies throughout most of the developed world in recent years have been overwhelmingly American.[25] Certainly in societies such as Hong Kong, and throughout much of Asia, the Japanese influence is very powerful as well; but when the people I interviewed equate the cultural supermarket with Westernization – when they think of "the West" as universal and "the East" as particular and threatened, they seem at least in part to be reflecting the reality they see before them.

The above analysis has emphasized how the cultural supermarket is predominant in the world today; but only a minority of the people I spoke with seemed to think of themselves primarily as consumers in the cultural supermarket. Ms. Clemens and Ms. Chan, as we saw, do think of themselves as living within the world described by Von Laue and Lyons; but most of the people of our earlier chapters don't seem altogether to live in that postmodern world. They live within their particular national culture as well as the global cultural supermarket, and may, like Ms. Ōkubo and Mr. Leung, define themselves primarily in terms of their belonging to their particular culture.

Just as there has been an explosion of books on globalism over the past few years, so too has there been an explosion of books on nationalism. Nationalism was assumed to be a dead subject in the 1950s, but academic interest in the subject has swelled, just as has nationalism in the world: "We inhabit a late twentieth-century world in which many of the old nostrums and doctrines have withered. Socialism has gone; fascism has gone. Nationalism has survived and prospers,"[26] as can be seen in ethnic flashpoints across the globe, ethnic groups seeking to become nations. The nationalism to be seen in this book is more gentle than that to be seen in the newspaper headlines in all their reports of atrocities; but in that it seeks to assert that a culture belongs to a given people more than to any other people, it is indeed a form of cultural nationalism.

There has been considerable academic debate as to whether nationalism is primarily the product of a modernity that manufactures the myth of a common national past, as Ernest Gellner argues, or whether, on the other hand, nationalism rests on the basis of premodern myths, symbols, memories, and roots, as Anthony Smith maintains.[27] This question does not directly relate to this book's investigation; but it does seem likely that the more convincing one's claim of linkage to a past tradition is, the more persuasive one's present identity claims will be. We heard in Chapter 2 from Japanese artists who maintain that their arts represent Japan's roots, two thousand years of Japanese history in the Japanese unconscious. We discussed in Chapter 3 the

American Christians who claim that the United States was founded on Christian principles from which it has strayed, and the American Buddhists who claim that Buddhism embodies the dream of American Jeffersonian democracy. We explored in Chapter 4 the fundamentally different versions of Hong Kong history supporting Hong Kong as a part of China as opposed to Hong Kong as apart from China.

These different historical claims are using their construction of the past to bolster their legitimacy in the present: their drawing power within the cultural supermarket of their societies. If their claims were wholly bogus, then perhaps they would be rejected – there are journalists and academics in all three societies ready to debunk national myths whose invention is overly obvious. But their claims finally do not concern the past's truth, but the present's construction of truth – they are attempting to sell national cultural identity in the cultural supermarket. And as the words of a number of people in this book attest, they are often quite successful in this effort to create a sense of cultural identity that its adherents believe transcends the cultural supermarket.

Scholars in recent years have argued much about the future of national cultural identity. Anthony Smith asserts that national identity "is likely to continue to command humanity's allegiances for a long time to come"; Ulf Hannerz writes that although "there are now various kinds of people for whom the nation works less well as a source of cultural resonance," global culture provides no obvious alternative locus of loyalty; Arjun Appadurai argues that nationalism today is profoundly receding before a range of postnational, decentered identities and social forms.[28] My own view, based on my research and interviews for this book, is closest to that of Hannerz: the nation will remain for the foreseeable future, for lack of any alternative. The people in this book belong to the cultural supermarket but often seek a belonging beyond it, a home; national cultural identity is, for most, the prime locus for such a home. But any such primordial home may be increasingly difficult to believe in, and this is the source of the contradiction most of the people I spoke with are attempting in various ways to overcome. Perhaps the nation is weakening in its hold: but where else can home be found, or imagined?

The conflict between particular culture and global cultural supermarket that we've explored in this book is a conflict over cultural identity, over who people believe themselves to be. But this conflict is paralleled by that of tribalism/nationalism vs. globalism in the realm of politics and state vs. market in the realm of economics. These conflicts are explored in several notable recent popular books. In *The Commanding Heights* Yergin and Stanislaw examine, as the book's subtitle tells us, "the battle between government and the marketplace that is remaking the modern world."[29] Since the 1970s, there has been a shift away from the state as the locus of economic control and toward the market: "All around the globe, socialists are embracing capitalism, governments are selling off companies they had previously nationalized, and countries are seeking to entice back multinational corporations that they had expelled just two decades earlier."[30] This shift has taken place because governments have proved ineffective, they say, in managing the market instead of serving as a referee, their more appropriate role; across the globe, the state has proved less effective than the market in raising standards of living and justly allocating resources. Misgivings remain: "For many countries, participation in the new global economy is very much a mixed blessing. It promotes economic growth and brings new technologies and opportunities. But it also challenges the values and identities of national and regional cultures."[31] But as, most notably among recent events, the East Asian economic crisis has shown, the global economy sweeps over nations like floods over levees.

Another recent book, Benjamin Barber's *Jihad vs. McWorld*, examines, as its subtitle tells us, "how globalism and tribalism are reshaping the world."[32] McWorld, in Barber's formulation, consists of consumer capitalism – "fast music, fast computers, and fast food – MTV, Macintosh, and McDonald's – pressing nations into one homogenous global theme park . . . tied together by communications, information, entertainment, and commerce."[33] Jihad, in contrast, is tribal, racial, and religious fundamentalism, of the kind that is shaking the world from Serbia to Afghanistan. Barber sees both of these forces at war with his ideal, that of liberal democracy: "Belonging by default to McWorld, everyone is a consumer; seeking a repository for identity, everyone belongs to some tribe. But no one is a citizen. Without citizens, how can there be democracy?"[34] He speaks of a possible world in which "the only available identity is that of blood brother or solitary consumer,"[35] and worries how democratic nations can survive between the forces of Jihad and McWorld.

Barber recognizes that McWorld and Jihad are not simply opposites: "Human beings are so psychologically needy, so dependent on community, so full of yearning for a blood brotherhood commercial consumption disallows . . . that McWorld has no choice but to service, even to package and market Jihad."[36] He suggests that we may have, in his evocative terms, not Jihad vs. McWorld – not tribalism vs. globalism – but rather Jihad via McWorld, as market transmits and hardens particular allegiances. This is what we have seen throughout this book: particular culture, in a world of the cultural supermarket, must sell itself within the cultural supermarket to remain viable. There is no tribal or national home apart from the cultural supermarket; rather, that home must be searched for from within the cultural supermarket, and then presented as a home that transcends the cultural supermarket.

I am skeptical about Barber's ideal of democracy between Jihad and McWorld: hasn't democracy itself in today's world become one more form of marketing? Hasn't McWorld, through political advertising and constant polling, rendered partially obsolete the very idea of the citizen over the consumer? But both these books are highly interesting in the ways that they present in economic and political terms the conflict that this book has been exploring in cultural terms.

In fact, the forces of state vs. market, or nationalism vs. globalism are by no means in opposition. As the authors of *The Commanding Heights* indicate, the state is at best a referee and adjudicator of the market; as the author of *Jihad vs. McWorld* tells us, "via" may be as true as "vs." in exploring the relation between the two forces. At the level of discourse, however – at the level of how people comprehend their relation to the world – this opposition remains. Do people feel that they belong to a particular culture, that is their roots and home? Or are people happy to be homeless, floating within the world of the cultural supermarket? This is a central issue raised by the people whose voices we have heard in this book. But before turning to this question, let me consider briefly the shifting nature of anthropology.

Anthropologists and the study of culture

I began this book by discussing the changing meaning of culture in anthropology: the earlier generally accepted definition of culture as "the way of life of a people" is fading in anthropology, I wrote, in that it is no longer fully clear, in today's world of global flows and interactions, how much there really are independent "ways of life of a people." I countered this conception of culture with another: culture as "the information and identities available from the global cultural supermarket". I then sought to combine these two conceptions of culture by focusing on the self and its cultural shaping: on the basis of their taken-for-granted shaping, and the *shikata ga nai* imperatives of the world around them, selves shape themselves from the global cultural supermarket, as channeled and constrained by the people around them.

It seems clear, from the vantage point of our ethnographic chapters, that the taken-for-granted realm among the people we interviewed is only rarely that of particular cultural roots. Even those who spent their early childhoods in a taken-for-granted particular cultural milieu, like the *koto* teacher mentioned in Chapter 2 who grew up surrounded by *koto* music, were thereafter in their lives exposed to different cultural worlds, and thus different cultural choices. Particular cultural roots, at least within the fields of art, religion, and cultural identity, can at present only be chosen from the cultural supermarket by members of our three groups. The taken-for-granted realm in their lives is the principle of free choice from the cultural supermarket; their choices of particular culture they may sometimes seek to justify as roots but these are in fact choices, self-constructions among many that they might have taken from the cultural supermarket. The only thing that is taken for granted, we may say, is that nothing is taken for granted. This is an exaggeration when stated so broadly (one's language is a particular cultural manifestation that is indeed taken for granted by its native speakers), but seems very much true in the three fields we have examined in this book. If particular culture is supplanted by the cultural supermarket, and roots are supplanted by choice, what, then, does this mean for anthropology, the study of culture?

It may be that the idea of distinct, separate cultures, forming a coherent "way of life of a people" always was to some degree an anthropological myth. Perhaps the Zuñi, the Dobu, and the Kwakiutl so vividly depicted by Benedict in *Patterns of Culture*[37] never really did exist in accordance with the neat patterns she offers; perhaps, across much of the globe, anyway, there never really were such clear and stark patterns, neatly defining one group in contradistinction to another. Anthropologists once wrote books such as Radin's *The World of Primitive Man*; now they write books such as Kuper's *The Invention of Primitive Society*,[38] claiming that there never was such a thing as "primitive society," except in anthropologists' illusions. By the same token, anthropologists once wrote books (and to a degree still do) detailing the culture of the Kaluli, the Navajo, the Japanese, the Americans; now they write books such as Wagner's influential *The Invention of Culture*:[39] culture as the invention of symbol-using human beings, but also of the anthropologists themselves in representing and objectifying the cultural worlds they encounter. Another influential recent work, *Writing Culture*,[40] explores in its contributors' various essays how ethnographies, the written descriptions of cultures and societies that are anthropology's basic currency, have by no means been transparent windows into other societies, but have been partial and opaque, shaped by literary genres, institutional boundaries, and inequalities of power, among other factors. All these anthropologists seem to be saying in various ways that anthropologists never really have been able to understand the "way of life" of the people they study in any objective sense:

they are imagining it, inventing it, describing it in conventionalized ways to match the expectations of their Western audiences.

I believe that contemporary critiques such as these have gone too far. In accordance with contemporary postmodern theory, based in "incredulity toward metanarrative" and refusal to believe in any basis for objective truth, contemporary critiques sometimes seem to make cultural knowledge as anything other than solipsism all but impossible (and indeed, in accordance with this, it is a common gibe that some contemporary ethnographies speak more about the subjectivities of the anthropologist than about the lives of the people being studied). The basic question from which these critiques proceed, however, is certainly worth asking: did culture as "the way of life of a people" ever really exist with the degree of objectivity and coherence and homogeneity that earlier anthropologists assumed, and described in their books? Probably not, I would guess, although the question is certainly debatable. In any case, today such culture exists no more for most people in the world.

What, then, should anthropologists study? Some anthropologists study the global flows of culture in conjunction with the real or imagined way of life of a particular people, for example, Japanese and Indian immigrants in California envisioning an Asian home, Sri Lankan Tamil refugees preserving, recreating, and imagining through videotape the home they have left, and the latter-day construction of local identity in cosmopolitan Belize.[41] Other anthropologists have been studying the global flow of commodities, and the meanings they take in different locales, for example the meaning of McDonald's within five different East Asian cities, Japan's remaking of worldwide commodities within its own cultural context, and Australian aboriginal art and the meanings it takes on in the contemporary global artistic market.[42] Other anthropologists have been examining the struggle for particular cultural identity within the contemporary political world, for example, cultural identities in "post-Yugoslavia," and the discourse of race and culture among minority groups in the US[43] – efforts to create and assert a "way of life of a people" from the highly politicized cultural supermarket's shelves.

These books and book chapters – just a few among hundreds that might have been mentioned, for these are dominant themes in anthropology today – are all highly interesting and well worth reading; but even some of their authors might agree that their cultural basis is fragile. (Indeed, the introductions to two recent collections of essays ask exactly this question of how anthropology is to proceed in a world of transnational global flows, in which culture and place are to a large degree unlinked.[44]) Bronislaw Malinowski, anthropology's pre-eminent ethnographer, in 1922 uttered this famous lament:

> Ethnology is in the sadly ludicrous, not to say tragic, position, that at the very moment when it begins to put its workshop in order, to forge its proper tools, to start ready for work on its appointed task, the material of its study melts away with hopeless rapidity. Just now, when the methods and aims of scientific field ethnology have taken shape, when men fully trained for the work have begun to travel into savage countries and study their inhabitants – these die away under our very eyes.[45]

Within a few decades of Malinowski writing this, anthropologists began to turn their attention not just to "savage countries" but to contemporary societies as well. However, Malinowski's lament rings true today, in an even more fundamental sense. Anthropologists have, in the 120 years of the discipline's development, learned how to describe with great subtlety and suitable ambiguity the "ways of life" of different peoples across the globe; but those distinct "ways of life" are now in part vanishing or vanished, swallowed by the cultural supermarket.

If anthropologists today study culture less as "the way of life of people" than as "the imagined way of life of a people," if we study culture not as how people live in their own unique ways, but rather how people use in their own ways common global commodities, if we study not particular cultures but rather particular interest groups in the global cultural supermarket, then it is difficult to avoid the conclusion that the subject and content of anthropology have become quite murky. It is an interesting exercise to ask laypeople what they think cultural anthropology is. Some say that it involves the study of rain dances and headhunters and "primitive peoples," but more often I am told that it involves the study of contemporary cultural difference, for example "how Japanese are different from Americans": the comparison, in other words, of "ways of life of peoples." The new versions of anthropology described above have yet to attain much popular resonance, and indeed, how could they when their focus is so difficult to grasp? If anthropology becomes not the study of "the ways of life of peoples" but rather, "choices from the global cultural supermarket," then the discipline may be in danger of becoming not the study of culture but of fashion – as if a subset of the dreams of marketers and advertising agencies.

A number of anthropologists have attempted to create a theoretical basis for a new anthropology. Eric Wolf and Sidney Mintz have both long advocated that anthropologists be concerned with political economy, the global diffusion of cultural forms as linked to the West's political and economic colonization of much of the rest of the world.[46] Arjun Appadurai seeks to replace the center-periphery model of the West dominating "the rest" with a more decentered model, of the global cultural flows of what he terms "ethnoscapes, mediascapes, technoscapes, finanscapes, and ideoscapes," cultural flows that are not isomorphic but in relations of complex disjuncture.[47] Ulf Hannerz has proposed comprehending global cultural processes through four frames: "forms of life," culture as shaped through everyday life; "the state," culture as transmitted from the state to its citizens; "the market," commodified culture passing from seller to buyer; and "movements," through which people are proselytized and converted to various forms of belief.[48] Hannerz's formulations are similar to those in this book not simply through the prominence given to state and market, but more, because they imply not the large-scale global view of culture, but how people may actually receive and experience culture. Daniel Miller has attempted to redefine culture in terms of consumption. "People are often suspicious of culture defined as a process of consumption, seeing it as somehow less authentic or worthy given its comparative transience and lack of roots"; but this, he maintains, is the most apt definition of culture today: "culture . . . has become increasingly a process of consumption of global forms."[49] Miller, as in different ways do all of the anthropologists cited above, advocates a new anthropology, of comparative modernity and capitalism: of comparative nodes of the cultural supermarket.

In my own small way, I too have been trying to reformulate "culture": in this book I have been attempting to explore the changing nature of culture by looking not at large-scale global flows but at individual people in their formulations of who they are between a particular national culture and the global cultural supermarket. Whether or not I have been successful in this endeavor is for the reader to decide; but the fundamental problems facing anthropology, as a discipline whose subject-matter has become fragmented, remain. What is it that anthropologists study today? The above theorists are all trying, in different ways, to reformulate anthropology's focus, but their impact in reshaping the discipline remains to be seen. While anthropologists struggle to reconceive of culture, cultural studies theorists, most often from disciplines such as English and comparative literature, explore themes such as race and class and gender in the context of domination and resistance in contemporary societies; their mode of investigation has become celebrated, at least in academic circles, but most of them never specify what they mean by culture. And all the while, when one goes to large commercial bookstores and looks in their anthropology sections, one sees books on myths of the American Indians and travelers' tales in Amazonia, but very little that is written by anthropologists; it is as if our abstract musings and theorizings on culture have walled us off from the larger world beyond the academy.

Anthropology, I argue, must be returned to the world if it is to retain its liberating potential. We need another Ruth Benedict, to write a *Patterns of Transnational Culture* for our time. But because of the increasingly elusive nature of culture today, making such a book extraordinarily difficult to write, because voices as persuasive as Benedict's appear only very rarely in this world, and because of the structure of the academic world, where social scientists are rewarded for writing abstract tomes for their peers but not for writing to inform a larger public, this may not happen. I commented to one celebrated young anthropologist, whose recent book is a monument of clever opacity, that ordinary people would probably not understand what she was saying. "I don't write for ordinary people!" she exclaimed, with what seemed to be a sneer. In computer science or engineering or medicine, the theories arrived at by scientists will eventually benefit everyone, but this is not true of anthropology: if anthropologists don't do their best to communicate with the world at large, then they will be ignored by the world at large. This is unfortunate: anthropology, in its descriptions of how culture is being transformed in the world today, continues to be of remarkable importance, I believe. What anthropologists are now discovering about culture and its transmutations needs to be known by everyone in today's world.

For indeed, the transmutations of culture that I've been describing in this book have a direct impact, not just for students of anthropology but on everyone. Where, in this uprooted world of ours, are we to find any sense of home?

Where in the world is home?

"What does it mean, at the end of the twentieth century, to speak . . . of a native land?" asks James Clifford.[50] What does it mean to have a cultural home?

We earlier examined the people portrayed in our three ethnographic chapters, in their senses of belonging to a particular national culture or to the global cultural supermarket. But "native land," "home," "roots," have an emotional resonance that we've not yet considered: one's home is where in the world one most truly belongs. This emotional resonance, this yearning for home if not experience of home, was apparent in a number of the people whose voices we've heard over the last three chapters. Some Japanese traditional artists, like Ms. Ōkubo, feel rooted in a home that their fellow Japanese have forgotten; while contemporary artists like Mr. Kobayashi try to delve beneath a lifetime of foreign cultural influences to find or imagine finding their Japanese roots and home. As long as Japanese nature isn't altogether destroyed, one artist said, at least some sense of Japaneseness can remain; but in a world of concrete expressways and apartment blocks, his Japanese home may be no more than a sliver of nature preserve. Mr. Sasaki was the reverse of this, in wishing his home were elsewhere, wishing that he might have been born in a place that would have allowed him to become a real artist: his Japaneseness he seems to see as a sort of exile from his real artistic home. In their daily commonsensical world, these artists would undoubtedly maintain that of course they have a Japanese home; but in their arts, as we have seen, this becomes far more problematic – many of these artists were indeed searching through their arts for where in the world they truly belong.

Many of the American religious seekers seemed to feel less of a need for home than the Japanese artists, since for them the cultural supermarket may seem synonymous with home. Indeed, it seemed that some American Christians and Buddhists sought to distance themselves from the homes and roots of their childhoods, to formally embrace a new religion and a new home: to be "born again," in a sense, whether as Christian or as Buddhist, in a home of one's own making rather than of one's parents and background. Although the Christians and some of the Buddhists as well might not admit it, it seems that their adult spiritual homes are constructions from the cultural supermarket, which they deny are constructions by seeing them not as matters of personal taste but of ultimate truth. But yearning for home remains: Mr. Sasaki's American equivalent was the young American Zen student who wished she were Japanese. That she and Mr. Sasaki both imagine a home that in reality may not exist is in this context beside the point: the point is that they both dream of a particular home, one that is far from their actual home. Other American religious seekers, such as Ms. Clemens, seek no particular home; or rather, for them having the American cultural supermarket as home means that all the world is home.

Some Hong Kong Chinese seem to feel the need for home with particular poignancy. Mr. Wong's home is Hong Kong, in all its transience,

but Hong Kong was not home for his parents and perhaps cannot be
home for his children either, as it becomes increasingly Chinese. China
can be home for people like Mr. Leung, but not for many of his fellow
Hong Kong intellectuals; it is too alien in its values to serve as home.
Home is thus a problem for many I spoke with, "What do I belong to?
I don't know; I don't know where home is," as one person in Chapter 4
said; another said, as we've seen, that because of his Western education,
it is impossible for him ever to return home – with education, home in
a taken-for-granted world becomes foreclosed. If home is yearned for
by most, for a few homelessness is accepted as a good thing, or at least
as a given. As Ms. Chan tells us with a laugh, "Yeah, I guess I'm homeless. That's a very sad thing, isn't it?" – her professional role may be to
create a sense of national home in young people's minds, but her
personal home is nothing but the world.

Social critics have long commented on the erosion of senses of home in
the contemporary world, and on the need for home. "Modern man,"
write Berger, Berger, and Kellner,

> has suffered from a deepening condition of homelessness. . . . It goes
> without saying that this condition is psychologically hard to bear.
> It has therefore engendered . . . nostalgias . . . for a condition of
> "being at home" in society, with oneself and, ultimately, in the
> universe.[51]

They describe "the pluralization of lifeworlds" that has taken place in
contemporary modernity – or, for that matter, postmodernity[52] –
whereby the multiplicity of lives and identities one might conceivably
hold relativizes any particular identity that one happens to hold: all
cultural homes are in this sense rendered no more than choices from
the cultural supermarket.

Another critic, John Berger, defines home as that place on earth one
was "nearest to the gods in the sky and to the dead in the under-
world":[53] one's roots in this world, and in the world beyond as well.
Home, according to Berger, roots one not just in place but in time as
well: it is one's particular point of being *vis-à-vis* friends, neighbors, and
strangers in space, and ancestors and descendants in time. In today's
world, he writes, this is gone; in a world flooded with choice, "what has
been lost irretrievably is the choice of saying: this is the center of the
world."[54] It is, according to Berger, impossible to return: there can be
no center, in a world of a multiplicity of potential centers; there can be
no home in a world of the cultural supermarket. In a similar vein,
Simone Weil has written that "to be rooted is perhaps the most

important and least recognized need of the human soul":[55] without roots, one cannot be fully human – roots that at the time she was writing she saw as atrophied, vanishing, as is no doubt all the more the case today. "Ours is a century of uprootedness," writes Michael Jackson, in his book *At Home in the World*. "Perhaps it is the pace of historical change that makes a mockery of any expectation that one might ever live, as W. B. Yeats put it, 'like some green laurel/Rooted in one dear perpetual place.'"[56]

Other analysts look upon this nostalgia for home with skepticism. Liisa Malkki has discussed "the romantic vision of the rooting of peoples," a rooting that she argues is patronizing, as if to say, those tribal peoples are rooted to their land, as we modern people are not: "the 'natives'" are thereby "incarcerated in primordial bioregions and . . . recolonized."[57] Zygmunt Bauman has written of the privileged position that those who feel nostalgia for home may occupy:

> In [today's globalized era] so many . . . wonderful and untried sensations beckon from afar, that "home," though as always attractive, tends to be enjoyed most in the bitter-sweet emotion of homesickness. In its solid, brick-and-mortar embodiment, "home" breeds resentment and rebellion. If locked from outside, if getting out is a distant prospect or not a feasible prospect at all, the home turns into jail.[58]

Nostalgia for home, these comments indicate, may be the prerogative of cosmopolitan elites, not shared by the many in the world who are stuck at home. Nostalgia for home and roots, by this interpretation, may serve as an advertisement of one's privileged position in not having home and roots, but being able to consume as one wishes from the cultural supermarket, as most people in the world cannot.

This interpretation has considerable truth to it. Certainly the people in this book who yearn for roots and home are privileged consumers in the cultural supermarket. However, I don't think that their yearning can be wholly explained away by their privilege. The pain that many of these people have felt in their search for home and roots is too real to be thought of as merely privileged nostalgia, the imagined heartburn of affluence.

Some social critics discuss the political dangers of believing in a cultural home. John Berger, though lamenting the loss of home, as we have seen, writes that "the notion of *homeland* supplied a first article of faith for patriotism, persuading men to die in wars which often served no other interest except that of a minority of their ruling class."[59] The author Salman Rushdie argues that the search for cultural roots and home, to the extent that this reinforces notions of cultural boundaries of "us" versus "them," is an unmitigated evil:

> Do cultures actually exist as separate, pure, defensible entities? Is not melange, adulteration, impurity, pick'n'mix at the heart of the idea of the modern? . . . Doesn't the idea of pure cultures, in urgent need of being kept free from alien contamination, lead us inexorably toward apartheid, toward ethnic cleansing, toward the gas chamber?[60]

Rushdie has entitled one book of criticism *Imaginary Homelands*, in which he characterized his controversial novel *The Satanic Verses* as "a love-song to our mongrel selves."[61] Indeed, we are all mongrel selves, he seems to say, having inevitably mixed roots, from here, there, and everywhere; cultural purity, the idea of any pure cultural home, is a dangerous myth.

These political dangers are all too apparent in the world as a whole, as every day's newspaper headlines seem to attest. However, they are apparent in this book only in Chapter 4, where we saw how the Chinese government attempts to instill Chineseness in Hong Kong's people, who tend, at least at this early point in Hong Kong's history as part of China, to resist. Instead I have focused in this book on the phenomenological difficulties of belief in a particular cultural home. I argued in Chapter 2 that in Japan today Japanese roots are not *nō* theater but pizza and jazz, since this is what most Japanese have actually experienced in their lives, and this is true for almost everyone in this book. Japanese musical and artistic roots are now rock more than *koto*, oil painting more than ink painting; American religious roots may for some be Buddhist as much as Christian, just as American cuisine now may feature sushi as much as steak; Hong Kong's cultural mix seems Western and Japanese as much as Chinese in some senses, transnational more than particular. This seems to be the case to at least some degree throughout the developed world today. "You try and convince an Italian child . . . that Topolino – the Italian name for Mickey Mouse – is American"[62] – according to these words, Mickey Mouse, for Italian children, will be part of their Italian roots and home, just as McDonald's and Walkman and Nintendo are part of the cultural home of Japanese, American, and Hong Kong children in common. There is no longer any indisputable particular cultural home in a world of the cultural supermarket; as I have often expressed in these pages, one's particular cultural home can in most respects only be one more construction from the cultural supermarket.

However, as we've seen, one's cultural home and roots may be made as well as born into. We saw how Japanese traditional artists try to recreate Japanese tradition from their arts, just as contemporary artists may strive to recreate Japaneseness from within their imported artistic forms. We saw how American Buddhists strive to create an alternative American cultural home that is Buddhist, just as some American Christians struggle to mold America to fit their brand of Christianity. We saw how some historians strive to shape a version of Hong Kong that is rooted in Chinese culture, just as other historians try to preserve Hong Kong as having its own history apart from China. These different groups are all engaged in competitive rootmaking. They may never be wholly successful; but they are able to convince at least some people that they are indeed bearers of their societies' authentic roots. And people who become so convinced will indeed have a cultural home and roots, to the extent that they can believe in such a thing. In today's cultural supermarket, traditional roots may be uprooted; but there exists a vast array of materials through which roots may be reimagined, proffered in the social arena of their societies, and then, possibly, believed in.

It may be that roots and home will be felt as progressively less necessary in the world. This is the world of the cultural supermarket, the world in which Ms. Clemens and Ms. Chan apparently live, and also the world in which I myself live, as an American in Hong Kong and Japan, linked to the world through mass media and the Internet, having no particular desire to go home again, except for occasional visits. The yearning for home expressed by many of those I interviewed seems foreign to me (even though unwanted traces of American patriotism still seem to stick to me yet, as discerning Hong Kong and Japanese students occasionally point out to me). But then, in a sense I already am home. I am home because of the Americanization of much of the world, enabling me to go about most of my business in my own native language, as most others in the world at large cannot; and I am home because of contemporary technology.

One journalist recently wrote, "Thomas Wolfe said you can't go home again. He was wrong. In the era of the internet and globalization, in the era of . . . universal connectivity, you won't be able to leave home again"[63] – home, via your computer, represents your link to the globe. One's home is in this sense not one's particular ancestral place, but rather no more than a node from which to access the globe. John Berger has written that "only worldwide solidarity can transcend modern homelessness."[64] He presumably meant the solidarity of, for example, Amnesty International more than that of Global Shopping Network or worldporn.com; but all these are inseparably linked in the global world into which we have entered and, barring nuclear or environmental catastrophe, probably cannot leave.

Knowing this, one may spurn all ideas of cultural home, to revel in the global cultural supermarket, whereby all the world is, if not home, at least a home away from home. Or one may continue to dream of home, like some of the Japanese artists, American Christians, and culturally patriotic Hong Kong intellectuals we have seen. You may imagine home from within the cultural supermarket, and try to shut your own and others' eyes for long enough to make it real; and then, if enough people believe it, that vision may become real, until some other vision takes its place. But finally you can't go home again: there's no cultural home left to go back to. This situation may be celebrated or denied, raged at or reveled in; but this is the world in which more and more of us now inescapably live.

Notes

1 On the meanings of culture

1 In F. Baumer, *Main Currents of Western Thought*, fourth edition, New Haven, CN, Yale University Press, 1978, pp. 521, 523.

2 B. Berger, *An Essay on Culture: Symbolic Structure and Social Structure*, Berkeley, University of California Press, 1995, p. 17; emphasis in original.

3 C. Geertz, "The Impact of the Concept of Culture on the Concept of Man," in *The Interpretation of Cultures*, New York, Basic Books, 1973, pp. 46, 49.

4 For a fuller account of the changes in the concept of culture created by Boas against the legacy of Morgan and Tylor, see G. Stocking, *Race, Culture, and Evolution: Essays in the History of Anthropology*, Chicago, University of Chicago Press, 1982 [1968], pp. 110–233, or, more briefly, L. L. Langness, *The Study of Culture*, revised edition, Novato, CA, Chandler & Sharp, 1987, pp. 13–73.

5 A number of books discuss these debates over culture in the history of anthropology. See, to take just a few examples, E. Hatch, *Theories of Man and Culture*, New York, Columbia University Press, 1973; F. Gamst and E. Norbeck, *Ideas of Culture: Sources and Uses*, New York, Holt, Rinehart, & Winston, 1976; and S. Ortner, "Theory in Anthropology Since the Sixties," *Comparative Studies in Society and History*, 1984, vol. 26, no. 1, pp. 126–66.

6 This concept of culture has been stated in many places, but one classic formulation is that of M. Herskovits, *Man and His Works*, New York, Alfred A. Knopf, 1948, p. 29.

7 R. Benedict, *Patterns of Culture*, New York, Mentor, 1934; C. Geertz, "'From the Native's Point of View': On the Nature of Anthropological Understanding," in *Local Knowledge: Further Essays in Interpretive Anthropology*, New York, Basic Books, 1983.

8 British social anthropology, the other mainstream of anthropological thought in the first half of the twentieth century, tended to define itself not as the study of culture but of comparative social structure. As wrote the key figure in British social anthropology, "You cannot have a science of culture. You can study culture only as a characteristic of a social system" (A. R. Radcliffe-Brown, *A Natural Science of Society*, Glencoe, IL, Free Press, 1957, p. 106). In recent years, however, these different anthropological currents seem in large part to have merged.

9 M. Mead, "A New Preface," in R. Benedict, *Patterns of Culture*, Boston, MA, Houghton Mifflin, 1959, p. vii.

10 R. Brightman, "Forget Culture: Replacement, Transcendence, Relexification," *Cultural Anthropology*, 1995, vol. 10, no. 4, p. 510.
11 U. Hannerz, "Scenarios for Peripheral Cultures," in A. King (ed.), *Culture, Globalization, and the World System: Contemporary Conditions for the Representation of Identity*, Minneapolis, University of Minnesota Press, 1997, p. 107.
12 J. F. Lyotard, *The Postmodern Condition: A Report on Knowledge*, trans. G. Bennington and B. Massumi, Minneapolis, University of Minnesota Press, 1984, p. 76.
13 J. Forrester, "Harley Dreams," *Eastern Express*, 20 September 1994.
14 When I started thinking about the ideas in this book, I thought that the term "cultural supermarket" was my own, but I have since found it to have been used by others – hardly surprising, considering how aptly it describes aspects of the world today. Perhaps the earliest use of the term "supermarket" in relation to culture is that of T. H. Von Laue, in his *The World Revolution of Westernization: The Twentieth Century in Global Perspective*, New York, Oxford University Press, 1987, pp. 339, 341. The first direct use of the term "cultural supermarket" that I have come across is that of S. Hall, in "The Question of Cultural Identity," in S. Hall, D. Held, and T. McGrew (eds), *Modernity and its Futures*, Cambridge, Polity Press, 1992, p. 303. There are probably other places in which the term has been used that I have missed.
15 This important term is B. Anderson's, in his book *Imagined Communities*, revised edition, London, Verso, 1991.
16 Some theorists sidestep these conflicting concepts by defining culture as "the socially learned ways of living found in human societies" (M. Harris, *Theories of Culture in Postmodern Times*, Walnut Creek, CA, Altamira, 1999, p. 19) – a definition that encompasses both our concepts of culture. See U. Hannerz, *Transnational Connections: Culture, People, Places*, London, Routledge, 1996, pp. 30–43, for a discussion of the tension between concepts of culture as "enduring collectivities" – "ways of life of peoples," in our terms – and culture as what is universally human, which is what Harris's definition refers to.
17 E. Bruner and B. Kirshenblatt-Gimblett, "Maasai on the Lawn: Tourist Realism in East Africa," *Cultural Anthropology*, 1994, vol. 9, no. 4, p. 457.
18 C. Geertz, *After the Fact: Two Countries, Four Decades, One Anthropologist*, Cambridge, MA, Harvard University Press, 1995, p. 21.
19 R. Benedict, *The Chrysanthemum and the Sword*, Boston, MA, Houghton Mifflin, 1946.
20 Anderson, *Imagined Communities*; E. Hobsbawn and T. Ranger (eds), *The Invention of Tradition*, Cambridge, Cambridge University Press, 1983.
21 As quoted in F. Buell, *National Culture and the New Global System*, Baltimore, MD, Johns Hopkins University Press, 1994, p. 28. The argument that nationalism – the principle that "similarity of culture is the basic social bond" – is a product of the modern world that was largely lacking in earlier ages, is set forth forcefully by E. Gellner in his book *Nationalism*, London, Weidenfeld & Nicolson, 1997.
22 A. Shapiro, *We're Number One: Where America Stands – and Falls – in the New World Order*, New York, Vintage, 1992, p. 43.
23 E. Gellner, *Nations and Nationalism*, Oxford, Basil Blackwell, 1983, p. 6.
24 J. Weatherford, *Savages and Civilization*, New York, Crown, 1994, p. 236.

25 It is erosions such as this which lead A. Appadurai to write that "the nation-state, as a complex modern political form, is on its last legs" (in *Modernity at Large: Cultural Dimensions of Globalization*, Minneapolis, University of Minnesota Press, 1996, p. 19). Other analysts are more skeptical about the state's imminent demise; but certainly the power of the state is lessening, as we further discuss in Chapter 5.

26 C. Geertz, " 'From the Native's Point of View': On the Nature of Anthropological Understanding," in *Local Knowledge*, p. 59.

27 D. Kondo, *Crafting Selves: Power, Gender, and Discourses of Identity in a Japanese Workplace*, Chicago, University of Chicago Press, 1990, pp. 26, 37.

28 R. J. Lifton, *The Protean Self*, New York, Basic Books, 1993, pp. 1, 17.

29 M. Sarup, *Identity, Culture, and the Postmodern World*, Athens, GA, University of Georgia Press, 1996, p. 125.

30 P. Bourdieu, *Outline of a Theory of Practice*, trans. R. Nice, Cambridge, Cambridge University Press, 1977.

31 P. Berger and T. Luckmann, *The Social Construction of Reality: A Treatise in the Sociology of Knowledge*, New York, Doubleday Anchor, 1966, p. 59.

32 E. Becker, *The Birth and Death of Meaning*, second edition, New York, Free Press, 1971, p. 148.

33 S. Hall, "Introduction: Who Needs Identity?" in S. Hall and P. du Gay (eds), *Questions of Cultural Identity*, London, Sage, 1996, p. 6.

34 A. Giddens, *Modernity and Self-identity: Self and Society in the Late Modern Age*, Stanford, CA, Stanford University Press, 1991, pp. 53, 54.

35 D. Harvey, *The Condition of Postmodernity*, Oxford, Basil Blackwell, 1989, pp. 299–300.

36 R. Bocock, *Consumption*, London, Routledge, 1993, p. 10.

37 See D. Howes (ed.), *Cross-cultural Consumption: Global Markets, Local Realities*, London, Routledge, 1996. Doraemon, by way of explanation for Western readers, is a Japanese cartoon cat well known throughout East Asia.

38 P. Bourdieu, *Distinction: A Social Critique of the Judgement of Taste*, trans. R. Nice, London, Routledge & Kegan Paul, 1984.

39 At a few points in Chapters 2 and 3 I also bring in the words of Japanese artists and American religious seekers whom I interviewed in 1989–91, in my earlier research on what makes life worth living in Japan and the United States (G. Mathews, *What Makes Life Worth Living? How Japanese and Americans Make Sense of Their Worlds*, Berkeley, University of California Press, 1996). Indeed, several of the people I interviewed were the same in the two projects.

40 See A. Cohen, *Self Consciousness: An Alternative Anthropology of Identity*, London, Routledge, 1994, for a book-length argument as to the importance of the individual self in anthropological analysis.

41 See E. Goffman, *The Presentation of Self in Everyday Life*, New York, Doubleday Anchor, 1959.

2 What in the world is Japanese?

1 R. Smith, *Japanese Society: Tradition, Self, and the Social Order*, Cambridge, Cambridge University Press, 1983, p. 36.

2 R. Tsunoda *et al.* (eds), *Sources of Japanese Tradition*, vol. 1, New York, Columbia University Press, 1964 [1958], p. 92.

3   See P. Mason, *History of Japanese Art*, New York, Harry N. Abrams, 1993, among many other books describing the history of Japanese traditional art *vis-à-vis* China.

4   In Tsunoda *et al.*, *Sources of Japanese Tradition*, vol. 1, pp. 395, 397.

5   H. P. Varley, *Japanese Culture: A Short History*, Tokyo, Charles E. Tuttle, 1973, p. 155.

6   D. Waterhouse, "Music, Western," *Kodansha Encyclopedia of Japan*, Tokyo, Kodansha, 1983.

7   R. Smith, "The Moving Target: Japanese Culture Reconsidered," *Comparative Civilizations Review*, 1990, no. 23, pp. 15–16.

8   M. Creighton, "The *Depāto*: Merchandising the West While Selling Japaneseness," in J. Tobin (ed.), *Remade in Japan: Everyday Life and Consumer Taste in a Changing Society*, New Haven, CN, Yale University Press, 1992, p. 53.

9   M. Ivy, *Discourses of the Vanishing: Modernity, Phantasm, Japan*, Chicago, University of Chicago Press, 1995.

10 H. Befu, "Nationalism and *Nihonjinron*," in H. Befu (ed.), *Cultural Nationalism in East Asia: Representation and Identity*, Berkeley, University of California Institute of East Asian Studies, 1993.

11 See K. Yoshino, *Cultural Nationalism in Contemporary Japan: A Sociological Enquiry*, London, Routledge, 1992, for a discussion of how Japanese businessmen and educators, influenced by *nihonjinron*, conceive of their Japaneseness.

12 G. Mathews, *What Makes Life Worth Living? How Japanese and Americans Make Sense of Their Worlds*, Berkeley, University of California Press, 1996.

13 All names of people I interviewed in this book are pseudonyms.

14 Ms. Ōkubo was stared at in the morning, but not in the evening. This is because bar proprietors and bar hostesses often wear kimono, one of the few areas of Japanese life in which kimono are still worn; those who saw Ms. Ōkubo in the evening would assume that she was off to work at a bar.

15 D. Waterhouse, "Dance, traditional," *Kodansha Encyclopedia of Japan*, Tokyo, Kodansha, 1983.

16 Y. Aida, *Nihonjin no wasuremono* [The things Japanese have forgotten], Tokyo, PHP kenkyūjo, 1994.

17 E. Kikkawa, *Nihon ongaku no seikaku* [The character of Japanese music], Tokyo, Ongaku no tomosha, 1979.

18 This trend is mentioned in the most recent edition of W. Malm's well-known ethnomusicology textbook, *Music Cultures of the Pacific, the Near East, and Asia*, third edition, Upper Saddle River, NJ, Prentice Hall, 1996, p. 245.

19 K. Lawrence, "Modern composer instrumental in liberating the staid shakuhachi," *Japan Times*, 22 December 1995.

20 T. S. Lebra, *Japanese Patterns of Behavior*, Honolulu, University of Hawaii Press, 1976, p. 88.

21 K. Yoshino, in *Cultural Nationalism*, pp. 27–32, argues that the emphasis on "race" and "blood" among Japanese commentators does not necessarily indicate genetic determinism; "blood" may in their words serve more as a metaphor for culture than as a determinant of culture. This seems generally true; but at least a few of the artists I interviewed seemed to mean "blood" quite literally, as a genetic determinant of culture.

22 A. Kerr, *Lost Japan*, Melbourne, Lonely Planet, 1996, author's trans. of *Utsukushiki nippon no zanzo*, Tokyo: Shinchōsha.

23 M. Takeuchi and S. Kisaragi, *Hōgaku, hōbu* [Japanese music and dance], Tokyo, Iwanami shoten, 1996, pp. 80–1.

24 S. Yui, *Ikite iru jazu shi* [The living history of jazz], Tokyo, Shinko Music, 1988, pp. 294–5.

25 S. Nicholson, *Jazz: The 1980s Resurgence*, New York, Da Capo, 1995, p. 346.

26 S. Yui, *Ikite iru jazu shi*, pp. 277–80.

27 H. Becker, *Art Worlds*, Berkeley, University of California Press, 1982, pp. 331–2.

28 Y. Iwanami, *Kodawari "jazu" nōto* [Opinionated jazz notes], Tokyo, Rippū shobō, 1993, pp. 75–6.

29 M. Weber, *The Protestant Ethic and the Spirit of Capitalism*, trans. T. Parsons, New York, Charles Scribner's Sons, 1958 [1920–1], pp. 14–15.

30 As quoted in M. Kawakita, *Modern Currents in Japanese Art*, trans. C. Terry, New York, Weatherhill, 1974, p. 86.

31 Both quoted in N. Strauss, "Japan's Pop Music Scene: Tomorrow, the World?" *International Herald Tribune*, 15 July 1998.

32 As quoted in ibid.

33 K. Motoe, "Distance and Japanese Art," *Flash Art*, April–May 1985, no. 122, p. 61.

34 P. Fisher, "Music World of Asia Coming to You Live by Satellite," *Japan Times*, 9 June 1995.

35 G. Fazio, "Consciousness with a Beat," *Japan Times*, 30 November 1996.

36 K. Ohmae, *The Borderless World*, New York, HarperBusiness, 1990.

37 As quoted in A. Munroe, "*Hinomaru Illumination*: Japanese Art of the 1990s," in A. Munroe *et al.*, *Japanese Art After 1945: Scream Against the Sky*, New York, Harry N. Abrams, 1994, p. 347.

38 Ibid., p. 341.

39 Ibid., p. 342.

40 The Ainu are the aboriginal people who lived in northern Japan before the Japanese arrived; they now live primarily in Hokkaido, Japan's northern island. They are roughly comparable to the Native American Indians in the United States.

41 J. Pareles, "Where Music is a Chunk of Information," *International Herald Tribune*, 27 March 1996.

42 For a lengthy discussion of this, see *On stāji* [On stage], editorial staff, *Nihon rokku taikei* [A complete history of Japanese rock], two vols, Tokyo, Byakuya shobō, 1990.

43 Okinawan *min'yō* has of late had considerable impact on some forms of Japanese rock; but such folk music can't really be considered a marker of Japaneseness for most Japanese.

44 One highly interesting such work is Yamamoto Hōzan's 1984 recording "Breath" (Denon/Nippon Columbia 38C38-7281), available on CD.

45 S. Yui, *Ikite iru jazu shi*, pp. 295–6.

46 Ibid., p. 302.

47 As quoted in J. Clewley, "Enka, Okinawa, and the Masters of Clone: The Japanese are Coming!" in S. Broughton *et al.* (eds), *World Music: The Rough Guide*, London, Penguin, 1995, p. 465.

48 N. Wakabayashi, *Gendai bijutsu nyūmon* [An introduction to contemporary art], Tokyo, Takarajimasha, 1987, p. 188.

49 A. Munroe, "*The Laws of Situation*: Mono-ha and Beyond the Sculptural Paradigm," in A. Munroe *et al.*, *Japanese Art After 1945*, p. 266.

50 As recounted in R. McGregor, *Japan Swings: Politics, Culture and Sex in the New Japan*, Singapore, Butterworth-Heinemann Asia, 1996, pp. 38–9.

51 These terms are not fully translatable, but Japanese–English dictionaries offer these glosses: *iki* refers to "smartness; stylishness; chic"; *wabi* refers to "taste for simplicity and quiet"; and *sabi* refers to "patina; an antique look . . . elegant simplicity."

52 N. Sugawara, *Nihon no gendai bijutsu* [Contemporary Japanese art], Tokyo, Maruzen, 1995, p. 30.

53 Ibid., p. 105.

54 Ibid., p. 145.

55 Hokkaido is Japan's northernmost island. The fact that this artist would discuss Hokkaido's snow in the context of Japaneseness calls into question such common Japaneseness: in Japan's southern regions, it never snows. Thus, is there really a common Japanese climate and landscape, as opposed to everywhere else?

56 J. Watson (ed.), *Golden Arches East: McDonald's in East Asia*, Stanford, CA, Stanford University Press, 1997.

3 What in the world is American?

1 The term "America" is a misnomer in referring to the United States, since this term applies equally to Latin America. Nonetheless, this is the way in which the Americans I interviewed referred to their society. While being fully aware of the problems of this usage, I repeat it in this chapter. I don't seek to analyze the United States as an objective entity in this chapter; rather, I seek to understand the cultural conceptions of the people I interviewed of the society they live in, which they call "America."

2 H. Stout, "Work and Order in Colonial New England," in N. Hatch and M. Noll (eds), *The Bible in America: Essays in Cultural History*, New York, Oxford University Press, 1982, p. 19.

3 S. Bercovitch, *The Puritan Origins of the American Self*, New Haven, CN, Yale University Press, 1975, p. 108.

4 P. Miller quoted in N. Hatch and M. Noll (eds), "Introduction," in *The Bible in America*, pp. 5–6.

5 M. Noll, "The Image of the United States as a Biblical Nation," in N. Hatch and M. Noll (eds), *The Bible in America*, p. 39.

6 J. Turner, *Without God, Without Creed: The Origins of Unbelief in America*, Baltimore, MD, Johns Hopkins University Press, 1985, pp. 141, 171.

7 R. L. Moore, *Selling God: American Religion in the Marketplace of Culture*, New York, Oxford University Press, 1994, p. 43.

8 G. Wacker, "The Demise of Biblical Civilization," in N. Hatch and M. Noll (eds), *The Bible in America*, p. 121.

9 A. Shapiro, *We're Number One: Where America Stands – and Falls – in the New World Order*, New York, Vintage, 1992, p. 40 offers statistics showing that 98 percent of Americans believe in God; L. Harris, *Inside America*, New

York, Vintage, 1987, p. 67, shows that 95 percent of Americans believe in God; R. Stark and W. S. Bainbridge, in *The Future of Religion: Secularization, Revival, and Cult Formation*, Berkeley, University of California Press, 1985, p. 79, show that 84 percent of Americans believe in God. Much of this difference seems to relate to the particular way in which the question of belief is phrased.

10 A number of recent surveys have called into question the strength of American religious belief. See, for example, the research of C. K. Hadaway, P. L. Marler, and M. Chaves ("What the Polls Don't Show: A Closer Look at U.S. Church Attendance," *American Sociological Review*, 1993, vol. 58, pp. 741–52), which shows that despite the claims of the vast majority of Americans to believe in God, no more than 20 percent acually attend church or synagogue.

11 The phrase is R. Bellah's, from his well-known essay "Civil Religion in America," in *Beyond Belief: Essays on Religion in a Post-Traditional World*, New York, Harper & Row, 1970.

12 R. Stark and W. S. Bainbridge, *The Future of Religion*, p. 41.

13 This statement is from "Buddha in the Market: An Interview with Korean Zen Master Samu Sunim," *Tricycle: The Buddhist Review*, fall 1995, p. 91.

14 Quoted in R. L. Moore, *Selling God*, p. 249.

15 Ibid., p. 256.

16 B. Kosmin and S. Lachman, *One Nation Under God: Religion in Contemporary American Society*, New York, Crown, 1993, p. 20.

17 R. Bocock, *Consumption*, London, Routledge, 1993, p. 10.

18 H. Lindsey, *The Final Battle*, Palos Verdes, CA, Western Front, 1995, pp. 214–15.

19 M. Horton, *Made in America: The Shaping of Modern American Evangelism*, Grand Rapids, MI, Baker, 1991, pp. 15–37.

20 Both quotes are from J. D. Hunter, *Culture Wars: The Struggle to Define America*, New York: Basic Books, 1991, p. 113.

21 G. Bauer, *Our Hopes, Our Dreams: A Vision for America*, Colorado Springs, CO, Focus on the Family, 1996, p. 24.

22 See, for more comprehensive discussion of contemporary American religion, two earlier-cited books, R. Stark and W. S. Bainbridge, *The Future of Religion*, and B. Kosmin and S. Lachman, *One Nation Under God*.

23 P. Little, *Know Why You Believe*, third edition, Downers Grove, IL, Intervarsity Press, 1988, pp. 146, 147; emphasis in original.

24 B. Kosmin and S. Lachman, *One Nation Under God*, p. 158.

25 P. Little, *Know Why You Believe*, third edition, p. 144.

26 J. D. Hunter as quoted in M. Horton, *Made in America*, p. 56.

27 G. Jesson, "The Train Wreck of Truth and Knowledge," in A. Crippen II (ed.), *Reclaiming the Culture: How You Can Protect Your Family's Future*, Colorado Springs, CO, Focus on the Family, 1996, pp. 45, 63.

28 D. Groothuis, *Christianity That Counts: Being a Christian in a Non-Christian World*, Grand Rapids, MI, Baker, 1994, p. 87.

29 M. Marty, "Religio-secular Society," in W. T. Anderson (ed.), *The Truth About the Truth: De-confusing and Re-constructing the Postmodern World*, New York, G. P. Putnam's Sons, 1995, p. 217.

30 The line between evangelical Christians and liberal Christians is not always clear. Two people I interviewed straddled both camps, in seeming to

express, in various of their statements, both that Christianity offered the world's one truth, and that the world's religions all bore ultimate truth.

31 J. Hick, *Problems of Religious Pluralism*, New York, St. Martin's, 1985, p. 36.

32 See, for example, E. Holmes, *What Religious Science Teaches*, Los Angeles, Science of Mind, 1974, with its liberal sprinkling of quotations from the Bible, the Tao Te Ching, the Upanisads, the Kabbalah, the Bhagavad Gita, and the Koran, among other of the world's religious texts.

33 G. Burk, "Long Time Here!" *Science of Mind*, March 1996, p. 96–7.

34 "Personal Affirmations," *Science of Mind*, March 1996, p. 2.

35 One version is recounted in J. Kornfield, "Is Buddhism Changing in North America?" in D. Morreale (ed.), *Buddhist America: Centers, Retreats, Practices*, Santa Fe, NM, John Muir Press, 1988,pp. xi–xii.

36 Ibid., pp. xii–xvi.

37 R. Kornman, "Vajrayana: The Path of Devotion," in D. Morreale (ed.), *Buddhist America*, p. 200.

38 M. McLeod, "Himalayan Stories," *Shambhala Sun*, September 1994.

39 See, for example, D. Lopez Jr., *Prisoners of Shangri-la: Tibetan Buddhism and the West*, Chicago, University of Chicago Press, 1998.

40 C. Trungpa, *Cutting Through Spiritual Materialism*, Boston, MA, Shambhala, 1973.

41 "Power, Sex and Democracy: Modern Problems in the Teacher–Student Relationship," *Shambhala Sun*, May 1995, p. 35.

42 C. Trungpa, *Cutting Through Spiritual Materialism*, p. 63.

43 C. Trungpa, *Journey Without Goal: The Tantric Wisdom of the Buddha*, Boston, Shambhala, 1985, p. 5.

44 S. Butterfield, *The Double Mirror: A Skeptical Journey into Buddhist Tantra*, Berkeley,CA, North Atlantic, 1994, p. 10.

45 "Reincarnation: A Debate: Batchelor vs. Thurman," *Tricycle: The Buddhist Review*, summer 1997.

46 R. Thurman, "The Politics of Enlightenment," *Tricycle: The Buddhist Review*, fall 1992, pp. 29, 30, 31, 32.

47 D. J. Khyenstse, "Distortion," *Shambhala Sun*, September 1997, pp. 25, 26.

48 J. Lief, "Will the Vajrayana Make the Transition to the West?" *Shambhala News*, September 1996.

49 R. Fields, "Confessions of a White Buddhist," *Tricycle: The Buddhist Review*, fall 1994.

50 b. hooks, "Waking up to Racism," *Tricycle: The Buddhist Review*, fall 1994, p. 42.

51 M. Horkheimer and T. Adorno, *Dialectic of Enlightenment*, New York, Continuum, 1972 [1947], pp. 120–67.

52 V. S. Hori, "Sweet-and-Sour Buddhism," *Tricycle: The Buddhist Review*, fall 1994, pp. 50, 52.

53 "No Right, No Wrong: An Interview with Pema Chodron," *Tricycle: The Buddhist Review*, fall 1993, p. 18.

54 This comment is that of Numazaki Ichiro, in personal conversation. He made a similar point on an online posting: Numazaki, "Re: The West and the Rest," East Asia Anthropologists' Discussion Group, EASIANTH@VM.TEMPLE.EDU, 11 May 1997.

4 What in the world is Chinese?

1 These statements come from P. K. Choi, "Introduction," in P. Choi and L. S. Ho (eds), *The Other Hong Kong Report 1993*, Hong Kong, Chinese University Press, 1993, p. xxxiii; N. W. Kwok, *Hong Kong Braves 1997*, Hong Kong, Hong Kong Christian Institute, 1994, p. 111; K. C. Chan, "History," in P. K. Choi and L. S. Ho (eds), *The Other Hong Kong Report 1993*, p. 483 (emphasis in original); and M. Yahuda, *Hong Kong: China's Challenge*, London, Routledge, 1996, pp. 58–9. Actually, in response to Kwok's claim, only 93 percent of Hong Kong people are Chinese. Hong Kong had, as of March 1999, 485,000 expatriate residents – people with nationality other than that of Hong Kong or China – out of a population of 6.8 million. The largest proportion of these are Filipina, working for Chinese families as domestic helpers.

2 N. W. Kwok, *Hong Kong Braves 1997*, p. 24.

3 K. C. Fok, *Hèunggóngsí: gaauhohk chàamháau jìlíu* [Hong Kong history: teaching reference materials], vol. 1., Hong Kong: Joint Publishing Company, 1995, p. 33.

4 K. C. Chan, "History," in P. K. Choi and L. S. Ho (eds), *The Other Hong Kong Report 1993*, p. 457.

5 Ibid., p. 483.

6 The historian G. G. Siu, as quoted in C. F. Lam, "*Luhkchìnnìhnchìhn yíhyauh tóujyu gèuimàhn*" [Six thousand years ago, already there were native inhabitants of Hong Kong], *Sing Tao Daily*, 2 March 1996.

7 K. F. Au as quoted by A. Higgins, "One Territory But Two Histories," *Eastern Express*, 25/6 November 1995.

8 C. Hibbert as quoted in F. Welsh, *A History of Hong Kong*, London: Harper-Collins, 1993, p. 80.

9 F. J. Lo, *Ngàpín jinjàng yùh hèunggóng* [The Opium War and Hong Kong], Hong Kong, Jaahpyìhnsēh, 1983, p. 42.

10 J. Morris, *Epilogue to an Empire*, London, Penguin, 1993, pp. 194–5.

11 F. Welsh, *A History of Hong Kong*, p. 278; J. Morris, *Epilogue to an Empire*, p. 67.

12 S. M. Yu and S. W. Lau (eds), *Yihsahp saigéi dīk hèunggóng* [Twentieth-century Hong Kong], Hong Kong, Kéihléuhn syùying yauhahn gùngsì, 1995.

13 M. Turner, "Alterity and Abundance: Early Aspirations to Cosmopolitan Lifestyle and Consumer Culture in Hong Kong," paper presented at the Second Annual Symposium on Cultural Criticism, Chinese University of Hong Kong, 4–6 January 1996.

14 See K. C. Fok, *Lectures on Hong Kong History: Hong Kong's Role in Modern Chinese History*, Hong Kong, Commercial Press, 1990.

15 See, for example, S. K. Lau and H. C. Kuan, *The Ethos of the Hong Kong Chinese*, Hong Kong, Chinese University Press, 1988, p. 71, whose 1985 survey found that 45 percent of their Hong Kong respondents felt that politics was "dangerous" and close to 30 percent "dirty."

16 See, for example, M. Roberti, *The Fall of Hong Kong: China's Triumph and Britain's Betrayal*, New York, John Wiley & Sons, 1996.

17 T. Shan, "Tactics Will Backfire," letter to the editor, *South China Morning Post*, 11 August 1997.

18 C. K. Lau, "Visitors to China Find New Hazard," *South China Morning Post*, 22 June 1997.
19 K. Y. No, "New Status Inspires Little Pride," *South China Morning Post*, 1 October 1997; Hong Kong Transition Project, online, http://www.hkbu.edu.hk/-hktp, 1997–9.
20 R. Callick, *Comrades and Capitalists: Hong Kong Since the Handover*, Sydney, University of New South Wales Press, 1998, pp. 146–8.
21 S. Vines, *Hong Kong: China's New Colony*, London, Aurum Press, 1998.
22 "A City in Search of Leadership," *Asian Business*, Perspective, September 1998.
23 E. Gargan, "For Hong Kong, 'Just a Holiday,'" *International Herald Tribune*, 2 October 1997.
24 More than in the previous two chapters, the views expressed in this chapter could conceivably prove dangerous for their adherents in a future Hong Kong. Thus, aside from disguising names, as I have in all chapters, I add further disguise, including, in some cases, details about profession and age and other matters, to make certain that no speaker in this chapter can be identified from his or her words.
25 These survey results come from S. K. Lau and H. C. Kuan, *The Ethos of the Hong Kong Chinese*, p. 178; W. K. Fung, "Public Softens Stance on Handover but Rights Fears Remain," *South China Morning Post*, 17 February 1996; and J. Zhu, H. Chen, and Z. Guo, "Views Across Wide Divide," *South China Morning Post*, 8 July 1997.
26 "'Hong Kong' Identity Is Really a Non-issue," *Hong Kong Standard*, editorial, 3 October 1998.
27 Hong Kong Transition Project, online, http://www.hkbu.edu.hk/-hktp, 1997–9.
28 S. Kwok, "Welcoming Professor Erects Putonghua Language Barrier," *South China Morning Post*, 10 October 1998.
29 J. Watson, *Golden Arches East: McDonald's in East Asia*, Stanford, CA, Stanford University Press, 1997, p. 80; emphasis in original.
30 See, for example, C. Swindoll, *The Strong Family: Growing Wise in Family Life*, Portland, OR, Multnomah, 1991; and P. B. Wilson, *Liberated Through Submission: The Ultimate Paradox*, Eugene, OR, Harvest House, 1990.
31 K. Shek, "*Yáuh dò síugo jùngwok?*" [How many Chinas are there?], *Ming Pao*, 12 August 1995.
32 To refer only to my own institution, some types of training at Chinese University, such as that in Chinese philosophy and Chinese language and literature, seem to emphasize a common Chinese tradition, and the historical depth of that tradition. Other types of training, such as that in anthropology and sociology, may emphasize the invention of tradition, and the political uses to which tradition may be put. This variance is paralleled in the people we interviewed, some of whom saw Chineseness as their taken-for-granted essence, others of whom saw Chineseness as open to question.
33 These statistics are found in *Asiaweek* magazine, which provides every week, in its "Bottom Line" section, statistics for a range of countries on their per capita income adjusted in terms of purchasing power parity.
34 Hong Kong Transition Project, online, http://www.hkbu.edu.hk/-hktp, 1997–9.

35 A. So, "New Middle Class Politics in Hong Kong: 1997 and Democratiza-
    tion," in G. Schmutz (ed.), *Chinese Societies at the Dawn of the Third Millennium:
    Political, Social and Economic Transformations in China, Hong Kong, Taiwan and
    Singapore*, Bern, Peter Lang, 1995, p. 101.
36 Mr. Leung may simply have been trying to defuse potential social tension
    in maintaining that I too could become Chinese; and yet his views are not
    altogether idiosyncratic. Scholars have "often noted how culture, rather
    than ethnicity, features prominently in defining Chineseness" (W. M. Tu,
    "Cultural China," in W. M. Tu (ed.), *The Living Tree: The Changing Meaning
    of Being Chinese Today*, Stanford, CA, Stanford University Press, 1994, p. 3),
    and non-Chinese groups have been assimilated into Chineseness throughout
    history. Nonetheless, a white or black foreigner proclaiming Chineseness
    in Hong Kong or China today would certainly not be taken seriously; a
    basic prerequisite of Chineseness in these societies is that one must appear
    "physically Chinese."
37 In 1998, a Hong Kong legislator demanded that during the economic down-
    turn Filipina maids be made to work 16 hours a day. (See N. Constable,
    Maid to Order in Hong Kong: Stories of Filipina Workers, Ithaca, NY, Cornell
    University Press, 1997, for a detailed account of the difficult situation of
    Filipinas in Hong Kong.) A series of *South China Morning Post* articles in late
    1998 and early 1999 showed how at bars and nightclubs, Indians are
    charged more than Chinese or Caucasians. In March 1999, it was revealed
    that South Asians – Indians, Pakistanis, Nepalese, Bangladishis – were 367
    times more likely to be body-searched upon entering Hong Kong than
    were Westerners, despite the fact that the almost 9,000 searches conducted
    the previous year led to only three discoveries of drugs (G. Schloss,
    "Torment of Airport Body Searches," *South China Morning Post*, 21 March
    1999).
38 V. Chiu, "Vanguard of a Mainland Elite," *South China Morning Post*,
    4 August 1997. The article uses a different romanization system of Canto-
    nese to the one I use; I substitute the term "Ah Chan" for its "Ah Tsarn."
39 D. Ho quoted in S. Kwok, "Migrants From China Rude, Dirty: Poll," *South
    China Morning Post*, 10 March 1997.
40 A. Cheung, "Cultural Conflict," *Asiaweek*, 28 June 1996.
41 See C. K. Lau, *Hong Kong's Colonial Legacy: A Hong Kong Chinese's View of the
    British Heritage*, Hong Kong, Chinese University Press, 1997.
42 W. Szeto, "ICAC Teaches Migrants the Evils of Bribes," *South China
    Morning Post*, 2 August 1997.
43 S. Burton, "Hong Kong Surprise," *Newsweek* (Asia Edition), 6 July 1998.
44 The first of these quotations comes from K. L. Wong, *"Seui puihyéuhng
    hohksáang ngoigwok jìngsàhn"* [The need to develop students' patriotic spirit],
    Wen Wei Po, 26 September 1997. The second comes from F. Wong, "Citizens
    Unlikely to Seize the Day," *South China Morning Post*, 1 October 1997.
    Because I am citing articles from a variety of different sources, it is perhaps
    worth discussing the character of Hong Kong newspapers. Hong Kong
    English-language and Chinese-language newspapers parallel one another
    in their political coverage although definitely not in their coverage of
    popular Hong Kong culture. Among Chinese-language papers, *Apple Daily*
    is largely against the Chinese mainland government and today the
    Chinese-backed Hong Kong government, *Ming Pao* and the *Hong Kong*

Economic Times are centrist, and *Ta Kung Pao* and *Wen Wei Po*, economically supported by Beijing, are pro-China and supporters of the Hong Kong government. Among English-language papers, the *South China Morning Post* is somewhat more against the mainland Chinese government and the Hong Kong government today, and the *Hong Kong Standard* is somewhat more in favor of China and the Hong Kong government today. The English-language newspapers are, it is claimed, read more by Hong Kong Chinese than by foreigners in Hong Kong, which accounts for their comparatively local perspective.

45 H. Luk, "4 Percent Opt for Chinese Schools," *South China Morning Post*, 24 August 1998.

46 K. F. Cheng, "*Hònhéi siuhàahn lìhngting gwokgō yùléihbāthahp*" [Films are for enjoying leisure, not for listening to the national anthem], *Apple Daily*, 2 October 1997.

47 A. Ho, "Sense of Identity Lacking," *South China Morning Post*, 7 October 1997.

48 "*Jang yuhk-sìhng yúh hohksāang tàahmwah*" [Tsang Yok-sing in dialogue with students], *Ta Kung Pao*, 1 October 1997.

49 Y. L. Lee, "*Jànjing dīk gwokhing*" [The real National Day], *Apple Daily*, 3 October 1997.

50 C. Yeung, "Anson Tells of her Spiritual Return to China," *South China Morning Post*, 13 June 1998.

51 D. Gittings, "Agenda Behind the Patriotism," *South China Morning Post*, 14 June 1998.

52 F. L. Leung, "*Tàmùhn muhtyáuh jìgaak tàahm ngoigwok*" [They're not qualified to talk about patriotism!], *Apple Daily*, 10 July 1998.

53 Y. Lee, "*Wùihgwài jàunìhn*" [Anniversery of the handover], *Apple Daily*, 6 July 1998.

54 M. Pao, "Identity Crisis," *Far Eastern Economic Review*, 9 July 1998.

55 C. J. Lai, "*Ngóh sih jùnggwokyàhn: bātjoi gaamgaai!*" [It's no longer embarrassing to be Chinese!], *Wen Wei Po*, 1 October 1998; committee spokesperson quoted by S. Kwok, "Patriotism Lesson for Four-Year-Olds," *South China Morning Post*, 25 September 1998.

56 H. Ming, "*Jóugwok sàangyaht faailohk*" [Happy birthday, mother country], *Ta Kung Pao*, 1 October 1998; C. P. Ho, "*Fúsàm jihmahn*" [Ask ourselves with a true heart], *Wen Wei Po*, 1 October 1998.

57 F. Lo, "*Néih hing tà bāt hing, góngdahksīk gwokhing*" [You celebrate, he doesn't celebrate: National Day with Hong Kong character], *Apple Daily*, 2 October 1997.

58 R. Callick, *Comrades and Capitalists: Hong Kong Since the Handover*, Sydney, University of New South Wales Press, 1998, p. 85.

59 S. Shiu, "National Day Queues for the Dog-Tired," *South China Morning Post*, 2 October 1998; R. Mathewson and C. Lo, "Police Called to Prevent McSnoopy Stampede," *South China Morning Post*, 1 October 1998.

60 W. Wing, "*Héunggòng dīk yuhtleung*" [The moon in Hong Kong], *Ming Pao*, 2 October 1998.

61 V. Chiu, "Vanguard of a Mainland Elite," *South China Morning Post*, 4 August 1997.

62 As quoted in D. Elliot, "Built to Last," *Newsweek* (Asia Edition), 13 July 1999.

63 C. Y. Cheung, "*Mòhnggei 'daaih hèunggóng*'" [Forget about "great Hong Kong"], *Hong Kong Economic Times*, 22 January 1999.

64 "*Sàn yìhmàhn yìngòi taidouh*" [New immigrants should change their attitudes], *Apple Daily*, letter to the editor, 17 January 1999.

65 "*Sìhngsai hín gwoklihk maaihheung sànsaigéi*" [Prosperity reveals national power], *Wen Wei Po*, editorial, 1 October 1998; L. Chau, *Jànsìhng dīk jūkfūk* [A true blessing], *Ming Pao*, 2 October 1998.

66 J. Leung, "The End of a Free Market," *Asian Business*, October 1998.

67 K. Cooper, "Intervention a 'Blunder,'" *South China Morning Post*, 13 November 1998.

68 M. Ng, "The Dangers of Fealty to the Flag," *South China Morning Post*, 11 September 1998.

69 "O Sinsaang" [Mr. O: a pseudonym], "*Chòih hósāt seunsàm bāt hósāt*" [Money can be lost, confidence cannot be lost], *Hong Kong Economic Times*, 3 September 1998.

70 C. Yeung, "Intervention 'Damaged World Image,'" *South China Morning Post*, 15 September 1998.

71 J. Cheung, "Martin Lee Warns on 'Dangerous' Intervention," *South China Morning Post*, 14 September 1998.

5 Searching for home in the cultural supermarket

1 R. L. Moore, *Selling God: American Religion in the Marketplace of Culture*, New York, Oxford University Press, 1994.

2 T. Levitt, *The Marketing Imagination*, New York, Free Press, 1983, pp. 30–1.

3 T. H. Von Laue, *The World Revolution of Westernization: The Twentieth Century in Global Perspective*, New York, Oxford University Press, 1987, p. 339.

4 W. T. Anderson, "Introduction: What's Going On Here?", in W. T. Anderson (ed.), *The Truth About the Truth: De-confusing and Re-constructing the Postmodern World*, New York, G. P. Putnam's Sons, 1995, p. 2.

5 A. Giddens, *Modernity and Self-identity: Self and Society in the Late Modern Age*, Stanford, CA, Stanford University Press, 1991, p. 81.

6 J. Kahn, *Culture, Postculture, Multiculture*, London, Sage, 1995, p. 128.

7 See D. Lyon, *Postmodernity*, Minneapolis, University of Minnesota Press, 1994, for a good introductory discussion of what postmodernism means.

8 J. F. Lyotard, *The Postmodern Condition: A Report on Knowledge*, trans. G. Bennington and B. Massumi, Minneapolis, University of Minnesota Press, 1984, p. xxiv.

9 D. Lyon, *Postmodernity*, pp. 56, 55, 71.

10 Z. Bauman, *Globalization: The Human Consequences*, Cambridge, Polity Press, 1998, pp. 95, 2.

11 U. Hannerz, *Transnational Connections*, London, Routledge, 1996, p. 18.

12 R. Robertson, "Social Theory, Cultural Relativity and the Problem of Globality," in A. King (ed.), *Culture, Globalization and the World System: Contemporary Conditions for the Representation of Identity*, Minneapolis, University of Minnesota Press, 1997, p. 88.

13 J. Friedman, *Cultural Identity and Global Process*, London, Sage, 1994, p. 3; F. Braudel, *A History of Civilizations*, trans. R. Mayne, New York, Penguin, 1993.

14 Recently a number of books have been published on the cultural identities of ancient peoples: see, for example, R. Laurence and J. Berry (eds), *Cultural Identity in the Roman Empire*, London, Routledge, 1998. In part this may reflect the current academic preoccupation with cultural identity being extended to an earlier age; but this also may indicate a growing awareness that cultural identity was not simply a given in the past, but was in some ways perhaps as problematic as it is at present.

15 D. Morley and K. Robins, *Spaces of Identity: Global Media, Electronic Landscapes and Cultural Boundaries*, London, Routledge, 1995, p. 133.

16 P. Ricoeur, *History and Truth*, trans. C. Kelbley, Evanston, IL, Northwestern University Press, 1965, p. 278.

17 F. Jameson, *Postmodernism, or the Cultural Logic of Late Capitalism*, Durham, NC, Duke University Press, 1993, p. 36.

18 D. Harvey, *The Condition of Postmodernity*, Oxford, Basil Blackwell, 1989, pp. 62, 344.

19 K. Marx, "Manifesto of the Communist Party" [1848], in R. Tucker (ed.), *The Marx–Engels Reader*, second edition, New York, W. W. Norton, 1978, pp. 476, 477.

20 T. H. Von Laue, *The World Revolution of Westernization: The Twentieth Century in Global Perspective*, New York, Oxford University Press, 1987.

21 D. Morley and K. Robins, *Spaces of Identity*, pp. 108, 160, 164.

22 A. Appadurai, *Modernity at Large: Cultural Dimensions of Globalization*, Minneapolis, University of Minnesota Press, 1996,

23 As quoted in M. Van Elteren, "Conceptualizing the Impact of U.S. Popular Culture Globally," *Journal of Popular Culture*, 1996, vol. 30, no. 1, p. 56.

24 "To Paris, U.S. Looks Like a 'Hyperpower,'" *International Herald Tribune*, 5 February 1999.

25 B. Barber, *Jihad vs. McWorld: How Globalism and Tribalism are Reshaping the World*, New York, Ballantine, 1996, pp. 307–9.

26 D. McCrone, *The Sociology of Nationalism*, London, Routledge, 1998, p. vii.

27 Ibid., pp. 15–16.

28 A. Smith, *National Identity*, Reno, University of Nevada Press, 1991, p. 176; U. Hannerz, "The Withering Away of the Nation?" in *Transnational Connections: Culture, People, Places*, London, Routledge, 1996, p. 88; A. Appadurai, *Modernity at Large*.

29 D. Yergin and J. Stanislaw, *The Commanding Heights: The Battle Between Government and the Marketplace that is Remaking the Modern World*, New York, Simon & Schuster, 1998.

30 Ibid., p. 10.

31 Ibid., pp. 384–5.

32 B. Barber, *Jihad vs. McWorld*.

33 Ibid., p. 4.

34 Ibid., p. 8.

35 Ibid., p. 224.

36 Ibid., p. 155.

37 R. Benedict, *Patterns of Culture*, New York, Mentor, 1934.

38 P. Radin, *The World of Primitive Man*, New York, Grove Press, 1953; A. Kuper, *The Invention of Primitive Society: Transformations of an Illusion*, London, Routledge, 1988.

39 R. Wagner, *The Invention of Culture*, revised edition, Chicago, University of Chicago Press, 1981.
40 J. Clifford and G. Marcus (eds), *Writing Culture: The Poetics and Politics of Ethnography*, Berkeley, University of California Press, 1986.
41 K. Leonard, "Finding One's Own Place: Asian Landscapes Re-visioned in Rural California," in A. Gupta and J. Ferguson (eds), *Culture, Power, Place: Explorations in Critical Anthropology*, Durham, NC, Duke University Press, 1997; A. S. Preis, "Seeking Place: Capsized Identities and Contracted Belonging Among Sri Lankan Tamil Refugees," in K. F. Olwig and K. Hastrup (eds), *Siting Culture: The Shifting Anthropological Object*, London, Routledge, 1997; R. Wilk, "Learning to be Local in Belize: Global Systems of Common Differences," in D. Miller (ed.), *Worlds Apart: Modernity Through the Prism of the Local*, London, Routledge, 1995.
42 J. Watson (ed.), *Golden Arches East: McDonald's in East Asia,* Stanford, CA, Stanford University Press, 1997; J. Tobin (ed.), *Remade in Japan: Everyday Life and Consumer Taste in a Changing Society*, New Haven, CN, Yale University Press, 1992; H. Morphy, "Aboriginal Art in a Global Context," in D. Miller (ed.), *Worlds Apart*.
43 S. Jansen, "Homeless at Home: Narrations of Post-Yugoslav Identities," in N. Rapport and A. Dawson (eds), *Migrants of Identity: Perceptions of Home in a World of Movement*, Oxford, Berg, 1998; P. Dresch, "Race, Culture and – What?: Pluralist Certainties in the United States," in W. James (ed.), *The Pursuit of Certainty: Religious and Cultural Formulations*, London, Routledge, 1995.
44 K. F. Olwig and K. Hastrup (eds), *Siting Culture*; A. Gupta and J. Ferguson (eds), *Culture, Power, Place*.
45 B. Malinowski, *Argonauts of the Western Pacific*, Prospect Heights, IL, Waveland, 1984 [1922], p. xv.
46 E. Wolf, *Europe and the People Without History*, Berkeley, University of California Press, 1982; S. Mintz, *Sweetness and Power: The Place of Sugar in Modern History*, London, Penguin, 1985.
47 A. Appadurai, "Disjuncture and Difference in the Global Cultural Economy," in M. Featherstone (ed.), *Global Culture: Nationalism, Globalization, and Modernity*, London, Sage, 1990; A. Appadurai, *Modernity at Large*.
48 U. Hannerz, *Cultural Complexity: Studies in the Social Organization of Meaning*, New York, Columbia University Press, 1992; U. Hannerz, *Transnational Connections*, London, Routledge, 1996. The ideas mentioned in the text are discussed in both books, but for a concise summary see pp. 65–78 of *Transnational Connections*.
49 D. Miller, "Introduction: Anthropology, Modernity and Consumption," in D. Miller (ed.), *Worlds Apart*, pp. 4, 8. See also D. Miller, "Consumption as the Vanguard of History: A Polemic By Way of Introduction," in D. Miller (ed.), *Acknowledging Consumption: A Review of New Studies*, London, Routledge, 1995, pp. 1–57.
50 J. Clifford, *The Predicament of Culture: Twentieth-century Ethnography, Literature, and Art*, Cambridge, MA, Harvard University Press, 1988, p. 275.
51 P. Berger, B. Berger, and H. Kellner, *The Homeless Mind: Modernization and Consciousness*, New York, Vintage Books, 1974, p. 82.
52 Ibid., pp. 63–82. The reader may be confused by the fact that what one thinker calls postmodern, another calls modern. This terminological over-

lap stems partly from the fact that Berger, Berger, and Kellner were writing 25 years ago, before the term "postmodern" had sprung into its current vogue. These designations are not of crucial importance in the context of this book's discussion – they are finally no more than shorthand labels – but one way to think of them in terms of "home" is that if in the high modernity of the mid-twentieth century there was a nostalgia for a cultural home that was felt to be vanishing, in some quarters of late-twentieth-century post-modernity, there is instead a celebration of homelessness. Applying this to the people in this book, Mr. Kobayashi seems quintessentially modern in his search for a sense of home, while Ms. Chan seems quintessentially post-modern in her laughter over having no home.

53 J. Berger, *And Our Faces, My Heart, Brief as Photos*, New York, Vintage International, 1991 [1984], p. 56.
54 Ibid., p. 64.
55 S. Weil, *The Need for Roots*, London, Routledge & Kegan Paul, 1952, p. 41.
56 M. Jackson, *At Home in the World*, Durham, NC, Duke University Press, 1995, pp. 1, 2.
57 L. Malkki, "National Geographic: The Rooting of Peoples and the Reterritorialization of National Identity Among Scholars and Refugees," in A. Gupta and J. Ferguson (eds), *Culture, Power, Place*.
58 Z. Bauman, *Globalization: The Human Consequences*, Cambridge, Polity Press, 1998, p. 121.
59 J. Berger, *And Our Faces, My Heart, Brief as Photos*, p. 55; emphasis in original.
60 S. Rushdie, "Sneakers and Burgers Aren't the Real Enemies," *International Herald Tribune*, 6/7 March 1999.
61 S. Rushdie, *Imaginary Homelands*, London, Granta, 1991, p. 394.
62 The president of Euro Disneyland, as quoted in D. Morley and K. Robins, *Spaces of Identity*, p. 111.
63 T. Friedman, "You Can't Leave Home Again: Life With the Net," *International Herald Tribune*, 20 July 1998.
64 J. Berger, *And Our Faces, My Heart, Brief as Photos*, p. 67.

Select bibliography

Aida, Y., *Nihonjin no wasuremono* [The things Japanese have forgotten], Tokyo, PHP kenkyūjo, 1994.

Anderson, B., *Imagined Communities*, revised edition, London, Verso, 1991.

Anderson, W. T., *The Truth About the Truth: De-confusing and Re-constructing the Postmodern World*, New York, G. P. Putnam's Sons, 1995.

Appadurai, A., "Disjuncture and Difference in the Global Cultural Economy," in M. Featherstone (ed.), *Global Culture: Nationalism, Globalization, and Modernity*, London, Sage, 1990.

——, *Modernity at Large: Cultural Dimensions of Globalization*, Minneapolis, University of Minnesota Press, 1996.

Barber, B., *Jihad vs. McWorld: How Globalism and Tribalism are Reshaping the World*, New York, Ballantine, 1996.

Bauer, G., *Our Hopes, Our Dreams: A Vision for America*, Colorado Springs, CO, Focus on the Family, 1996.

Bauman, Z., *Globalization: The Human Consequences*, Cambridge, Polity Press, 1998.

Baumer, F., *Main Currents of Western Thought*, fourth edition, New Haven, CN, Yale University Press, 1978.

Becker, E., *The Birth and Death of Meaning*, second edition, New York, Free Press, 1971.

Becker, H., *Art Worlds*, Berkeley, University of California Press, 1982.

Befu, H. "Nationalism and *Nihonjinron*," in H. Befu (ed.), *Cultural Nationalism in East Asia: Representation and Identity*, Berkeley, University of California Institute of East Asian Studies, 1993.

Bellah, R., "Civil Religion in America," in *Beyond Belief: Essays on Religion in a Post-Traditional World*, New York, Harper & Row, 1970.

Benedict, R., *Patterns of Culture*, New York, Mentor, 1934.

——, *The Chrysanthemum and the Sword*, Boston, MA, Houghton Mifflin, 1946.

Bercovitch, S., *The Puritan Origins of the American Self*, New Haven, CN, Yale University Press, 1975.

Berger, B., *An Essay on Culture: Symbolic Structure and Social Structure*, Berkeley, University of California Press, 1995.

Berger, J., *And Our Faces, My Heart, Brief as Photos*, New York, Vintage International, 1991 [1984].

Berger, P. and Luckmann, T., *The Social Construction of Reality: A Treatise in the Sociology of Knowledge*, New York, Doubleday Anchor, 1966.

Berger, P., Berger, B. and Kellner, H., *The Homeless Mind: Modernization and Consciousness*, New York, Vintage, 1974.

Bocock, R., *Consumption*, London, Routledge, 1993.

Bourdieu, P., *Outline of a Theory of Practice*, trans. R. Nice, Cambridge, Cambridge University Press, 1977.

——, *Distinction: A Social Critique of the Judgement of Taste*, trans. R. Nice, London, Routledge & Kegan Paul, 1984.

Braudel, F., *A History of Civilizations*, trans. R. Mayne, New York, Penguin, 1993.

Brightman, R., "Forget Culture: Replacement, Transcendence, Relexification," *Cultural Anthropology*, 1995, vol. 10, no. 4, pp. 509–46.

Bruner, E. and Kirshenblatt-Gimblett, B., "Maasai on the Lawn: Tourist Realism in East Africa," *Cultural Anthropology*, 1994, vol. 9, no. 4, pp. 435–70.

Buell, F., *National Culture and the New Global System*, Baltimore, MD, Johns Hopkins University Press, 1994.

Butterfield, S., *The Double Mirror: A Skeptical Journey into Buddhist Tantra*, Berkeley, CA, North Atlantic, 1994.

Callick, R., *Comrades and Capitalists: Hong Kong Since the Handover*, Sydney, University of New South Wales Press, 1998.

Chan, K. C., "History," in P. K. Choi and L. S. Ho (eds), *The Other Hong Kong Report 1993*, Hong Kong, Chinese University Press, 1993.

Choi, P. K. and Ho, L. S. (eds), *The Other Hong Kong Report 1993*, Hong Kong, Chinese University Press, 1993.

Clewley, J., "Enka, Okinawa, and the Masters of Clone: The Japanese are Coming!" in S. Broughton *et al.* (eds), *World Music: The Rough Guide*, London, Penguin, 1995.

Clifford, J., *The Predicament of Culture: Twentieth-century Ethnography, Literature, and Art*, Cambridge, MA, Harvard University Press, 1988.

Clifford, J. and Marcus, G. (eds), *Writing Culture: The Poetics and Politics of Ethnography*, Berkeley, University of California Press, 1986.

Cohen, A., *Self Consciousness: An Alternative Anthropology of Identity*, London, Routledge, 1994.

Constable, N., *Maid to Order in Hong Kong: Stories of Filipina Workers*, Ithaca, NY, Cornell University Press, 1997.

Creighton, M., "The *Depāto*: Merchandising the West While Selling Japaneseness," in J. Tobin (ed.), *Remade in Japan: Everyday Life and Consumer Taste in a Changing Society*, New Haven, CN, Yale University Press, 1992.

Crippen, A. (ed.), *Reclaiming the Culture: How You Can Protect Your Family's Future*, Colorado Springs, CO, Focus on the Family, 1996.

Dresch, P., "Race, Culture and – What?: Pluralist Certainties in the United States," in W. James (ed.), *The Pursuit of Certainty: Religious and Cultural Formulations*, London, Routledge, 1995.

Fields, R., *How the Swans Came to the Lake: A Narrative History of Buddhism in America*, Boston, MA, Shambhala, 1992.

——, "Confessions of a White Buddhist," *Tricycle: The Buddhist Review*, fall 1994.

Fok, K. C., *Lectures on Hong Kong History: Hong Kong's Role in Modern Chinese History*, Hong Kong, Commercial Press, 1990.

——, *Hèunggóngsí: gaauhohk chàamháau jíliúh* [Hong Kong history: teaching reference materials], vol. 1, Hong Kong, Joint Publishing Company, 1995.

Friedman, J., *Cultural Identity and Global Process*, London, Sage, 1994.

Gamst, F. and Norbeck, E., *Ideas of Culture: Sources and Uses*, New York, Holt, Rinehart, & Winston, 1976.

Geertz, C., *The Interpretation of Cultures*, New York, Basic Books, 1973.

——, *Local Knowledge: Further Essays in Interpretive Anthropology*, New York, Basic Books, 1983.

——, *After the Fact: Two Countries, Four Decades, One Anthropologist*, Cambridge, MA, Harvard University Press, 1995.

Gellner, E., *Nations and Nationalism*, Oxford, Basil Blackwell, 1983.

——, *Nationalism*, London, Weidenfeld & Nicolson, 1997.

Giddens, A., *Modernity and Self-identity: Self and Society in the Late Modern Age*, Stanford, CA, Stanford University Press, 1991.

Goffman, E., *The Presentation of Self in Everyday Life*, New York, Doubleday Anchor, 1959.

Groothuis, D., *Christianity That Counts: Being a Christian in a Non-Christian World*, Grand Rapids, MI, Baker, 1994.

Gupta, A. and Ferguson, J. (eds), *Culture, Power, Place: Explorations in Critical Anthropology*, Durham, NC, Duke University Press, 1997.

Hadaway, C. K., Marler, P. L., and Chaves, M., "What the Polls Don't Show: A Closer Look at U.S. Church Attendance," *American Sociological Review*, vol. 58, 1993, pp. 741–52.

Hall, S., "The Question of Cultural Identity," in S. Hall, D. Held, and T. McGrew (eds), *Modernity and its Futures*, Cambridge, Polity Press, 1992.

——, "Introduction: Who Needs Identity?" in S. Hall and P. du Gay (eds), *Questions of Cultural Identity*, London, Sage, 1996.

Hannerz, U., *Cultural Complexity: Studies in the Social Organization of Meaning*, New York, Columbia University Press, 1992.

——, *Transnational Connections: Culture, People, Places*, London, Routledge, 1996.

——, "Scenarios for Peripheral Cultures," in A. King (ed.), *Culture, Globalization, and the World System: Contemporary Conditions for the Representation of Identity*, Minneapolis, University of Minnesota Press, 1997.

Harris, L., *Inside America*, New York, Vintage, 1987.

Harris, M., *Theories of Culture in Postmodern Times*, Walnut Creek, CA, Altamira, 1999.

Harvey, D., *The Condition of Postmodernity*, Oxford, Basil Blackwell, 1989.

Hatch, E., *Theories of Man and Culture*, New York, Columbia University Press, 1973.

Hatch, N. and Noll, M. (eds), *The Bible in America: Essays in Cultural History*, New York, Oxford University Press, 1982.

Herskovits, M., *Man and His Works*, New York, Alfred A. Knopf, 1948.

Hick, J., *Problems of Religious Pluralism*, New York, St. Martin's, 1985.

Hobsbawn, E. and Ranger, T. (eds), *The Invention of Tradition*, Cambridge, Cambridge University Press, 1983.

Holmes, E., *What Religious Science Teaches*, Los Angeles, Science of Mind, 1974.

Hong Kong Transition Project, online, http://www.hkbu.edu.hk/-hktp, 1999.

hooks, b., "Waking up to Racism," *Tricycle: The Buddhist Review*, fall 1994.

Hori, V. S., "Sweet-and-Sour Buddhism," *Tricycle: The Buddhist Review*, fall 1994.

Horkheimer, M. and Adorno, T., *Dialectic of Enlightenment*, New York, Continuum, 1972 [1947].

Horton, M., *Made in America: The Shaping of Modern American Evangelism*, Grand Rapids, MI, Baker, 1991.

Howes, D. (ed.), *Cross-cultural Consumption: Global Markets, Local Realities*, London, Routledge, 1996.

Hunter, J. D., *Culture Wars: The Struggle to Define America*, New York, Basic Books, 1991.

Ivy, M., *Discourses of the Vanishing: Modernity, Phantasm, Japan*, Chicago, University of Chicago Press, 1995.

Iwanami, Y., *Kodawari "jazu" nōto* [Opinionated jazz notes], Tokyo, Rippū shobō, 1993.

Jackson, M., *At Home in the World*, Durham, NC, Duke University Press, 1995.

James, W. (ed.), *The Pursuit of Certainty: Religious and Cultural Formulations*, London, Routledge, 1995.

Jameson, F., *Postmodernism, or the Cultural Logic of Late Capitalism*, Durham, NC, Duke University Press, 1993.

Jansen, S., "Homeless at Heart: Narrations of Post-Yugoslav Identities," in N. Rapport and A. Dawson (eds), *Migrants of Identity: Perceptions of Home in a World of Movement*, Oxford, Berg, 1998.

Jesson, G., "The Train Wreck of Truth and Knowledge," in A. Crippen II (ed.), *Reclaiming the Culture: How You Can Protect Your Family's Future*, Colorado Springs, CO, Focus on the Family, 1996.

Kahn, J., *Culture, Postculture, Multiculture*, London, Sage, 1995.

Kawakita, M., *Modern Currents in Japanese Art*, trans. C. Terry, New York, Weatherhill, 1974.

Kerr, A., *Lost Japan*, Melbourne, Lonely Planet, 1996; author's trans. of *Utsukushiki nippon no zanzo*, Tokyo, Shinchōsha, 1993.

Khyenstse, D. J., "Distortion," *Shambhala Sun*, September 1997.

Kikkawa E., *Nihon ongaku no seikaku* [The character of Japanese music], Tokyo, Ongaku no tomosha, 1979.

King, A. (ed.), *Culture, Globalization and the World System: Contemporary Conditions for the Representation of Identity*, Minneapolis, University of Minnesota Press, 1997.

Kondo, D., *Crafting Selves: Power, Gender, and Discourses of Identity in a Japanese Workplace*, Chicago, University of Chicago Press, 1990.

Kornfield, J., "Is Buddhism Changing North America?" in D. Morreale (ed.), *Buddhist America: Centers, Retreats, Practices*, Santa Fe, NM, John Muir Press, 1988.

Kornman, R., "Vajrayana: The Path of Devotion," in D. Morreale (ed.), *Buddhist America: Centers, Retreats, Practices*, Santa Fe, NM, John Muir Press, 1988.

Kosmin, B. and Lachman, S., *One Nation Under God: Religion in Contemporary American Society*, New York, Crown, 1993.

Kuper, A., *The Invention of Primitive Society: Transformations of an Illusion*, London, Routledge, 1988.

Kwok, N. W., *Hong Kong Braves 1997*, Hong Kong, Hong Kong Christian Institute, 1994.

Langness, L. L., *The Study of Culture*, revised edition, Novato, CA, Chandler & Sharp, 1987.

Lau, C. K., *Hong Kong's Colonial Legacy: A Hong Kong Chinese's View of the British Heritage*, Hong Kong, Chinese University Press, 1997.

Lau, S. K. and Kuan H. C., *The Ethos of the Hong Kong Chinese*, Hong Kong, Chinese University Press, 1988.

Laurence, R. and Berry, J. (eds), *Cultural Identity in the Roman Empire*, London, Routledge, 1998.

Lebra, T. S., *Japanese Patterns of Behavior*, Honolulu, University of Hawaii Press, 1976.

Leonard, K., "Finding One's Own Place: Asian Landscapes Re-visioned in Rural California," in A. Gupta and J. Ferguson (eds), *Culture, Power, Place: Explorations in Critical Anthropology*, Durham, NC, Duke University Press, 1997.

Levitt, T., *The Marketing Imagination*, New York, Free Press, 1983.

Lief, J., "Will the Vajrayana Make the Transition to the West?" *Shambhala News*, September 1996.

Lifton, R. J., *The Protean Self*, New York, Basic Books, 1993.

Lindsey, H., *The Final Battle*, Palos Verdes, CA, Western Front, 1995.

Little, P., *Know Why You Believe*, third edition, Downers Grove, IL, Intervarsity Press, 1988.

Lo, F. J., *Ngàpín jinjàng yùh hèunggóng* [The Opium War and Hong Kong], Hong Kong, Jaahpyìhnsēh, 1983.

Lopez, D. Jr., *Prisoners of Shangri-la: Tibetan Buddhism and the West*, Chicago, University of Chicago Press, 1998.

Lui, T. L., "Social Change: Post-1997 Uneasiness," in C. Yeung (ed.), *Hong Kong, China: The Red Dawn*, Sydney, Prentice-Hall, 1998.

Lyon, D., *Postmodernity*, Minneapolis, University of Minnesota Press, 1994.

Lyotard, J. F., *The Postmodern Condition: A Report on Knowledge*, trans. G. Bennington and B. Massumi, Minneapolis, University of Minnesota Press, 1984.

McCrone, D., *The Sociology of Nationalism*, London, Routledge, 1998.

McGregor, R., *Japan Swings: Politics, Culture and Sex in the New Japan*, Singapore, Butterworth-Heinemann Asia, 1996.

McLeod, M., "Himalayan Stories," *Shambhala Sun*, September 1994.

Malinowski, B., *Argonauts of the Western Pacific*, Prospect Heights, IL, Waveland, 1984 [1922].

Malkki, L., "National Geographic: The Rooting of Peoples and the Reterritorialization of National Identify Among Scholars and Refugees," in A. Gupta and J. Ferguson (eds), *Culture, Power, Place: Explorations in Critical Anthropology*, Durham, NC, Duke University Press, 1997.

Malm, W., *Music Cultures of the Pacific, the Near East, and Asia*, third edition, Upper Saddle River NJ, Prentice Hall, 1996.

Marty, M., "Religio-secular Society," in W. T. Anderson (ed.), *The Truth About the Truth: De-confusing and Re-constructing the Modern World*, New York, G. P. Putnam's Sons, 1995.

Marx, K., "Manifesto of the Communist Party" [1848], in R. Tucker (ed.), *The Marx–Engels Reader*, second edition, New York, W. W. Norton, 1978.

Mason, P., *History of Japanese Art*, New York, Harry N. Abrams, 1993.

Mathews, G., *What Makes Life Worth Living? How Japanese and Americans Make Sense of Their Worlds*, Berkeley, University of California Press, 1996.

Mead, M., "A New Preface," in R. Benedict, *Patterns of Culture*, Boston, MA, Houghton Mifflin, 1959.

Miller, D. (ed.), *Acknowledging Consumption: A Review of New Studies*, London, Routledge, 1995.

—— (ed.), *Worlds Apart: Modernity Through the Prism of the Local*, London, Routledge, 1995.

Mintz, S., *Sweetness and Power: The Place of Sugar in Modern History*, London, Penguin, 1985.

Moore, R. L., *Selling God: American Religion in the Marketplace of Culture*, New York, Oxford University Press, 1994.

Morley, D. and Robins, K. *Spaces of Identity: Global Media, Electronic Landscapes and Cultural Boundaries*, London, Routledge, 1995.

Morphy, H., "Aboriginal Art in a Global Context," in D. Miller (ed.), *Worlds Apart: Modernity Through the Prism of the Local*, London, Routledge, 1995.

Morreale, D. (ed.), *Buddhist America: Centers, Retreats, Practices*, Santa Fe, NM, John Muir Press, 1988.

Morris, J., *Epilogue to an Empire*, London, Penguin, 1993.

Munroe, A. *et al.*, *Japanese Art After 1945: Scream Against the Sky*, New York, Harry N. Abrams, 1994.

Nicholson, S., *Jazz: The 1980s Resurgence*, New York, Da Capo, 1995.

Ohmae, K., *The Borderless World*, New York, HarperBusiness, 1990.

Olwig, K. F. and Hastrup, K., *Siting Culture: The Shifting Anthropological Object*, London, Routledge, 1997.

On stāji [On stage] editorial staff, *Nihon rokku taikei* [A complete history of Japanese rock], two vols, Tokyo, Byakuya shobō, 1990.

Ortner, S. "Theory in Anthropology Since the Sixties," *Comparative Studies in Society and History*, 1984, vol. 26, no. 1, pp. 126–66.

Preis, A. S., "Seeking Place: Capsized Identities and Contracted Belonging among Sri Lankan Tamil Refugees," in K. F. Olwig and K. Hastrup (eds), *Siting Culture: The Shifting Anthropological Object*, London, Routledge, 1997.

Radcliffe-Brown, A. R., *A Natural Science of Society*, Glencoe, IL, Free Press, 1957.

Radin, P., *The World of Primitive Man*, New York, Grove Press, 1953.

Rapport, N. and Dawson, A. (eds), *Migrants of Identity: Perceptions of Home in a World of Movement*, Oxford, Berg, 1998.

Ricouer, P., *History and Truth*, trans. C. Kelbley, Evanston, IL: Northwestern University Press, 1965.

Roberti, M., *The Fall of Hong Kong: China's Triumph and Britain's Betrayal*, New York, John Wiley & Sons, 1996.

Robertson, R., "Social Theory, Cultural Relativity, and the Problem of Globality," in A. King (ed.), *Globalization and the World System*, Minneapolis, University of Minnesota Press, 1997.

Rushdie, S., *Imaginary Homelands*, London, Granta, 1991.

Sarup, M., *Identity, Culture, and the Postmodern World*, Athens, GA, University of Georgia Press, 1996.

Schmutz, G. (ed.), *Chinese Societies at the Dawn of the Third Millennium: Political, Social and Economic Transformations in China, Hong Kong, Taiwan and Singapore*, Bern, Peter Lang, 1995.

Shapiro, A., *We're Number One: Where America Stands – and Falls – in the New World Order*, New York, Vintage, 1992.

Smith, A., *National Identity*, Reno, University of Nevada Press, 1991.

Smith, R., *Japanese Society: Tradition, Self, and the Social Order,* Cambridge, Cambridge University Press, 1983.

——, "The Moving Target: Japanese Culture Reconsidered," *Comparative Civilizations Review*, no. 23, 1990, pp. 15–16.

So, A., "New Middle Class Politics in Hong Kong: 1997 and Democratization," in G. Schmutz (ed.), *Chinese Societies at the Dawn of the Third Millenium: Political, Social and Economic Transformations in China, Hong Kong, Taiwan and Singapore*, Bern, Peter Lang, 1995.

Stark, R. and Bainbridge, W. S., *The Future of Religion: Secularization, Revival, and Cult Formation*, Berkeley, University of California Press, 1985.

Stocking, G., *Race, Culture, and Evolution: Essays in the History of Anthropology*, Chicago, University of Chicago Press, 1982 [1968].

Stout, H., "Work and Order in Colonial New England," in N. Hatch and M. Noll (eds), *The Bible in America: Essays in Cultural History*, New York, Oxford University Press, 1982.

Sugawara, N., *Nihon no gendai bijutsu* [Contemporary Japanese art], Tokyo, Maruzen, 1995.

Swindoll, C., *The Strong Family: Growing Wise in Family Life*, Portland, OR, Multnomah, 1991.

Takeuchi, M. and Kisaragi, S., *Hōgaku, hōbu* [Japanese music and Japanese dance], Tokyo, Iwanami shoten, 1996.

Thomas, H., *An Unfinished History of the World*, revised edition, London, Pan Books, 1981.

Thurman, R., "The Politics of Enlightenment," *Tricycle: The Buddhist Review*, fall 1992.

Tobin, J. (ed.), *Remade in Japan: Everyday Life and Consumer Taste in a Changing Society*, New Haven, CN, Yale University Press, 1992.

Trungpa, C., *Cutting Through Spiritual Materialism*, Boston, MA, Shambhala, 1973.

——, *Journey Without Goal: The Tantric Wisdom of the Buddha*, Boston, MA, Shambhala, 1985.

Tsunoda, R. *et al.* (eds), *Sources of Japanese Tradition*, two vols, New York, Columbia University Press, 1964 [1958].

Tu, W. M. (ed.), *The Living Tree: The Changing Meaning of Being Chinese Today*, Stanford, CA, Stanford University Press, 1994.

Turner, J., *Without God, Without Creed: The Origins of Unbelief in America*, Baltimore, MD, Johns Hopkins University Press, 1985.

Van Elteren, M., "Conceptualizing the Impact of US Popular Culture Globally," *Journal of Popular Culture*, 1996, vol. 30, no. 1, pp. 47–90.

Varley, H. P., *Japanese Culture: A Short History*, Tokyo, Charles E. Tuttle, 1973.

Vines, S., *Hong Kong: China's New Colony*, London, Aurum Press, 1998.

Von Laue, T. H., *The World Revolution of Westernization: The Twentieth Century in Global Perspective*, New York, Oxford University Press, 1987.

Wacker, G., "The Demise of Biblical Civilization," in N. Hatch and M. Noll (eds), *The Bible in America: Essays in Cultural History*, New York, Oxford University Press, 1982.

Wagner, R., *The Invention of Culture*, revised edition, Chicago, University of Chicago Press, 1981.

Wakabayashi, N., *Gendai bijutsu nyūmon* [An introduction to contemporary art], Tokyo, Takarajimasha, 1987.

Waterhouse, D., "Dance, traditional," *Kodansha Encyclopedia of Japan*, Tokyo, Kodansha, 1983.

——, "Music, Western," *Kodansha Encyclopedia of Japan*, Tokyo, Kodansha, 1983.

Watson, J. (ed.), *Golden Arches East: McDonald's in East Asia*, Stanford, CA, Stanford University Press, 1997.

Weatherford, J., *Savages and Civilization*, New York, Crown, 1994.

Weber, M., *The Protestant Ethic and the Spirit of Capitalism*, trans. T. Parsons, New York, Charles Scribner's Sons, 1958 [1920–1].

Weil, S., *The Need for Roots*, London, Routledge & Kegan Paul, 1952.

Welsh, F., *A History of Hong Kong*, London, HarperCollins, 1993.

Wilk, R., "Learning to be Local in Belize: Global Systems of Common Differences," in D. Miller (ed.), *Worlds Apart: Modernity Through the Prism of the Local*, London, Routledge, 1995.

Wilson, P. B., *Liberated Through Submission: The Ultimate Paradox*, Eugene, OR, Harvest House, 1990.

Wolf, E., *Europe and the People Without History*, Berkeley, University of California Press, 1982.

Yahuda, M., *Hong Kong: China's Challenge*, London, Routledge, 1996.

Yergin, D. and Stanislaw, J., *The Commanding Heights: The Battle Between Government and the Marketplace That is Remaking the Modern World*, New York, Simon & Schuster, 1998.

Yoshino, K., *Cultural Nationalism in Contemporary Japan: A Sociological Enquiry*, London, Routledge, 1992.

Yu, S. M. and Low, S. W. (eds), *Yihsahp saigéi dīk hèunggóng* [Twentieth-century Hong Kong], Hong Kong, Kéihléuhn syùying yauhahn gùngsì, 1995.

Yui, S., *Ikite iru jazu shi* [The living history of jazz], Tokyo, Shinko Music, 1988.

Index

"East" 26, 59, 67–8, 76, 79, 108, 176, 183
"Easternization" in United States 119–20
Edwards, Jonathan 77
e-maki 32
Emerson, Ralph Waldo 79
English language, in Hong Kong 125, 131–3, 150, 153, 156, 160, in names 145–8
ethnic identity 8–9, 18–19, 83, 178, 183; in American religion 116–17; "ethnic individuality" 66; "ethnic memory" 71; in Hong Kong 124, 136–8; in Japanese arts 45–8, 51–2, 55–8
ethnographic method used in book, 28
evangelical Christians 80, 82, 83–93

Falwell, Jerry 80–1
flexible accumulation 181
flower arranging 42
Fordism 181
Foucault, Michel 13
Franklin, Benjamin 77
French Enlightenment 77, 80
French Revolution 7
Freud, Sigmund 13
Friedman, Jonathan 179

Geertz, Clifford 2, 3, 6, 11
Gellner, Ernest 8, 183
Giddens, Anthony 16, 178
Ginsberg, Allen 79
global cultural supermarket: *see* cultural supermarket
globalization 177, 179, 183, 185
God 53, in American Christianity 76–95
Gods Must be Crazy, The 13
Graham, Billy 80
Great Britain, in Hong Kong 123–8, 139, 149–50
Guangdong Province 144, 148, 150
Guernica (Picasso) 69
Gurdjieff, G. I. 97–8

habitus (Bourdieu) 11
Hall, Stuart 16
handover, Hong Kong 128–9, 138, 153, 155, 163
Hannerz, Ulf 4, 179, 184, 190
Haring, Keith 48
Harvey, David 19, 181, 190
heaven 88

hell 84, 86, 88, 91–2
Hendrix, Jimi 30
Herder, Johann Gottfried 7
hèunggóngyàhn 135
Hick, John 94
Hinduism 76, 89, 94
Hiroshige 33
Hokkaido 72
Hokusai 33
Holocaust, the 101
home, senses of 24, 176, 186, 191–7; cultural supermarket as 119–20; as fiction 16; in Hong Kong 121, 123, 143, 153–4, 165; in Japan 63–4, 74–5; in United States 115, 118–20; transcendence of 119
Hong Kong, as research site 27, 122, 130–31
Hong Kong intellectuals and cultural identity 121–65; archeological evidence 124; as Chinese 134–43; as Chinese cultural values 137–8; as "race" 136; Chinese and Western histories of 122–30; as "Chineseness plus" 144–52; and colonialism 127, 150; and economic downturn 129, 161–2; and English language 125, 131–3, 150, 153, 156, 160; and Guangdong Province 144, 148, 150; and handover to China 128–9, 138, 153, 155, 163; as Hongkonese 127, 143–54; and Mandarin 129, 136–7; and mother-tongue [Cantonese] education 156; and mainland Chinese immigration 148; and names 145–8; and National Day 158–9; and resistance to Great Britain 127; and rule of law 150–1; and schooling 123; and state vs. market 155–64; surveys of identity 123, 134; and Westernness 144–5
Hong Kong Economic Times 162
Horkheimer, Max 117
Hoshi, Shin'ichi 36
Hosono, Haruomi 67
human rights 19, 140–1, 143, 150–1
Hunter, James Davison 81

identity (*see also* cultural identity, national identity, ethnic identity) definition 16–17; ethnic identity 8–9; market-based identity 9–10, 17–19; national identity 6–8; personal, collective 17–19
iemoto seido 44–5, 47, 51